# Learn SQL Server 2000 Administration

**Jeffrey Garbus**

**with Alvin Chang and Penny Garbus**

**Wordware Publishing, Inc.**

**Library of Congress Cataloging-in-Publication Data**

Garbus, Jeffrey R.
    Learn SQL server 2000 administration / by Jeffrey Garbus.
      p.  cm.
    Includes index.
    ISBN  1-55622-814-7 (pbk.)
    1.  SQL server.   2.  Client/server computing.    I.  Title.
    QA76.9.C55 G37    2001
    005.75'85—dc21                       00-069315
                                              CIP





ISBN 1-55622-814-7

10 9 8 7 6 5 4 3 2 1

0101




All inquiries for volume purchases of this book should be addressed to Wordware Publishing, Inc.,
at the above address. Telephone inquiries may be made by calling:

(972) 423-0090

# Dedication

For my parents and grandparents, my biggest literary fans; but most of all, for my love.

J.G.

For my family

A.C.

For my parents, sister Chris, wonderful children, and the best husband ever, Jeff.

P.G.

# Acknowledgments

Thanks to everybody who sent tips (look for your names in the appendix!); my coauthors Alvin and Penny, without whose help this book would not have been completed on time; and my son Brandon for helping reorganize Chapter 6.

Most of all, I'd like to thank my family, without whose support I might never have slept. Thank you all.

Jeff Garbus

I would like to thank Jeff Garbus for providing me the opportunity to contribute to this book. Thanks to Basil, my brother and sounding board, who keeps my phone bills high. And thanks to my parents, Yuling and Yuching Chang, who started me on computers in the first place.

Alvin Chang

I would like to thank Alvin Chang, Jim Hill, and Jeff Garbus.

Penny Garbus

# Contents

# Contents

Contents

# About the Authors

## Jeff Garbus

Jeff Garbus's background includes a B.S. degree from Rensselaer Polytechnic Institute, and work experience from PCs to mainframes and back again. He has many years of Microsoft and Sybase SQL Server experience, with a special emphasis on assisting clients in migrating from existing systems to pilot and large-scale projects. He is well known in the industry, having spoken at user conferences and user groups for many years and written articles and columns for many magazines nationally and internationally, as well as having written several books. Recently his focus has been on Very Large Databases, data warehousing, training, and remote database administration.

Jeff currently is CEO of Soaring Eagle Consulting, Ltd., an RDBMS consulting and training firm based in Tampa, which specializes in solving business problems as well as performance problems. Soaring Eagle now offers remote database administration services.

He can be reached at jeffg@soaringeagleltd.com.

## Alvin Chang

Alvin Chang is a consultant, technical trainer, and author working for Soaring Eagle Consulting, Ltd., a Tampa-based consulting and training firm. A Microsoft Certified Professional for SQL Server, he has taught SQL Server and consulted throughout the United States. Currently specializing in Microsoft and Sybase system administration, Alvin started as a technical trainer for products such as Microsoft Office, Lotus SmartSuite, and Lotus Notes before moving into RDBMSs.

Alvin can be reached at alvin@soaringeagleltd.com.

## Penny Garbus

Penny Garbus is a technical writer who has been involved in SQL Server training for over five years. She has written several thousand pages of materials on topics including introductory Transact-SQL, systems administration, advanced SQL techniques, and performance and tuning. She has been writing about Microsoft SQL Server since release 6.

Penny is president of Soaring Eagle Consulting, Ltd. She can be reached at penny@soaringeagleltd.com.

# Introduction

Have you suddenly been given responsibility for the maintenance of a Microsoft SQL Server?

There is an abundance of products on the market that use Microsoft SQL Server, and more are on the way every day. There is also a shortage of experienced database administrators (DBAs) on the market. It seems inevitable that some businesses and organizations end up purchasing a sophisticated system that they do not have the staff or background to maintain.

For these organizations, the question becomes: Now that we've got it, what do we need to do to keep it up and running smoothly? There is also an underlying question that we hope does not need to be answered and which we may not voice, in denial: What do we do if something goes wrong?

This book is written for any person who is about to embark upon the task of maintaining a SQL Server. It answers the first question in detail, with the hope that this will prevent the need to answer the second question.

## About This Book

Microsoft SQL Server 2000 is a sophisticated piece of software designed to store and retrieve data. For the latest release, Microsoft has upgraded the server to be as maintenance free as is possible with current technology.

But this does not absolve the systems administrator (SA) or database administrator (DBA) of the responsibility of making sure that the server has the resources it needs in order to function and continue to store data. The best definition this author has ever heard of a great DBA (or SA) is one who you never know is there, because everything is always running smoothly.

This book is geared towards making your SQL Server run as smoothly as it can to make your system as resilient as possible; and in a situation which requires action, teaching you what action to take, based on preparations we'll teach you to make. These teachings are based on the authors' real-life experience, as well as tips and tricks gathered from other experienced production DBAs.

Chapters 1 and 2 of this book discuss basic concepts, and list and describe the tasks you need to perform in order to successfully ensure ongoing system reliability, performance, and preparedness for disaster recovery. The remaining chapters tell you what you are doing and why.

Based on the definition we've given for a great administrator, you can become a great systems administrator on most small-scale applications by simply reading the first two chapters. If you need clarification, or want an in-depth understanding of a particular subject, simply jump to the chapter that explains that subject in detail.

The only assumptions we make are that you know enough about the hardware to turn the machine on and that you know enough about your environment to use a mouse.

Good luck, and have fun!

# Chapter 1

# Definitions and Concepts

In this chapter, we introduce some of the concepts that you will be exploring in the balance of this book. This includes client/server computing, the branch of computing that uses Microsoft SQL Server, what Microsoft SQL Server really is (a database engine), and basic systems administration concepts.

## Client/Server Concepts

Client/server computing is the branch of computer science in which we try to divide processing into hardware and software modules that may scale and perform their tasks independently. Stated differently, it is the architecture in which client processes (programs run from your PC) request work or data from a server process or processes, which is the SQL Server in your case.

The *client* is the hardware and software combination which shows you data and interfaces with the database. For example, your client workstation may be running Excel, Visual Basic, or a custom application on Windows 95, Windows 98, or Windows 2000 on some Intel- or Celeron-based desktop or laptop computer.

The *server* is the hardware and software combination that runs the database. For example, you might be running Microsoft SQL Server on Windows 95, Windows 98, Windows NT 4, Windows NT 5, or Windows

2000. This may be on the same hardware (PC) that is running your client, but that is not the usual setup in a production environment. Normally, the server software runs on a separate machine for scalability (so that if you need more processing power on the server, you only have to worry about buying more/faster memory for the one task).

The software you are going to be maintaining is the server software (Microsoft SQL Server) running on your physical server.

# Database Management System (DBMS)

A *database management system* is a software program that exists for the purpose of storing and retrieving data. It will deal directly with the operating system to manage disk space, it will keep the users that are accessing the data from modifying the same information at the same time (*lock management* or *transaction management*), and it will guarantee that information that is stored has permanence.

# SQL Server

Microsoft SQL Server is a *relational* DBMS (or *RDBMS)*. Relational means that we store the data in *tables*, using *rows* of data, and we relate the information within the tables with *keys*. For example, you may have a table that has a row for each customer (or client or patient). You may have another table that contains invoice information for each billing item for the client. The tables are related together by the customer; the key may be the customer's social security number, or other unique information.

# Systems Administration

*Systems administration* is the task of maintaining the physical environment, trying to ensure stability, and monitoring growth to ensure sufficient resources for the database management system.

# Database Administration

*Database administration* is the task of ensuring the smooth running of the DBMS. This includes running those tasks that ensure good performance, monitoring the changes in the system over time, and everything listed in Chapter 2 of this book.

# Enterprise Manager

The Enterprise Manager is a graphical tool used to assist in the tasks of systems administration and database administration. It allows the database to be controlled and maintained from a single, consistent, easy-to-use interface. It has features that are used in the development and modification of databases and their designs. This includes but is not limited to the development and modification of the database tables. The Enterprise Manager also contains helpful wizards to assist in the development of a maintenance schedule to keep a database running smoothly. These maintenance schedules are a series of database and system administration tasks that are run periodically to ensure that the database will run reliably. These maintenance tasks will be discussed in upcoming chapters.

The Enterprise Manager can be found on the Start menu under Microsoft SQL Server (see the figure at the top of the following page).

1.  Click the **Start** button.
2.  Click on **Programs**.
3.  Select **Microsoft SQL Server**.
4.  Select **Enterprise Manager**.

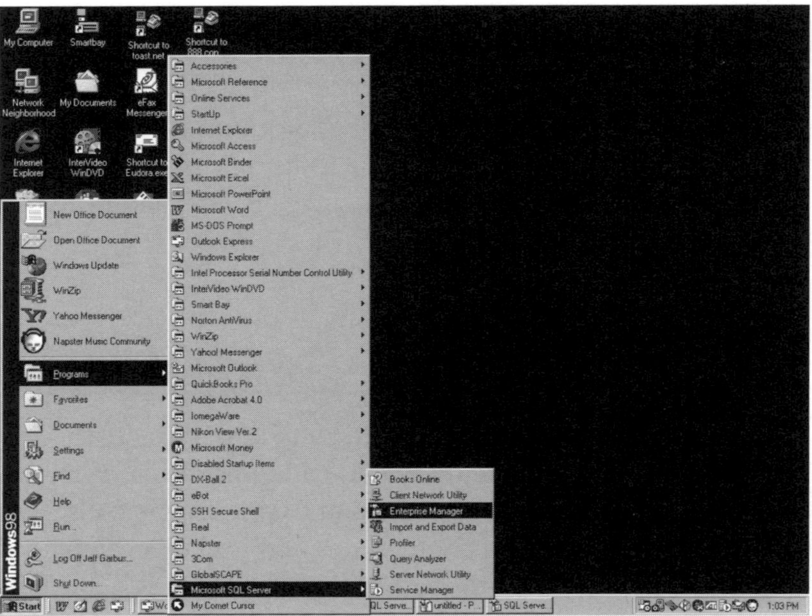

The Enterprise Manager contains lists of SQL Servers including older versions of SQL Server if they are still available and running. Access to most of the configurable items will be displayed in the tree on the left side of the screen.

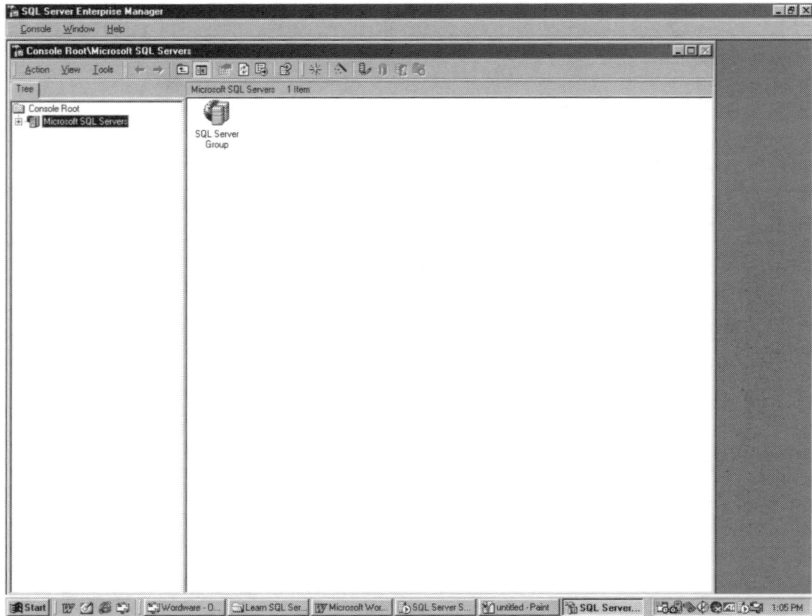

To access the servers click the plus sign (+) beside Microsoft SQL Servers to expand it. Then click on the plus sign (+) beside SQL Server Group to expand it. On the right side of the screen, you will find the taskpad that contains access to many of the necessary administration tasks.

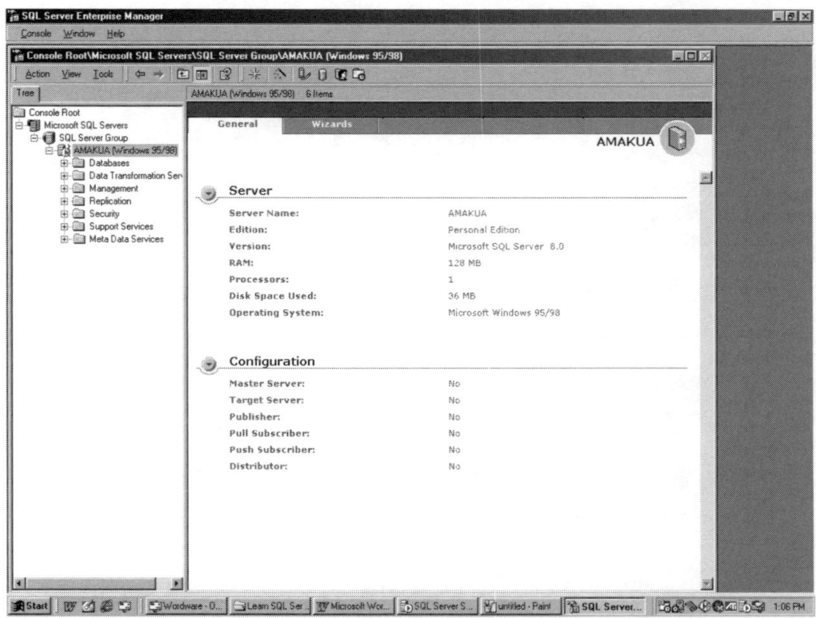

(Note that the version listed here is "8", not 2000. This was a prerelease version of the new SQL Server, and had the old name; yours may say SQL2000.)

Now that we have discussed the basic concepts and definitions we need, let's move on to putting them into practice. The next chapter introduces the set of tasks you need to perform to keep your system up and running.

# Chapter 2

# A Preventive Maintenance Regimen

In this chapter, we begin to look at the focus of this book. We will talk about what needs to be maintained, and what you need to do to maintain it. At the end of this chapter, you will find a checklist of recommended tasks categorized by how often they should be performed. Later chapters will look at the importance and frequency of various maintenance tasks in greater detail.

## What Needs to Be Maintained?

We break down the list of tasks to be performed based on scope. Some tasks take place at the server level, meaning that your tasks involve resources which affect the entire server.  For example, memory is a shared resource among all the tasks running on a SQL Server. Other tasks take place at the database level. The database is SQL's unit of backup and recovery, so we perform database backups (making a copy of the database) and other types of care and maintenance we'll discuss in a bit. Finally, at the table level (the table is what contains your data), you do things to help ensure database performance; that is, fast access to the data.

We divide tasks at these levels for purposes of comprehension. For a more practical approach to maintenance, at the end of the chapter we will change the order around a bit as we discuss the frequency of the tasks and put together a maintenance schedule.

## Server-level Maintenance

The word "server" is used in a variety of ways in literature, from a file server, which manages disks, to a Windows NT Server, which manages your hardware, to the SQL Server, which interfaces with each to manage your data. Here, we focus on the SQL Server.

Part of systems administration is disaster preparedness. Under some circumstances, you may need to reinstall your entire server. Earlier versions of SQL Server required a significant amount of configuration of the memory parameters, but with Microsoft SQL Server 2000, almost all parameters are set dynamically and automatically by the server. You may override these, and in fact, the vendor from whom you bought your software may have set some of these parameters to take advantage of SQL Server features for its own software. With Microsoft SQL Server 2000, you do not need to set any of these parameters yourself, and you should not do so without careful consideration and reading of the SQL Server manuals on the topic. What you should do, though, is make a permanent record of these parameters, and stash it somewhere you can find it if you need it in a stressful situation. If you never need it, fine. However, if one day you do need it, you'll be glad you took the time. This is a one-time action. To find the current configuration values, use Enterprise Manager like this:

1.    Click on the appropriate server name.

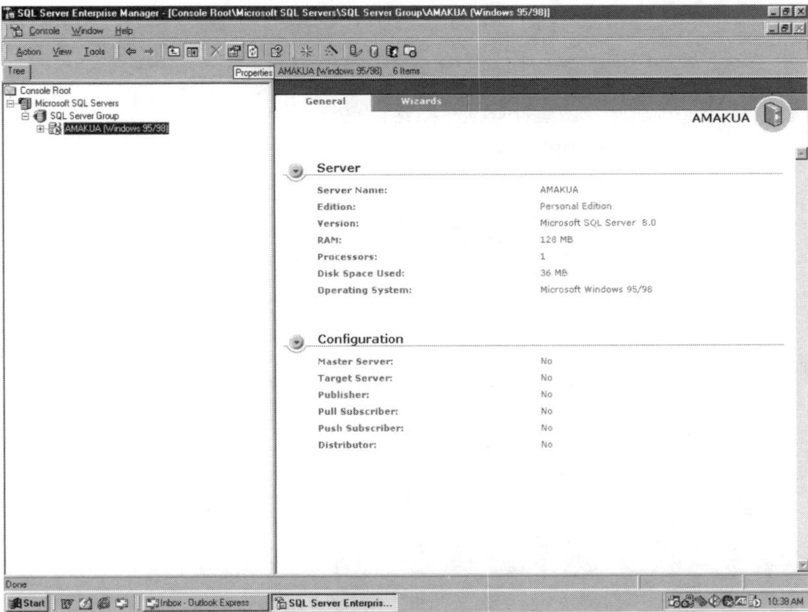

2. Right-click on the server name, then choose **Properties**.

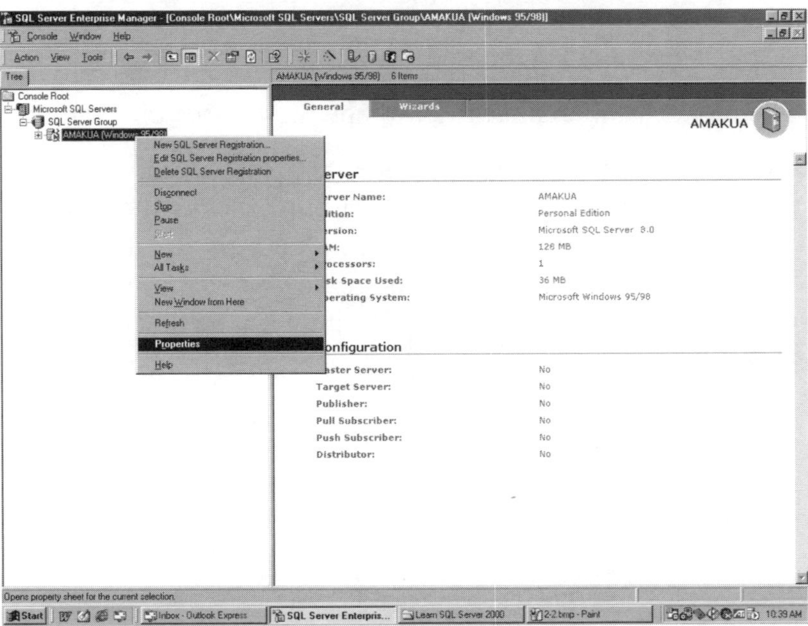

Alternatively, click on **Tools** on the menu bar, then click on **SQL Server Configuration Properties**.

3.  Click on the appropriate tab and make modifications as shown in the following figures. Look at the General tab first:

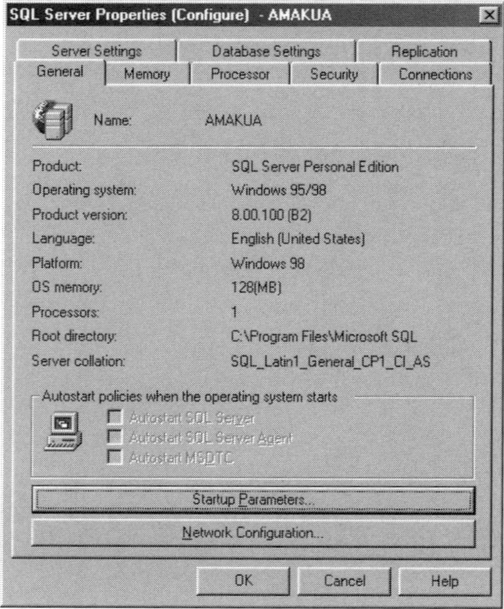

We recommend you set the SQL Server to start automatically when the operating system is rebooted.

The Memory tab defines the way the server uses the memory on the box.

You should allow the SQL Server to dynamically allocate memory to make use of any changing server resources. Note the running values vs. the configured values radio buttons. This tells you if you are looking at the changes you just made (configured), or what the server was set to when it was started (running). To run with the newly configured values, recycle the server.

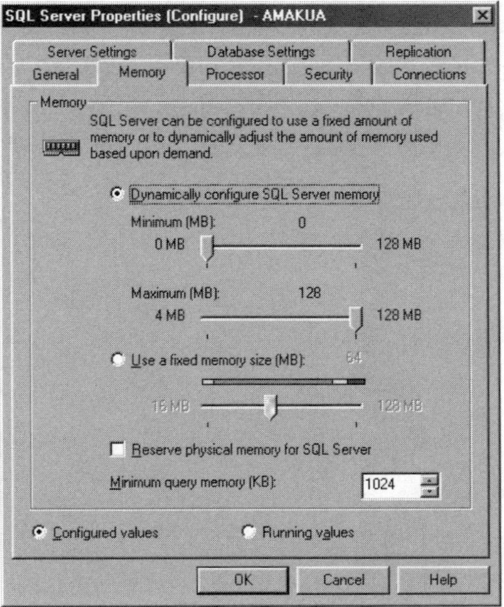

In the Processor tab, set the system to use all available processors, unless your application vendor has instructed you otherwise.

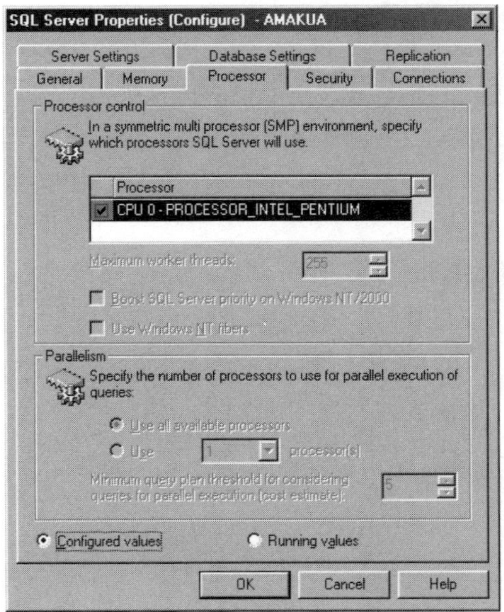

There are situations where using all the processors for a parallel query can drain resources from the rest of the system, so in a multi-cpu system you may end up setting this to less than the number of CPUs.

The next tab is Security. You should leave auditing off unless your site security requires that you track failed attempts at access. You can leave the startup SQL Server account on the default unless you want to change the security from the NT administrator.

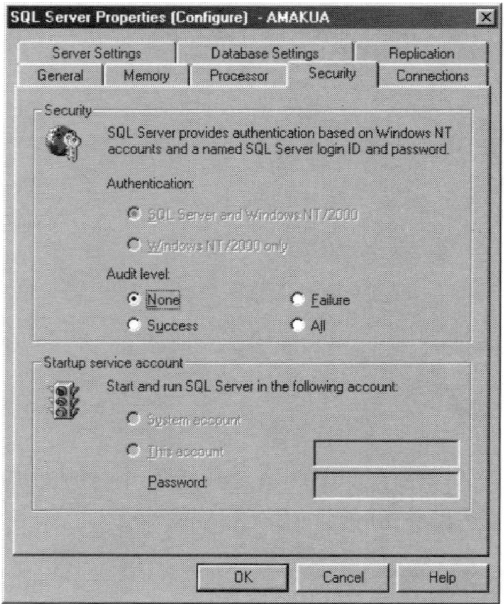

If you have other SQL Servers that need to communicate with this one, make sure the Allow other SQL Servers option is checked in the Connections tab. If not, make sure it is unchecked, as you will save some memory resources.

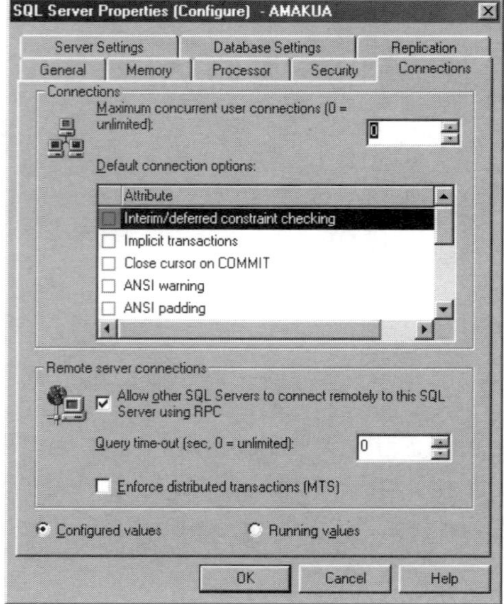

Leave all the defaults on in the Server Settings tab; changing these may affect the behavior of your application in unexpected ways.

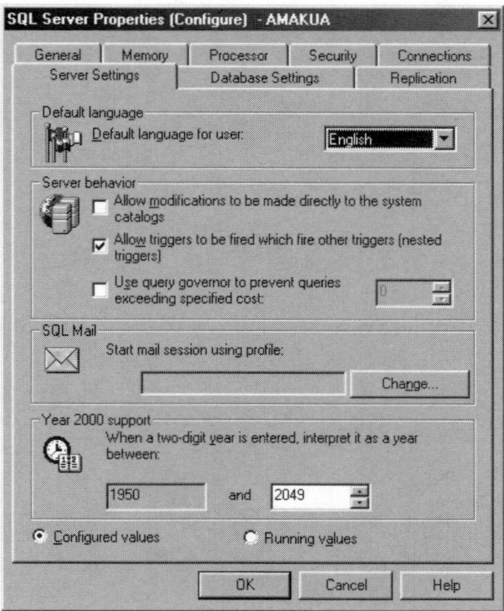

Leave the defaults on in the Database Settings tab as well; this affects administrative tasks, which we will be automating later in this chapter.

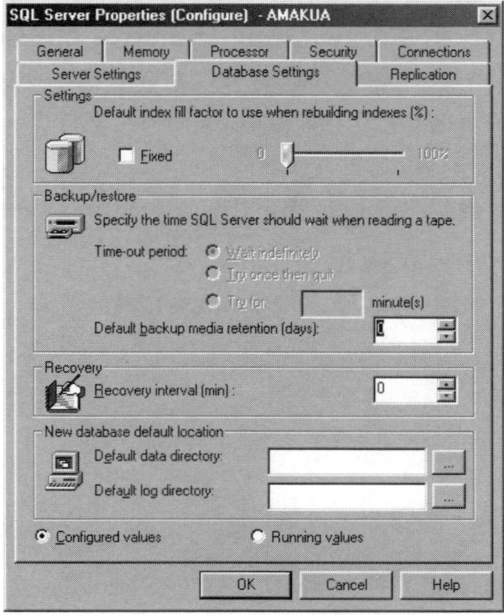

The Replication tab is for configuring automated data transfer from one database to another. Unless your vendor has configured this, we recommend you leave it alone.

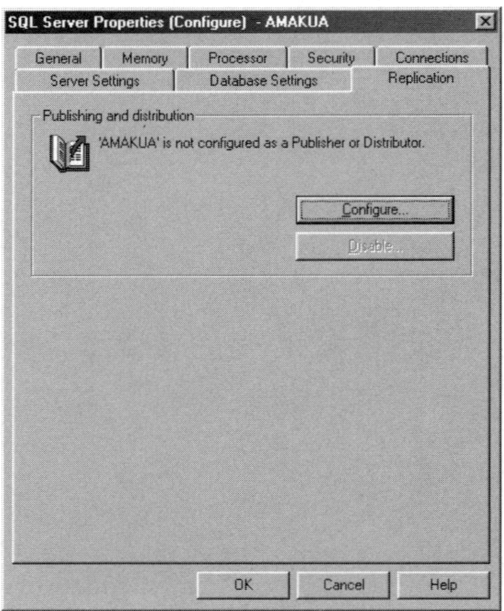

At the server level, you also need to monitor the messages that the server records in the activity log. This will contain information on everything from when the server was started, to warning and error messages of a sufficient severity that the server needs to alert you to them. You can look at the activity log using the following procedure; be sure to do this at least once daily:

1.  Open the **Management** folder for the appropriate server.

2.  Expand the **SQL Server Logs** item. This will give you your list of log files, archived each time you cycle your servers.

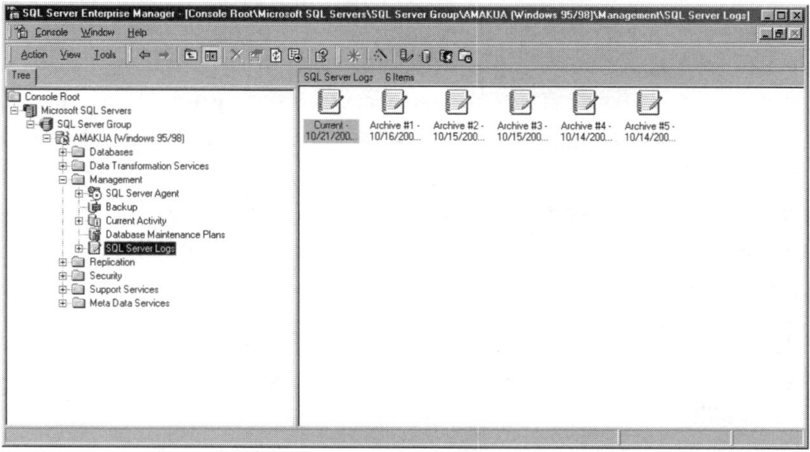

3.    Click on the appropriate log file.

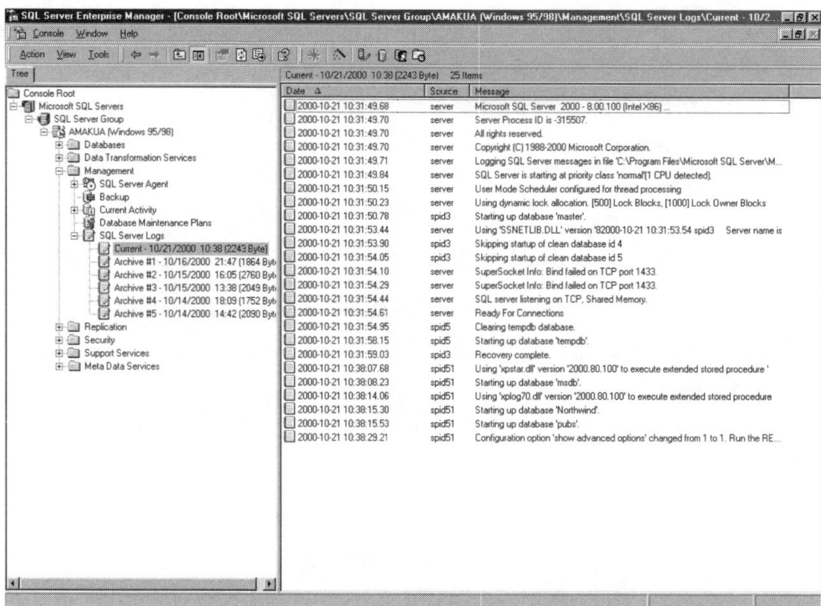

Messages tend to be self-explanatory (they have improved dramatically over the years). A low-volume system may rarely get messages other than the standard messages identifying that the server is starting or has started. You should check the log periodically, but at least once a day.

One of the most difficult parts of being a systems administrator, which requires the most thought and planning and which you hope is a waste of your time, is to devise a disaster recovery scheme. What happens if somebody steals the machine upon which your server resides? What if a disgruntled employee sets off the automatic sprinkler system, destroying the hardware? What if there is a fire that destroys the hardware? You must give serious consideration to anything that might interrupt your processing, for instance:

- **Loss of Hardware**  Plan for a way of getting a new box quickly, if necessary, and a means for loading your server software and database back on it.

- **Loss of Power**  A UPS (uninterruptible power supply) is essential; in case of a loss of power, you do <u>not</u> want your server to suddenly shut down. This can cause data loss or database corruption. You can get a UPS from any computer supply shop or, these days, office supply store.

- **Loss of Data**  You may experience loss of data for a variety of reasons, largely due to user error. (For example, perhaps somebody accidentally deleted an entire table rather than a single row.) Many shops do not bother to devise a recovery plan at this level, but you should carefully consider the possible consequences of your decision not to.

Database corruption is unusual (you may never experience this), but if it does occur, you must restore the database from your backup. You should always restore a database in its entirety; partial database restorations should be left to seasoned professionals. This is the quickest and most sure route to a functioning SQL Server.

Finally, in the server-level category for Microsoft SQL Server, keep an eye on overall resources. The server will do much of this for you, but it has no idea what to do when you run out of disk space, so plan ahead. Calculate how much space you need for data, figure out when you will need more disk space, and have an extra disk ready in advance.

# Database-level Maintenance

*Database-level maintenance* refers to the tasks we perform on <u>each</u> database as a whole. Note the stress on the word "each"; there is a reason for this. Many sites forget that it is important to maintain <u>every</u> database, not just the production databases. There are also several system databases you need to maintain. Make sure that you pay attention to <u>every</u> database listed in Enterprise Manager. Likewise, every maintenance task is important, and skipping any specific task runs the risk of jeopardizing your production system.

## Database Backups

A *database backup* is a copy of all of the used data pages that are stored on disk in the database. The database is the basic unit of recovery for a SQL Server. This means that in case of disaster, you may have to take this backup, replace the current damaged database or database device, and work from that point forward. This is not a situation you want to encounter, but it is an important one for which to prepare.

**Note:** The phrase *database backup* is used interchangeably with the phrase *database dump*. With the advent of Microsoft SQL Server 7.0, Microsoft changed the terminology (and syntax) from dump to backup. Because our focus is on Microsoft SQL Server 2000, we will endeavor to use the word backup.

Backing up your database is important, largely because bad things happen at the worst possible time. However, this precaution is not enough; you need to do two more things to guarantee that your backup will be useful in case of a disaster. First, you need to make sure that the backup will actually load. Second, you need to keep a copy of the backup off-site.

Why might the backup fail to load? The most common reason (and unfortunately, this does happen) is a failure in the backup media. For example, a floppy disk, Zip drive, tape, etc., has a physical flaw, which makes the disk unreadable. If this happens, you could end up with a box full of bad tapes and several months' worth of backups that don't work.

Why do we need to get a copy of the backup off-site? This is because some types of disaster are site-specific. Some examples: theft of equipment, flood, fire, hurricane, earthquake, mudslide, automatic sprinkler failure.... We're sure you can think of others. Any of these situations, which can and do occur, will make you glad you can order another physical server, take your backup devices out of the vault, load the SQL Server, and load from your backups.

As far as backups go, you can back up a database at any time. You do not need to wait until your system is inactive. Backups are performed like this:

1.    Choose the appropriate database.

You will see information on the database displayed to the right.

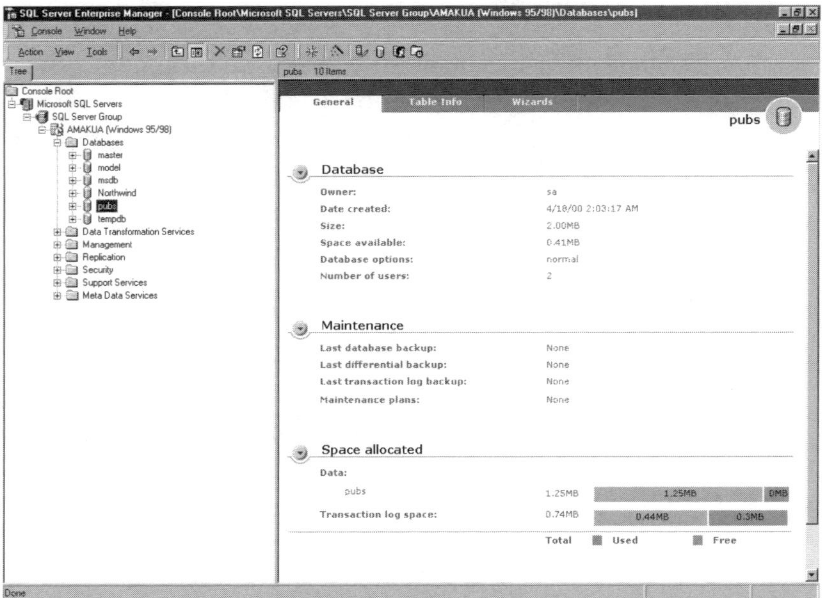

2.    Right-click on the database, and click **All Tasks**. Click on **Backup Database** in the pop-up menu.

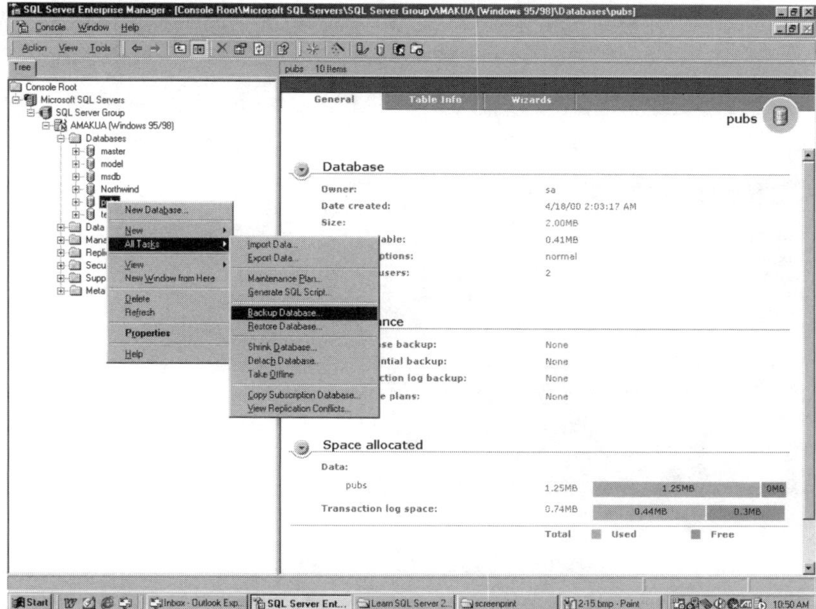

3.    Choose the appropriate database from the database list.

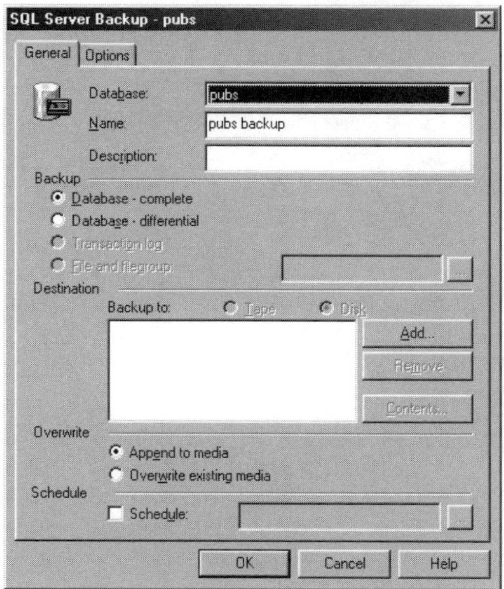

4.  The backup will go into a file on your disk (or tape). You will need to set up a target file for the backup by clicking on **Add**.

5.  Type a name for the backup file in the Filename box, or specify the location of the backup device (tape, for example). Then click **OK**.

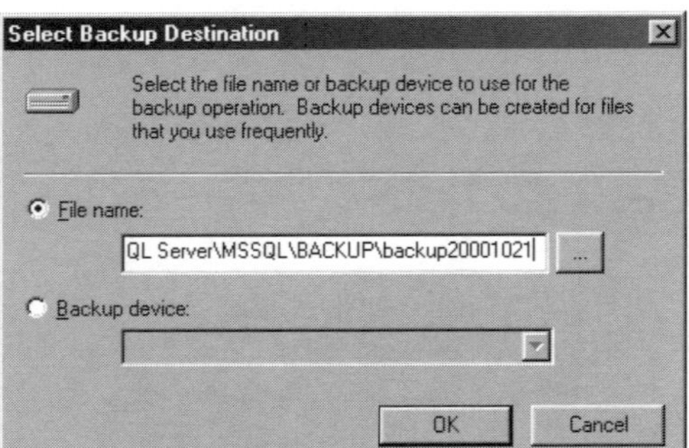

6.  Now, you can select a specific target for your backup:

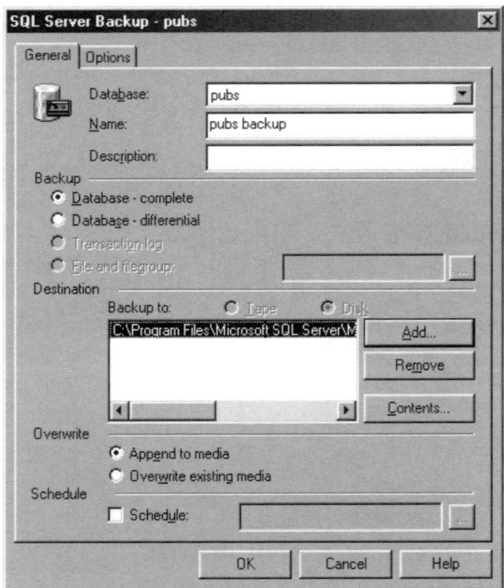

7.    Click on the **Options** tab, and make sure that Verify backup upon completion is checked. This will help make sure that the backup you create is valid.

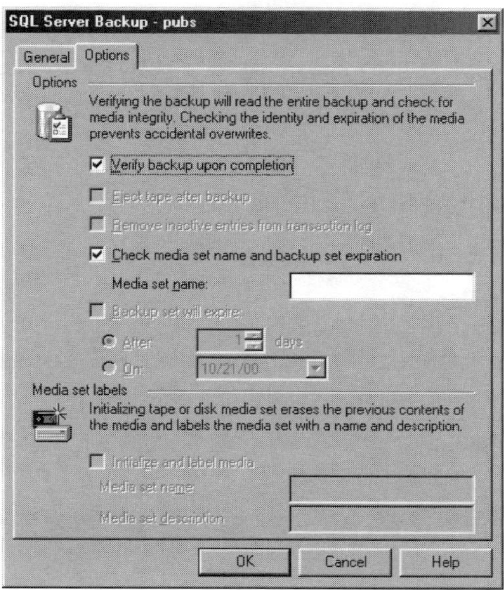

8.    Click **OK** to start the backup. You'll get this screen showing the progress of your backup:

And when it's done, this one:

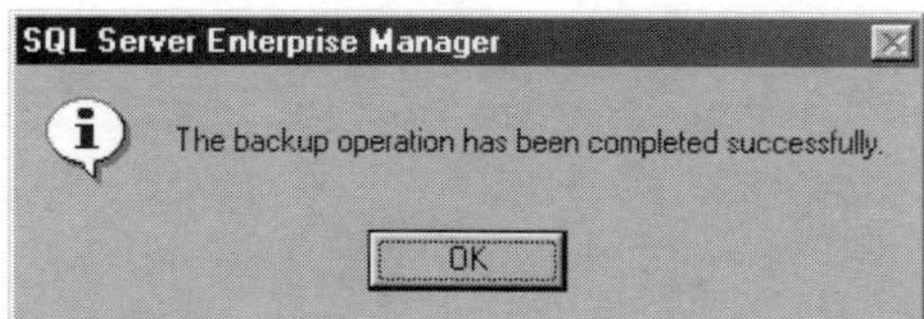

Now that the backup seems successful, try to load the database. This is important to test on occasion, because if you cannot load from the dump, your backup is useless.

If your database was live (in use) when you created the backup, be sure to load to a database other than your live production database (for example, if you backed up *accounting_prime* you should load to something like *accounting_test*).

You can test your backup by restoring it like this:

1.  Click on the **Tools** menu.

2.  Select **Restore Database**.

Alternatively, right-click on the database, and select **All Tasks|Restore Database**.

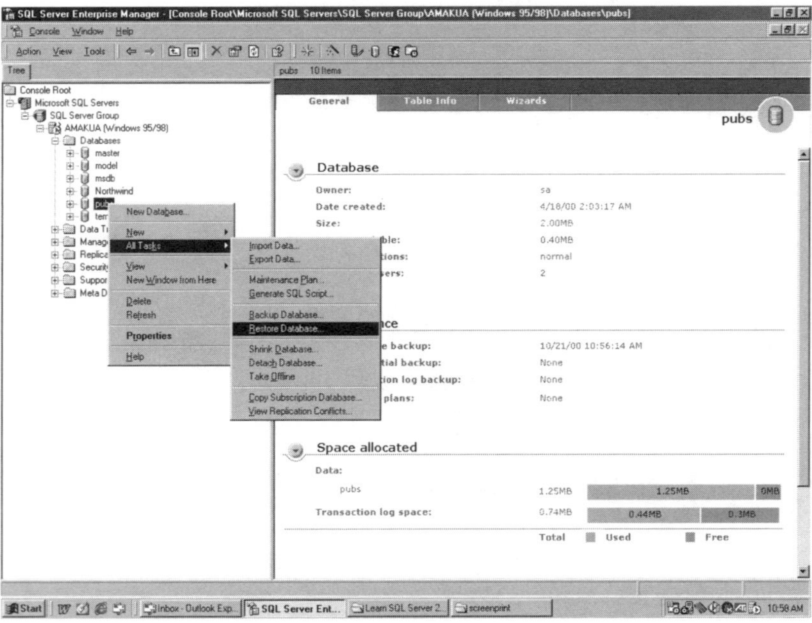

3.  Enter the name of the database to be restored.  Since the original is still here, we will have to name it something different. We don't want to overlay our current database.

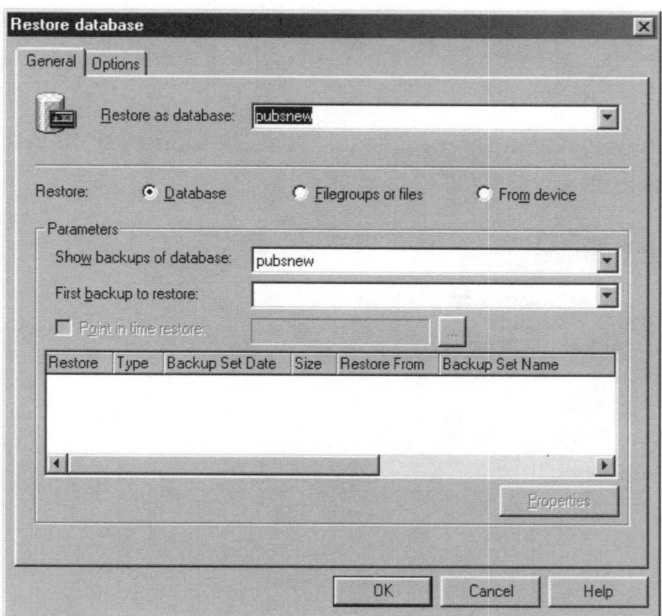

4. Select the name of the database that was backed up from the Show backups of database list.

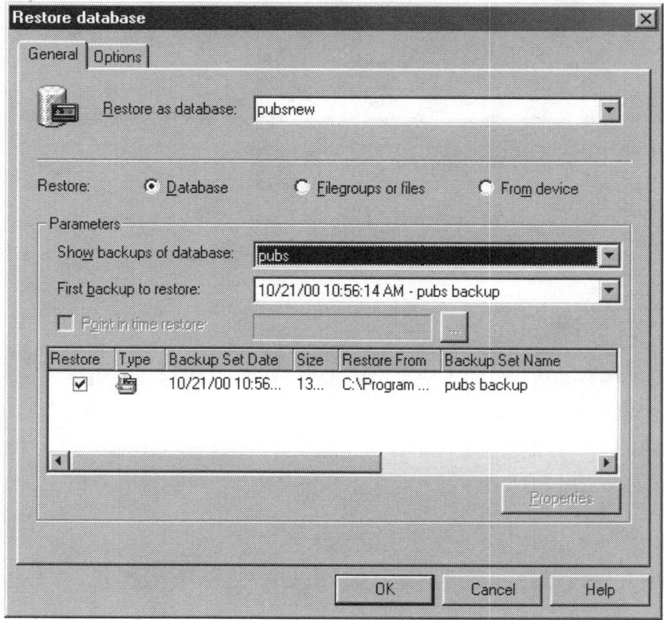

5.  Now select the database backup that was just made from the set of provided backups by checking the appropriate box in the Restore column.

6.  Click the **Options** tab and make sure the database files are being restored to the appropriate location.

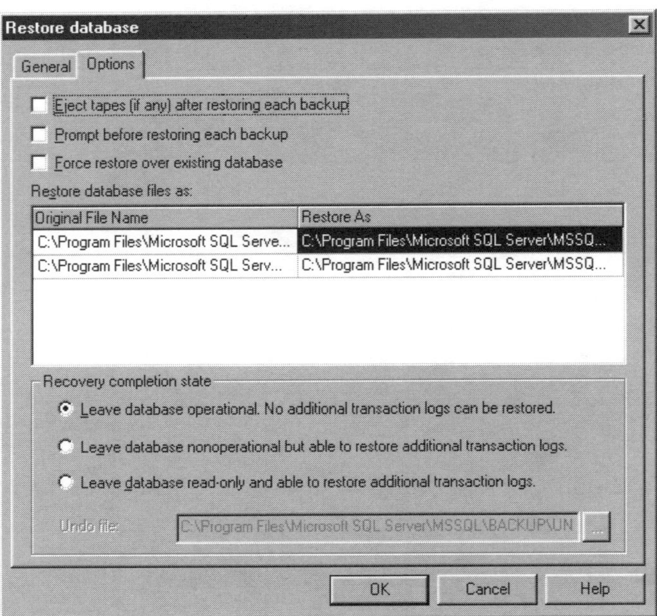


**Note:** Because our original database still exists, we need to make sure we do not inadvertently overlay information we care about; once a database is loaded, the old one is gone forever. This is normally done automatically by Enterprise Manager, but DBAs tend to spell things out for safety's sake.

7.  Click **OK** to start the restoration.

The new database should now be in place. Getting a copy off-site will depend on the security restrictions of your particular site. Check with a decision-maker at your company and determine whether it should go into a vault, a safety deposit box, or a shoe box in your bedroom closet.

The process of reusing your backup storage media (whether it be floppies, tapes, Zip disks, or Jaz drives) is called *aging out* the old media. For example, if you have 10 tapes, you might make daily backups, and transfer the whole week's backups onto one tape after the week is up. For example, if today is 3/30/2000, your tapes might correspond with these dates:

Tape 1:    3/30/2000
Tape 2:    3/29/2000
Tape 3:    3/28/2000
Tape 4:    3/27/2000
Tape 5:    3/26/2000
Tape 6:    3/25/2000
Tape 7:    3/24/2000
Tape 8:    3/17/2000
Tape 9:    3/10/2000
Tape 10:  3/03/2000

The idea is to pick a pivotal date, keep some backups for a period of time, and age them out as your business rules/policies deem them useless.

## Transaction Log Backups

A database management system is transactionally based. This means that any specific action you take, from adding a new customer to marking an invoice paid, needs to finish completely. You do not want, for example, your money account to be updated with a paid invoice, but have the invoice left marked unpaid due to a sudden power outage. This leads to unhappy customers and a lot of work by your bookkeepers.

To avoid this, Microsoft SQL Server keeps a transaction log of all changes to the database, as well as whether multiple modifications belong together in a single transaction. This transaction log will grow until it is truncated, unless you have the database option Truncate log on check-point turned on. Which is best for you? If your application needs up-to-the-second recovery, use transaction logging, and do not use the database option. If you do not have the resources to back up the transaction logs, then turn the option on, because otherwise your server will stop processing new transactions when the log fills up. You back up your transaction logs like this:

1.    Choose the appropriate database.

2.    Right-click on the database, and select **All Tasks|Backup Database**.

3.    On the General tab, select **Transaction log** under Backup.

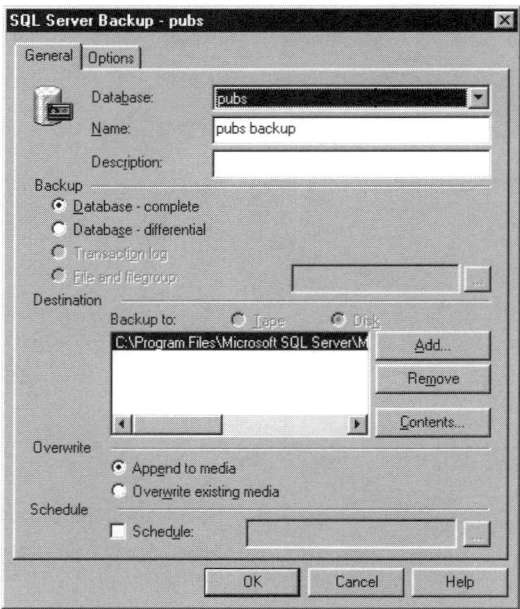

Add a new device if necessary (you may also choose to append the backup to any existing files).

## DBCC

The Database Consistency Checker (DBCC) is a tool that verifies the integrity of your database. The tables and indexes on your system reside on disk in complex structures that are fine most of the time. You may run for years without a problem, but on the off chance that a problem shows up, it is better to identify it with DBCC, which may repair the problem, than to find out about it when a query fails.

For each database, you have to run the following:

- DBCC CHECKCATALOG
- DBCC CHECKDB

## DBCCs are performed using the Query Analyzer:

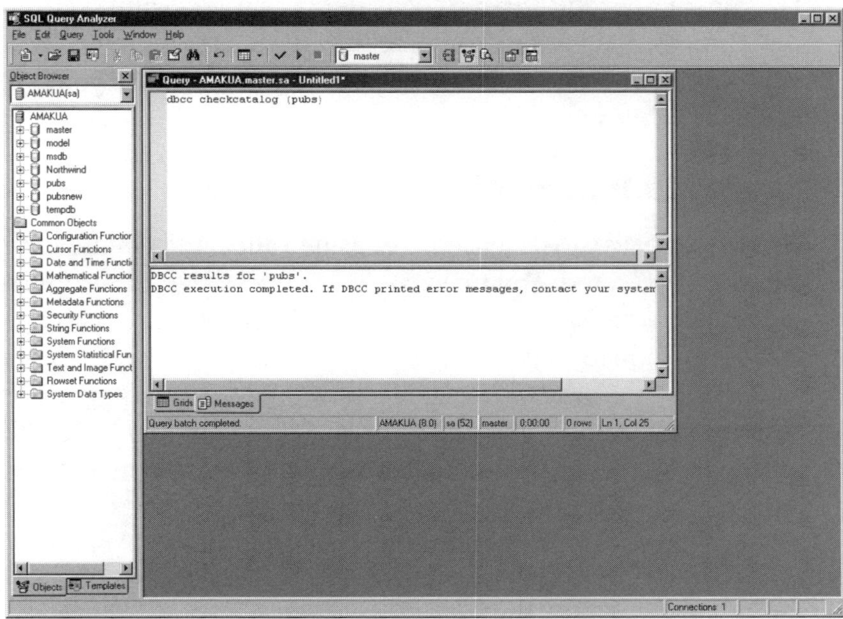

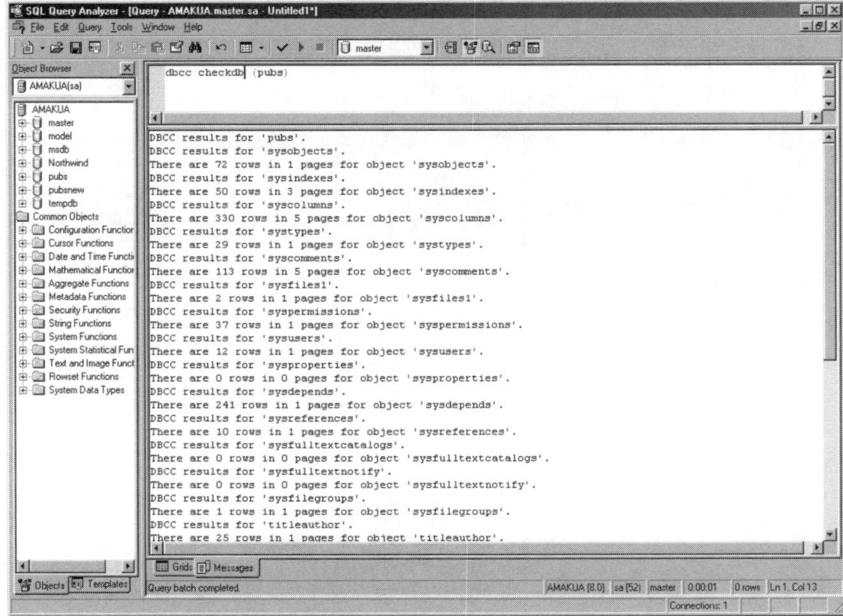

Ideally, you should run DBCCs before you perform your database backup. The most important thing to consider is that you should be sure you run DBCCs before aging out your backups, because running DBCCs are the only way to guarantee that the data you are storing is going to be of value when you choose to load it.

## Space Management

On a SQL Server, disk space is set aside (allocated) immediately when the database is created. You need to make sure of two things: First, make sure too much space isn't allocated. It unnecessarily uses up your disk resources and slows down your database loads (it won't slow down the backups because the server only backs up used data pages). Secondly, and of more importance, you need to make sure that you have sufficient room for the database to grow. Microsoft SQL Server has an auto-grow (and auto-shrink) option with database creation. This gives you the ability to instruct the database to shrink to a size that makes backups and restorations as quick as possible, and to grow automatically when extra disk space is needed. All you have to do is tell the server where to go for the extra disk space.

First, you determine how much space you have allocated, and how much is in use by selecting the database and looking to the right.

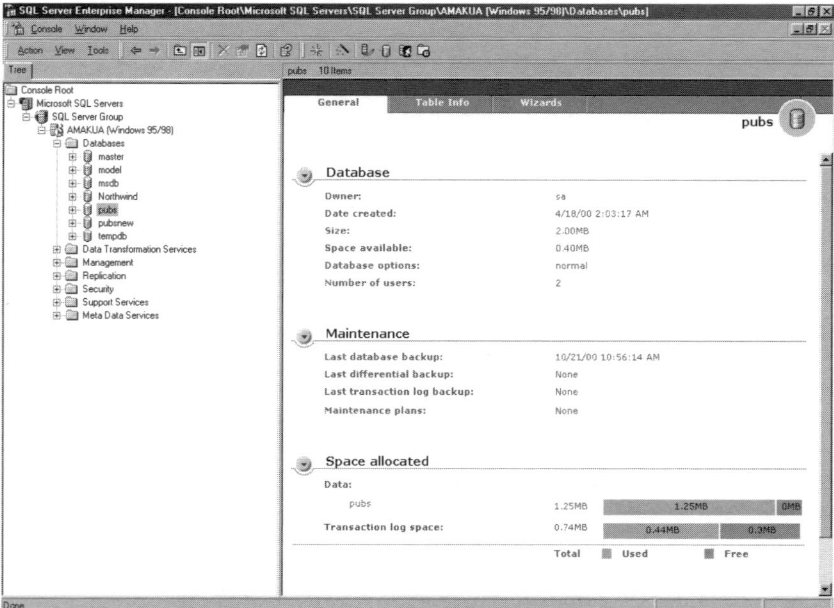

To set your database up for auto-grow/auto-shrink:

1.   Right-click the database and select **Properties** from the menu. Alternatively, click on the Properties button.

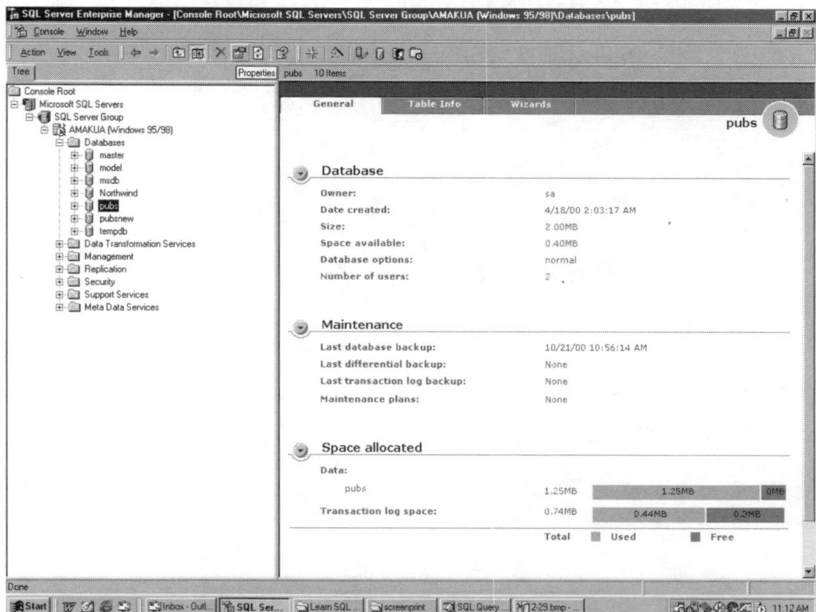

2.   Click on the **Data Files** tab.

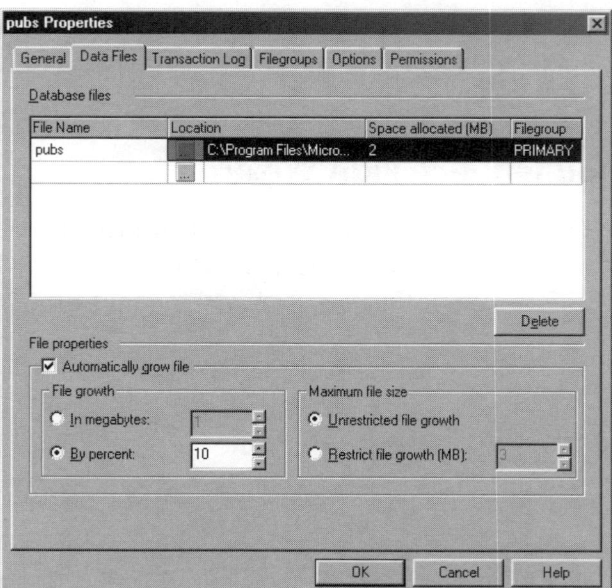

Check **Automatically grow file** in the dialog box. (This option also exists on the Transaction Log tab so transaction log files can also be set to auto-grow.)

3.    Click the **Options** tab. Check **Auto shrink** to enable the option.

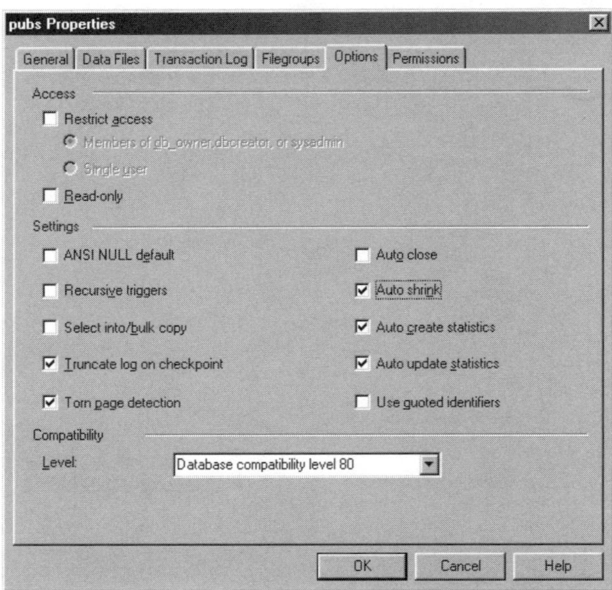


4.    Click **OK** to set the options.

You should monitor the space growth of your database(s). It is a good idea to check the allocated space once a week, every week, and chart the growth.

## Database Maintenance Plan Wizard

You can use the Database Maintenance Plan Wizard to automate many of the database-level tasks we've described. You can find this by looking at the bottom of your Console Root tree, and clicking on Database Maintenance Plans.

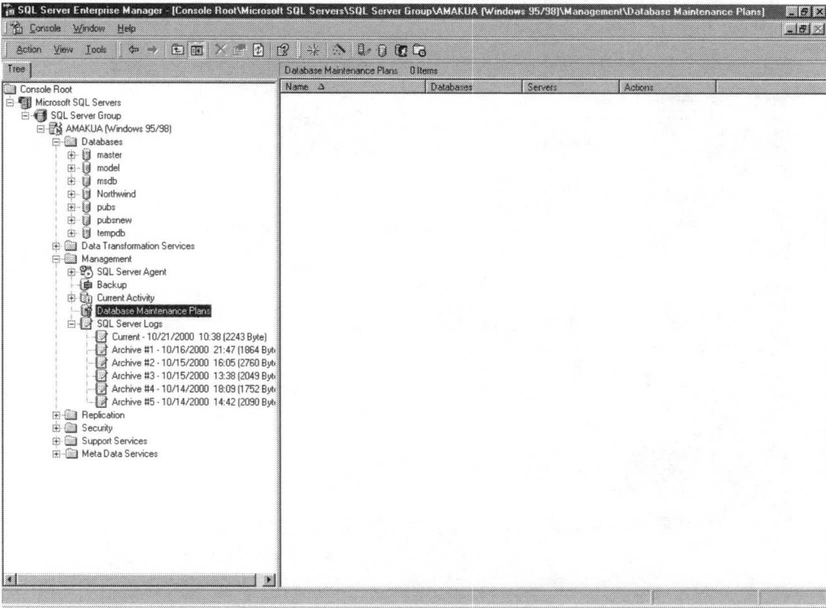

To create a new plan:

1.  Right-click on **Database Maintenance Plans** and select **New Maintenance Plan**.

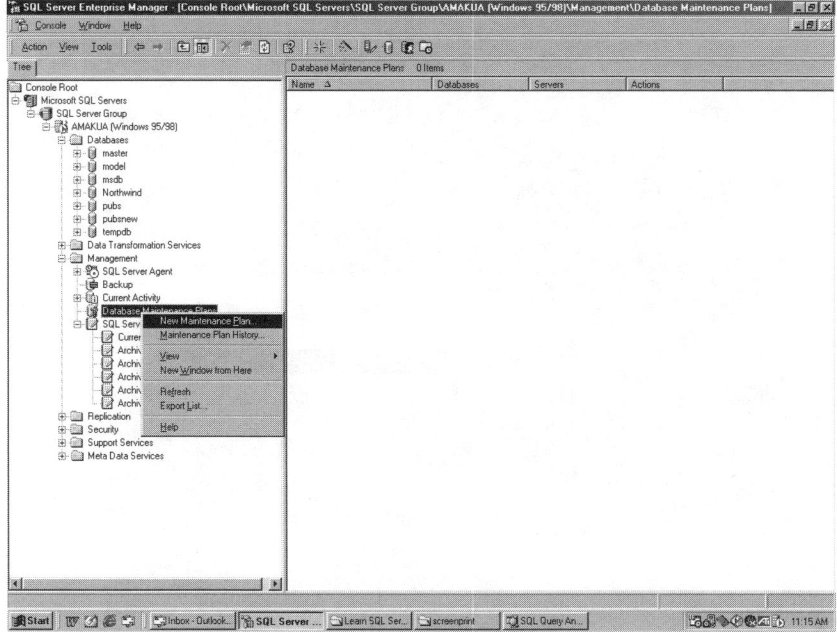

The wizard opens:

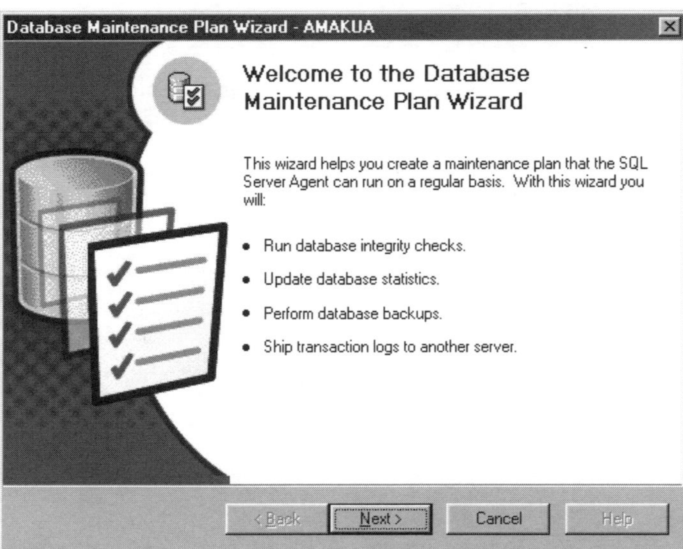

Click **Next**.

2.    Choose the databases for which you want to create a maintenance plan, and click **Next**.

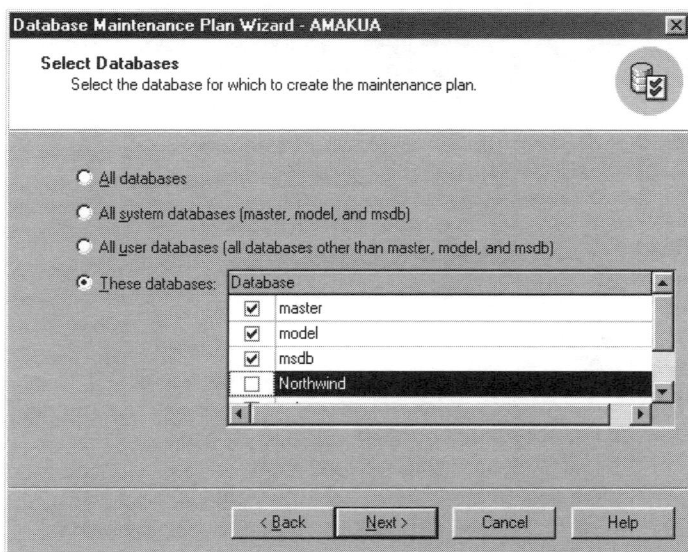

Decide on the appropriate schedule for your databases.

3.  If you select Reorganize data and index pages, then you can skip the index rebuild section of this chapter; this is a new SQL 2000 feature.

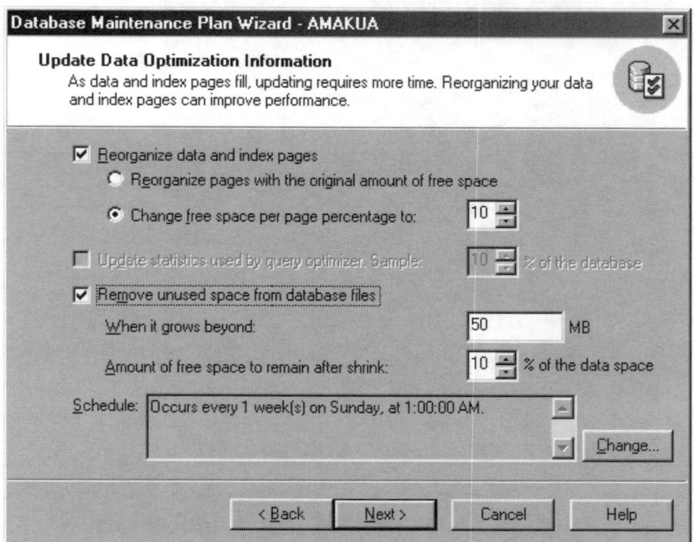


> **Note:** We recommend that you do all the system databases together (master, model, and msdb), and your user databases separately. Don't be shy about letting the server do all the work listed, and about checking all the boxes you see. In fact, we recommend you check the box labeled All databases. That way, you will even maintain newly created databases. Otherwise, you will need an additional plan each time you add an additional database.

4.  If you want to modify the schedule, click **Change** to open the Edit Recurring Job Schedule dialog box.

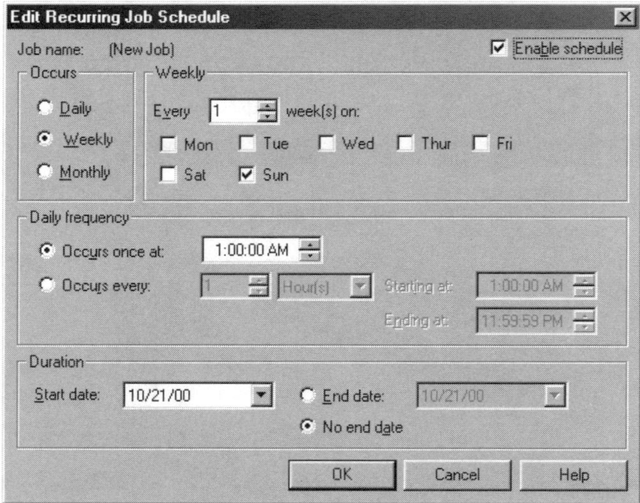

5.    Click **OK** followed by **Next** to continue with the wizard.

**Note:** We recommend backing up all of your databases every night, so we're making it part of the maintenance plan. Make sure you have enough space to back up your databases on your target devices. If not, the backup will not complete, and you will be at risk for data loss.

6.    In the Data Integrity Check dialog box, check all appropriate boxes; here, we've chosen to run integrity tests to check the data and the system tables.

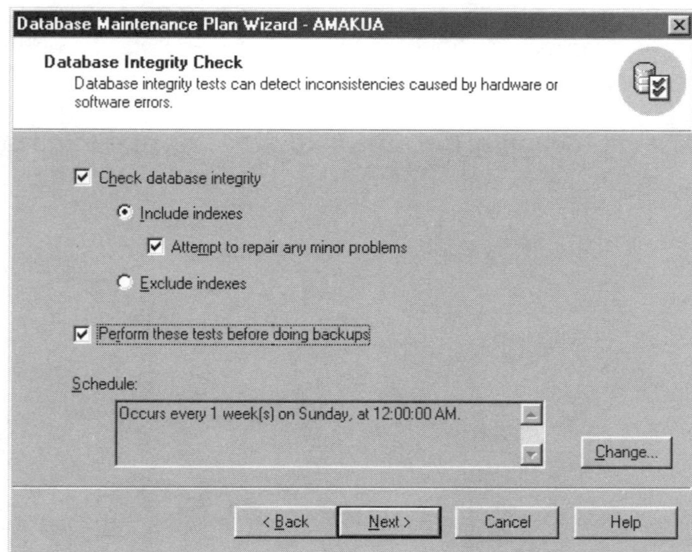

7.  Specify backup frequency. (The following figure says every week, but we recommend <u>daily</u>.) Clicking on the Change button will allow you to set a different schedule for database backups.

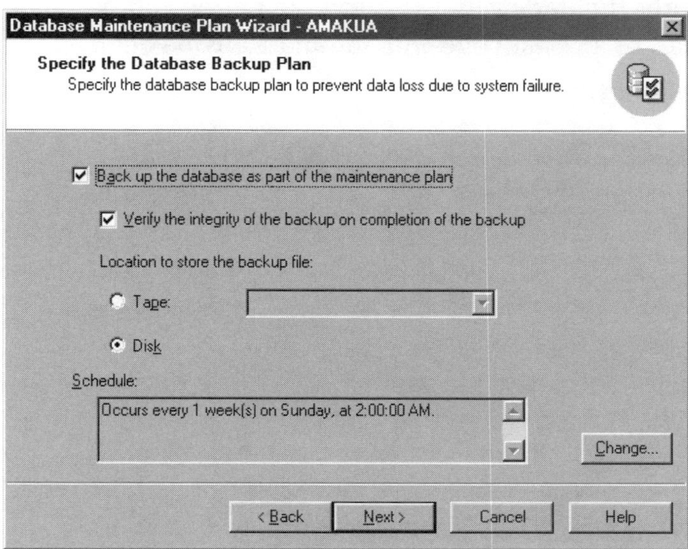

8.  Click **Next**. This screen allows you to determine how the backups will be stored on disk. By default, SQL Server will place all backup files in its own backup directory. This can be changed if necessary by changing the Use this directory option and entering a new location in the box.

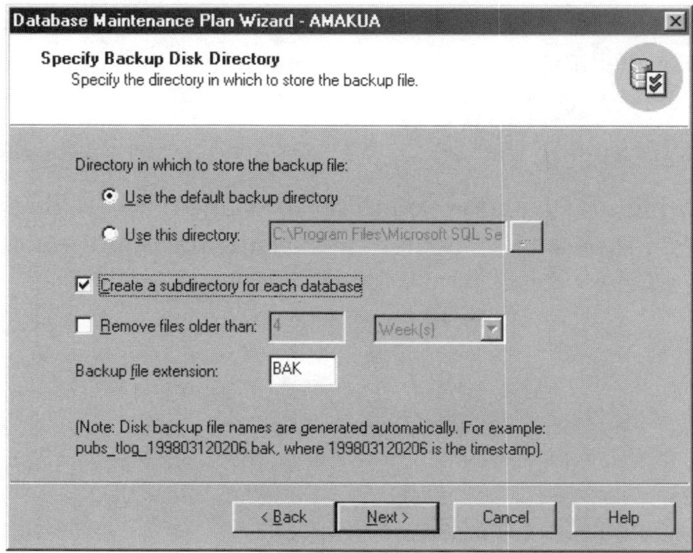

If the Create a subdirectory for each database option is checked, SQL Server will separate backups for different databases by automatically putting the files in separate directories. If you don't want to keep the backups permanently, the Remove files older than option can be changed so that backup files of a certain age will automatically be deleted.

9.   Click **Next**.

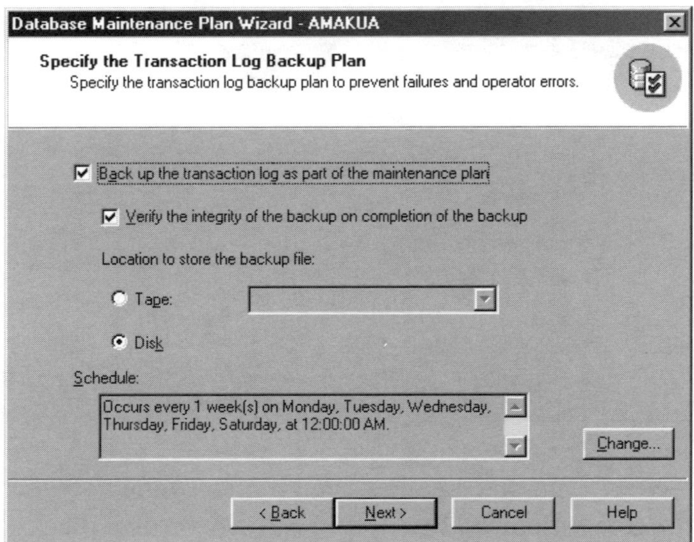

We recommend backing up the transaction log as well; remember, this cleans out the log and keeps its size manageable. Most of the options for transaction log backups are the same as database backups, but they may need to be scheduled more frequently and must work in conjunction with a full database backup.

10.   Click **Next**.

The following screen allows you to set the same types of file options for a transaction log backup as a database backup. Make sure your target directory has sufficient space before you decide to use it.

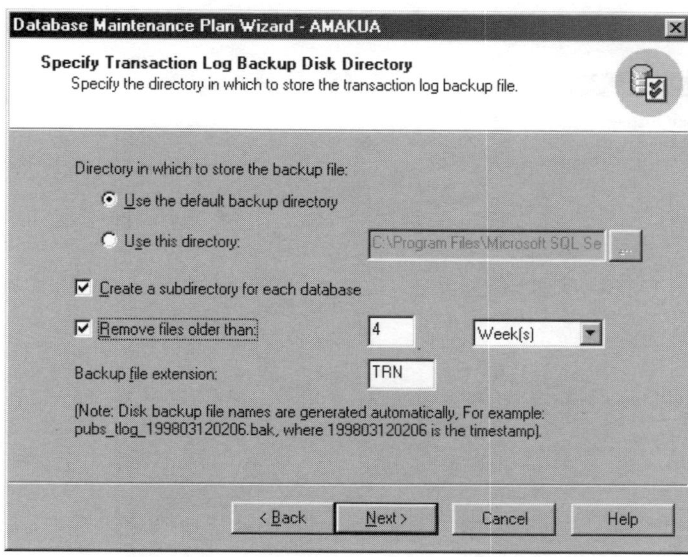

11.  Click **Next**.

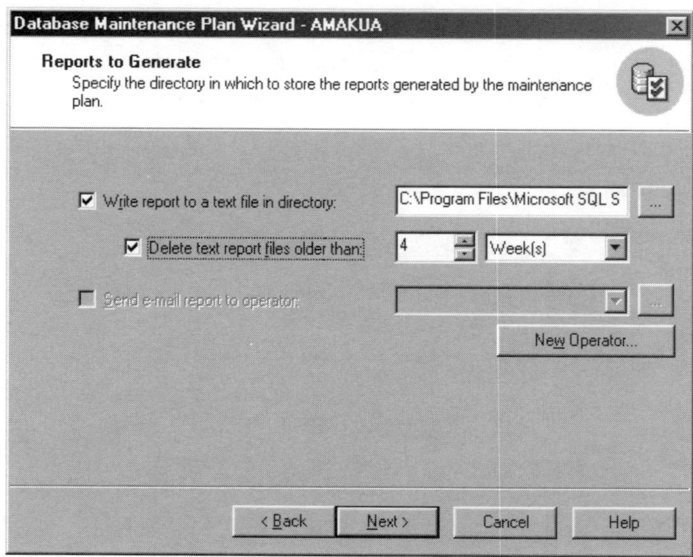

You do want reports written, to either a text file or HTML, depending on where it will be easiest for you to check it.

12. Click **Next**.

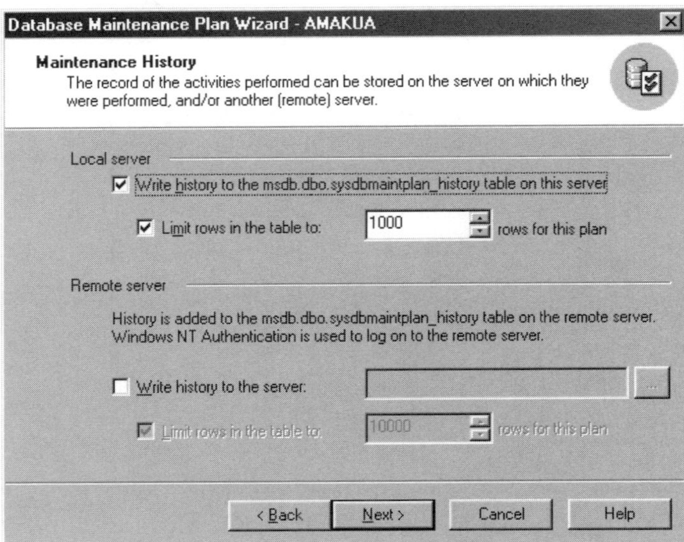

The plan records its actions in a database table. If the table is stored on a different server, you should specify the remote server on which the history will be stored, otherwise choose the default and store the history in its own server.

13. Click **Next**.

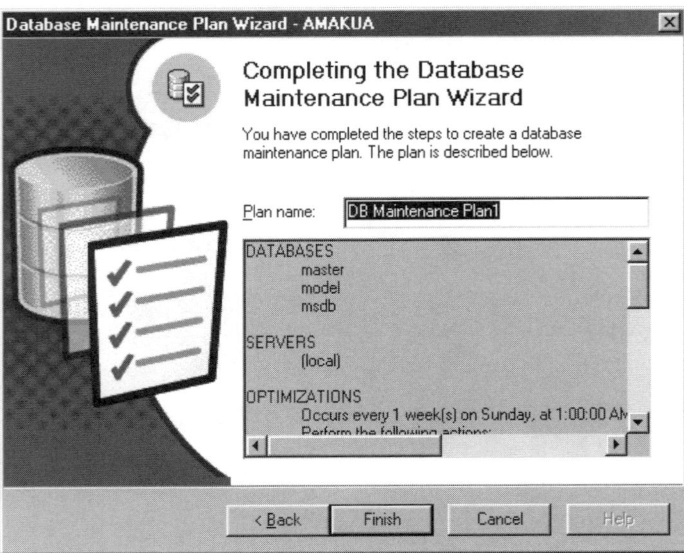

Here you can name your plan.

14.   Click **Finish** to display your plan in the Enterprise Manager window.

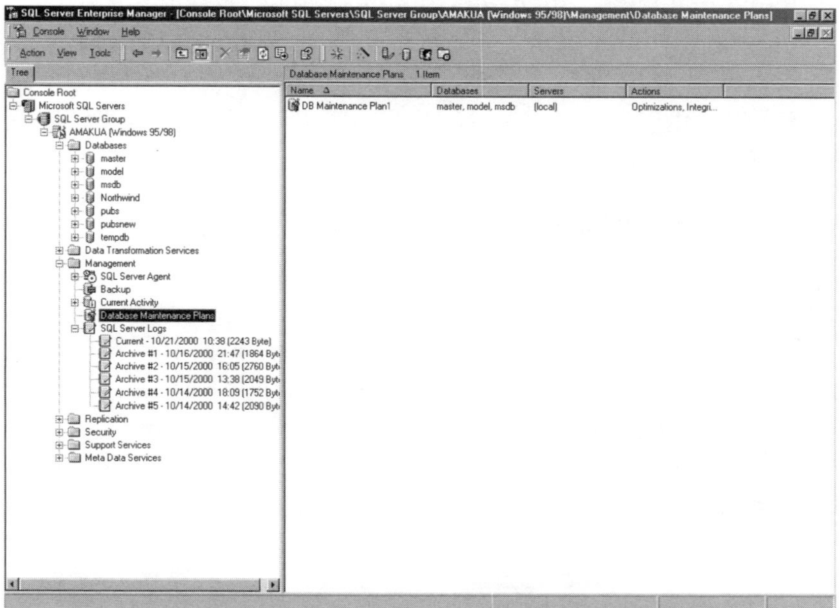

> **Note:** If it looks like your plan is not running, make sure the Agent is running; this is a requirement for the plans to execute. (The SQL Server Agent is an NT process and is described in Chapter 13.)

## Table-level Maintenance

Tables are what contain data in a relational database. When you add a customer to your database, you are actually inserting a row (instance) of data into a table. (You would be amazed at the percentage of databases that have a table named Customer!)

In addition to the tables themselves, the tables usually have other objects that are assigned to them called *indexes*. The purpose of an index is to improve performance of your database. If, for example, you have a million rows in a table, and you want to retrieve one of them, it is not efficient to read all the rows of the table in order to get the row you are looking for. The index dramatically reduces the number of page requests it takes to find the row you want.

## Monitor Growth Changes

If you know enough about your data to understand the growth of the individual tables, then you should keep an eye on the growth rates of these individual tables. If not, it may be good enough for you to track the overall database size instead. Sudden growth or shrinkage merits investigation. Also, if any of your tables are especially volatile, keep a close eye on them.

## Update Statistics

Microsoft SQL Server has a cost-based optimizer. The optimizer itself is the part of the DBMS which determines the approach the server will use to retrieve your data. *Cost-based* means that the server determines at query time how it will try to retrieve the information you request. In order for the server to estimate which indexes to use, it looks at a *statistics page*. The statistics page contains information that describes to the Microsoft SQL Server how those data are distributed so that it can appropriately match an index to a query. Stated another way, if your statistics are up to date, the optimizer is much more likely to pick the best plan for your query, and you will get your results back faster.

Here's the good news: The updating of statistics is now automatic and happens over the course of the utilization of the table; this feature was introduced in Microsoft SQL Server 7.0. If your system is older than version 7.0, you will have to update statistics manually and regularly (as often as weekly or daily!). Even though updating statistics over time is automatic, you may need to perform this task manually anyway, as the index's distribution skews ahead of the automatic update process (the distribution may change faster than the automatic update process can keep up). Also, after your initial data load, you may want to update the statistics to give the optimizer a head start. You can update the statistics manually (but this is not something you necessarily need to do very often).

Open the Query Analyzer program:

1. Click the **Start** button.

2. Select **Microsoft SQL Server**.

3. Select **Query Analyzer**.

To execute the UPDATE STATISTICS command:

4.    Type the command in the query window.

5.    Click the **Execute** button (looks like a green Play button).

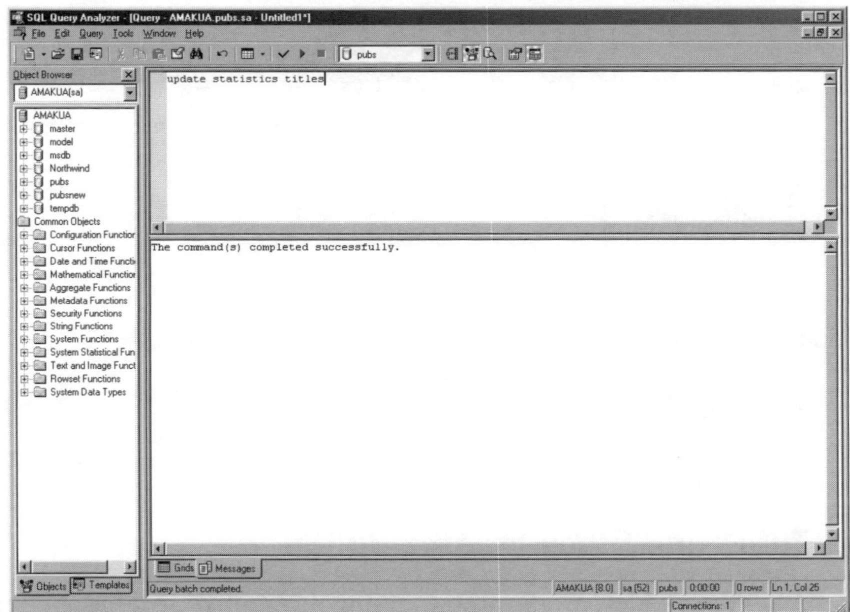

If you want to get a step ahead of your data, you can monitor data distribution changes using SP_STATISTICS, like this:

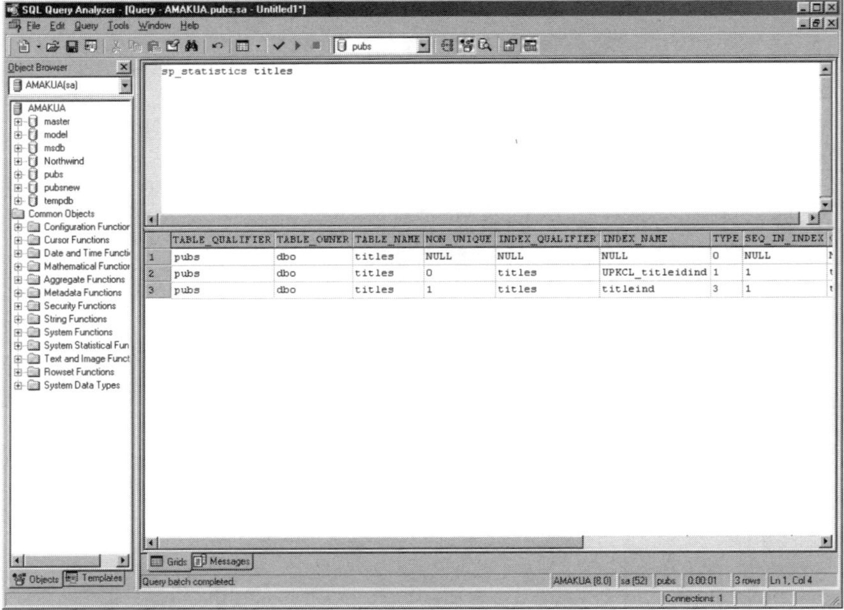

## Table and Index Fragmentation

As data is added to your table, removed from your table, updated, and moved around in your table, and index entries are rearranged accordingly, it is possible to get into a situation where your data is poorly organized in storage. More specifically, the pages (the basic physical storage units) that the data is stored on may become underutilized or spread out too far on the disk to be sequentially retrieved optimally. Said another way, sometimes you have to reorganize the way the data is stored on the disk. You can check the level of contiguity using the DBCC SHOWCONTIG function.

```
DBCC SHOWCONTIG scanning 'authors' table...
[SHOW_CONTIG - SCAN ANALYSIS]

Table: 'authors' (117575457) Indid: 1 dbid:5
TABLE level scan performed.
- Pages Scanned...............................: 2
- Extents Scanned............................: 2
- Extent Switches............................: 1
```

```
- Avg. Pages per Extent........................: 1.0
- Scan Density [Best Count:Actual Count].......: 50.00% [1:2]
- Logical Scan Fragmentation ..................: 0.00%
- Extent Scan Fragmentation ...................: 50.00%
- Avg. Bytes free per page.....................: 7051.0
- Avg. Page density (full).....................: 12.89%
(11 row(s) affected)
DBCC execution completed. If DBCC printed error messages, contact your
system administrator.
```

This tells you how full the pages are. A page contains 8,192 bytes. (Think of a byte as one character of information.) If your pages are under 50% utilized, you are probably wasting space, and should consider dropping and rebuilding your clustered indexes in order to clean up the data. (We will discuss how to do this in the following section.)

## Indexes

Indexes are the physical implementation of performance design for SQL Server tables. The index information is stored on pages just as data pages are, and can become fragmented in the same way that data pages do. If an index becomes fragmented, your only option is to drop it and rebuild it.

A shortcut to dropping and rebuilding all indexes for a table, as well as reorganizing the data for the table, is to drop and rebuild the clustered index on the table. Each table in a production database has at most one clustered index. In addition, each table in a production database should have a clustered index. In fact, if you have tables that do not have a clustered index, you should contact the person or organization responsible for the database design and ask for an explanation.

Prior to dropping the index, record the index type and column order. You will want this information when you re-create the index.

You can drop a clustered index like this:

1.   Right-click on a table in the Enterprise Manager.

2.   Select **All Tasks**.

3.   Select **Manage Indexes**.

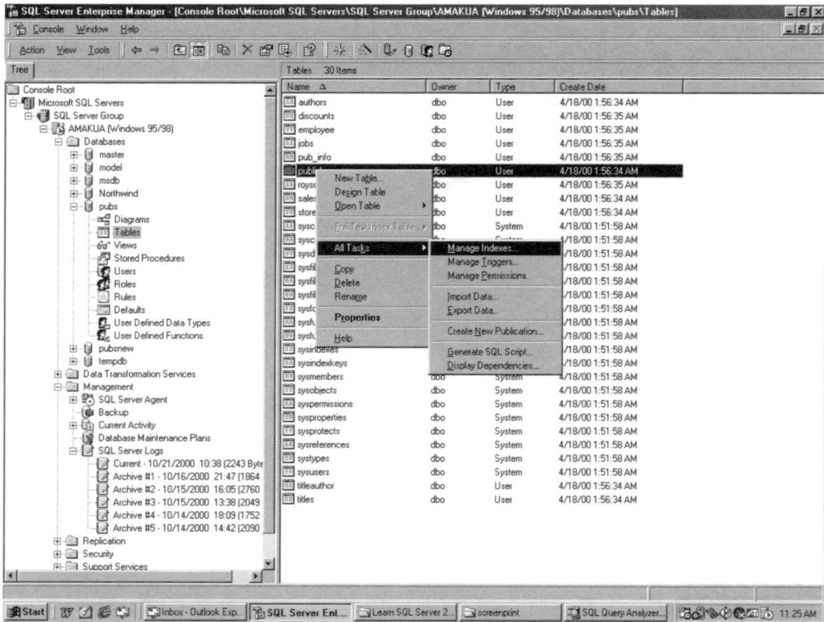

4. Click on the index to be deleted.

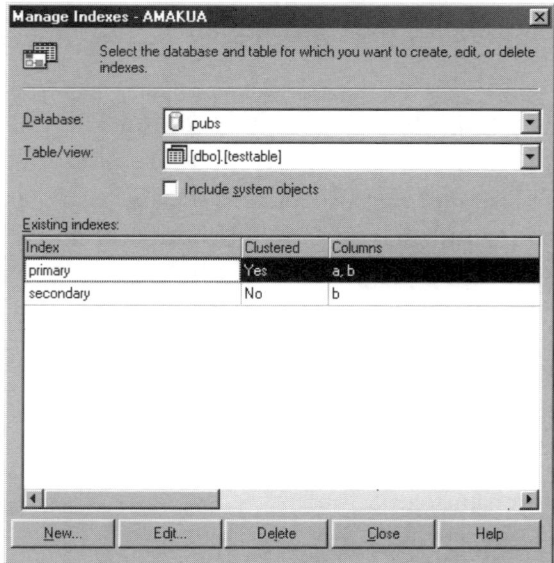

5. Click the **Delete** button.

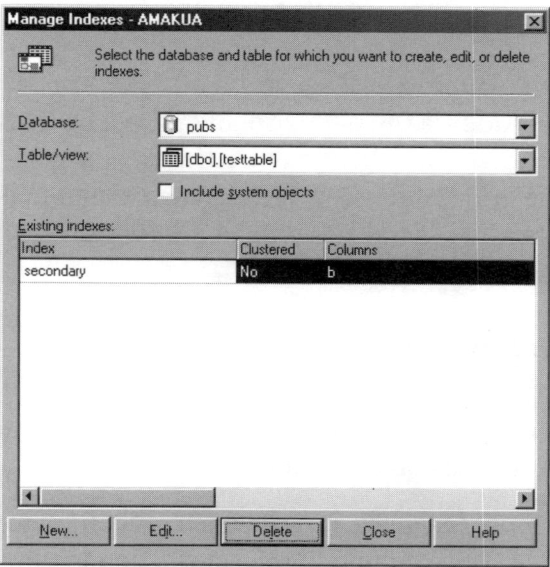

To create a new index:

1.  Click the **New** button in the Manage Indexes dialog.

2.  Type a unique name for the index in the Index name box.

3.  Check the columns to be indexed and check the Clustered index option if desired.

4.  Click **OK**.

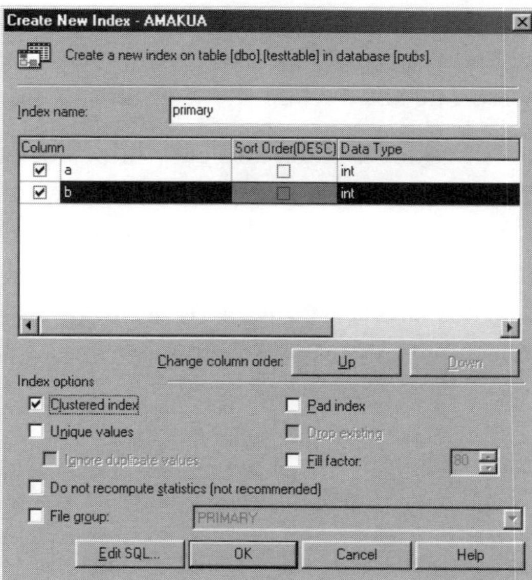

### Index Tuning Wizard

This wizard allows the Enterprise Manager to analyze your databases to determine from what indexes the database might benefit. This is based on allowing SQL Server to analyze the database and the usage of the database. With this information, the Index Tuning Wizard will make recommendations about what indexes will be necessary.

# Alerts, Jobs, and Operators

If you would like to get proactive about maintaining your system, you can do so by defining alerts, jobs, and operators.

An *alert* is an event on the SQL Server for which an automated response (job) may be triggered. For example, if the transaction log fills up, you may want to empty it and send an e-mail to yourself so that you are aware that it happened.

A *job* is the task we perform when an alert event occurs. Job steps can be:

- Executable programs
- Operating system (usually Windows NT) commands
- Transact-SQL statements
- Active scripts

An *operator* is an individual responsible for the maintenance of the SQL Server(s), and is the person notified when the job runs.

The Enterprise Manager provides a quick and easy interface to define alerts so when a specific error occurs the appropriate operator is notified of the problem. That way many errors can be prevented from escalating into disasters. This same interface will also be able to react to an alert by executing a job. This may often resolve the error before the operator gets the message. For more complete information on alerts, jobs, and operators, see Chapter 13.

# Your Maintenance Checklist

This is a recommended task list, and will serve the maintenance purposes of most installations. You should take a look at this list within the scope of your own application(s), and look at the documentation for your own product as well as the business requirements of your organization to decide whether this specific schedule works for you.

### One-time only:

- Store your memory configuration parameters someplace permanent.
- Devise and test your disaster recovery scheme.

### On-demand:

- Update the table statistics if/when the situation warrants.
- Predefine auto-grow/auto-shrink for your databases.

### Daily:

- Check the server activity log.
- Back up your database and transaction logs.
- Get the backups off-site.
- Run the preventive maintenance DBCC list. (This is a good thing to run overnight or when a low volume of processing is occurring.)

### Weekly:

- Check space utilization of your databases to make sure that the growth you are getting is the growth you expect. Also, verify that the amount of free space is what you expect.
- Store current table information (like the number of rows in each table) so that you can track growth.
- Check/correct table and index fragmentation.

## As often as you are able:

- Periodically, shut down and restart the server. It doesn't matter too much if this is daily, weekly, or monthly, but it is important to not only shut down the SQL Server, but also to shut down and restart the physical server. This is primarily to clean up memory.

# Chapter 3

# Configuration Values

Configuration options exist to allow you to tune Microsoft SQL Server 2000's performance by changing memory or I/O (physical input/output) settings. With newer releases, more and more experienced production DBAs are simply installing the server and letting it reconfigure itself (Microsoft SQL Server 2000 is self-tuning). There are a few configuration options that you may want to understand, on the chance that you want to second-guess the server. However, it is highly recommended that the default settings be retained, so that the server may tune itself. We categorize the configuration parameters as server, memory, or operating system (usually Windows NT) specific.

## Server Configuration Options

We have a host of configuration options available to the server. To see what is configurable, right-click on the server in Enterprise Manager, and select Properties:

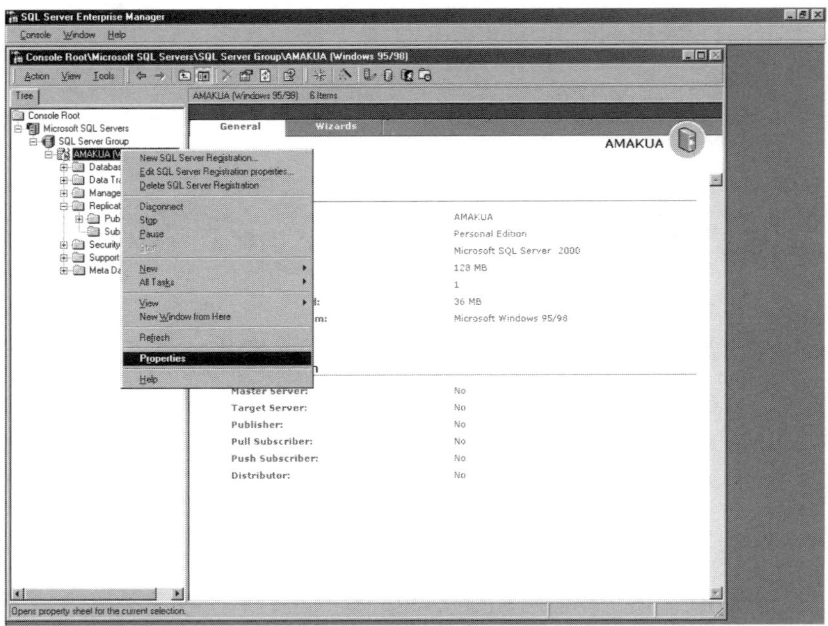

That will bring up this window:

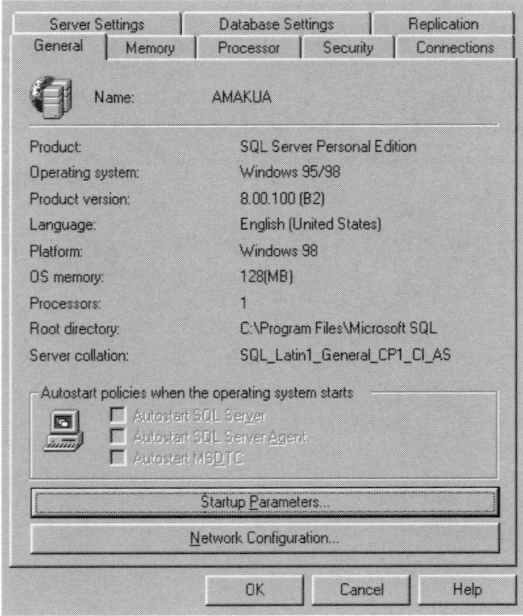

This General tab mostly repeats information you've seen on the previous screen, but it also gives you access to two more features: startup parameters and network configuration.

Startup parameters gives you the ability to control server-wide behavior at startup time. Microsoft Technical Support may ask you to put something here to, for example, control deadlocking behavior (what happens when two processes contend for the same resources and conflict).

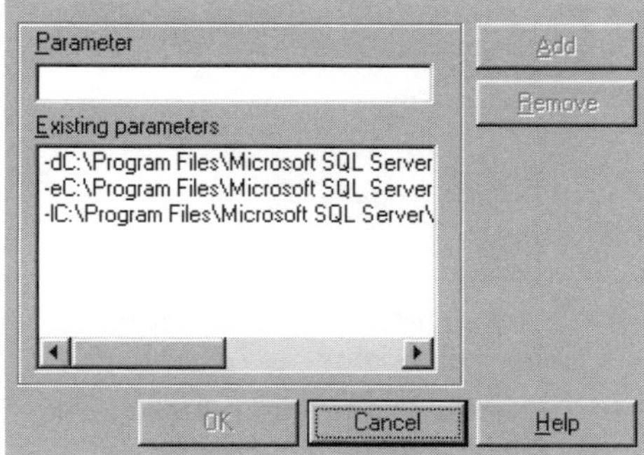

Leave all the network settings alone; these are for somebody who has read a book much thicker than this one on network services.

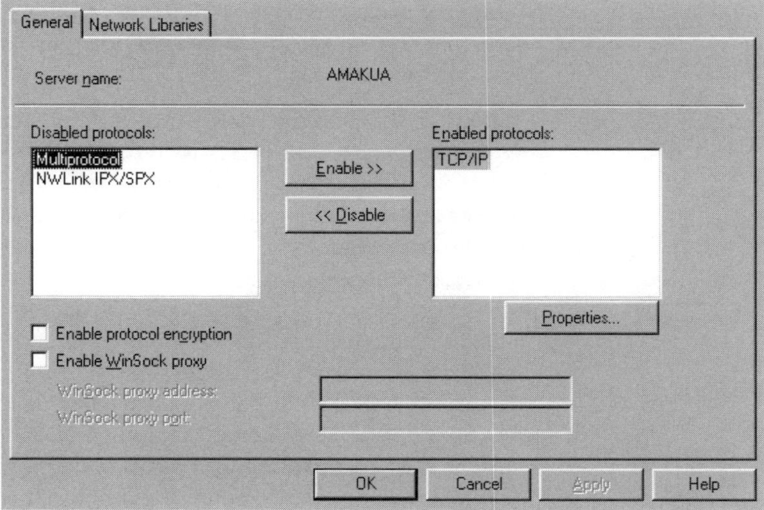

# Memory Configuration Options

The memory manager component of SQL Server allows self-configuration of memory for SQL Server. When SQL Server starts, it determines how much memory it may allocate based on how much memory the operating system and other applications are currently using. Note that this implies that the more you are running on that (presumably NT or Windows 2000) server, the fewer resources are available for Microsoft SQL Server 2000. As the load on the computer and SQL Server changes, so does the allocated memory.

The following memory configuration options are available for tuning:

| | |
|---|---|
| Min server memory | This memory option requires the server to start with this minimum amount of memory, as opposed to the default that allows the server to start with all available memory. It can be set to a specific value based on the amount of physical memory and level of activity on your SQL Server. Make sure that this minimum memory is set low enough that it does not suck all available memory from other OS level tasks, as that may also negatively affect Microsoft SQL Server performance. The default setting for min server memory is 0. We recommend the automatic setting, which will always allow NT to operate with as little paging as possible. |
| Max server memory | This option specifies the maximum amount of memory SQL Server can allocate when it starts and while it runs. It can be set to a specific value if you know there are multiple applications running at the same time as SQL Server and you want to ensure that these applications have sufficient memory to run. If the other applications request memory only as needed, then do not set this server configuration option, because SQL Server will release memory to them as needed. Remember that applications often use whatever memory is available when they start and do not request more if needed. If an application that behaves this way runs on the same computer as Microsoft SQL Server at the same time as SQL Server, set the max server memory server configuration option to a value that guarantees that the memory the application needs is not set aside for SQL Server. |
| | The default setting for max server memory is 2147483647. The minimum amount of memory you can specify for max server memory is 4 MB. |

You must set the max server memory option manually if you are running the full-text search (also called MSSearch) to ensure that the server leaves enough memory for the MSSearch service to run. It must be adjusted in conjunction with the Windows NT virtual memory size to ensure that the virtual memory remaining for full-text search is 1.5 times the physical memory (exclude the virtual memory requirements of the other services on the computer).

Try this formula:

Total virtual memory – (SQL Server maximum virtual memory + virtual memory requirements of other services) must be greater than or equal to 1.5 times the physical memory.

**Max worker threads**

Threads are operating system specific processes that enable parallel processing and multi-tasking. This configuration option can be used to specify the number of threads used to support the processes that will be run by users connected to SQL Server. The default setting of 255 can be slightly high for some configurations, depending on the number of concurrent users. Because each worker thread is preallocated, even if it is not being used, memory resources that might be better utilized by other operations, such as the buffer cache, can be unused. Generally, this configuration value should be set to the number of expected concurrent connections. The maximum value for max worker threads is 1024. Finally, note that this parameter has no effect when SQL Server is running on Windows 95/98.

**Index create memory**

This option controls the amount of memory used by sort operations during index creation. Creating an index on a production system is usually an infrequently performed task, often scheduled as a job to execute during off-peak time. While increasing this number can improve the performance of index creation, if you are not creating indexes, this is a waste of resources. We recommend you keep the min memory per query configuration option at the default, however, so the index creation job will still start even if all the requested memory is not available.

| | |
|---|---|
| Min memory per query | This configuration option can be used to specify the minimum amount of memory that will be allocated for the execution of any specific query. When many queries are executing concurrently in a system, increasing the value of this parameter can help improve the performance of memory-intensive queries. Do not set the min memory per query server configuration option too high, especially on very busy systems, because the query will have to wait until it can grab the minimum memory requested. If more memory is available than the specified minimum value required to run the query, the query may make use of the additional memory, provided that the additional memory will be used effectively by the query. |

You should not set the min server memory and max server memory configuration options to the same value. This would make the amount of memory allocated to SQL Server permanent. Dynamic memory allocation gives you the best overall performance.

You set these options as follows:

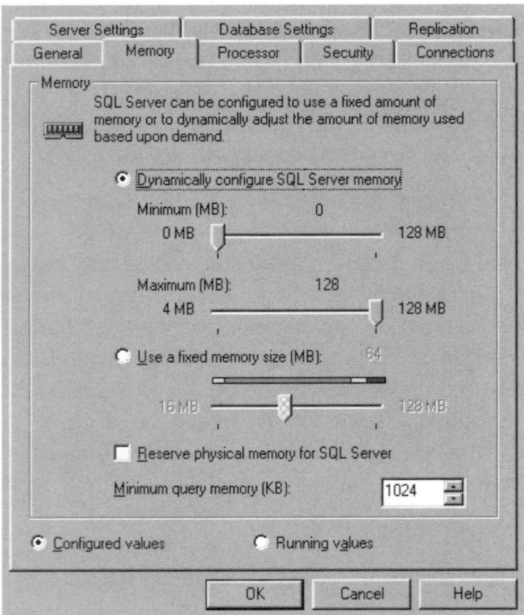

> **Note:** The radio button at the bottom identifies configured vs. running values. Memory parameter changes require shutting down and restarting the server, so this gives you the option of viewing either the settings the server is currently running with or those you have changed it to, and which will take effect on the next startup.

## Processor Options Tab

We recommend checking the Boost SQL Server priority check box, as well as the Use all available processors radio button on multi-processor boxes.

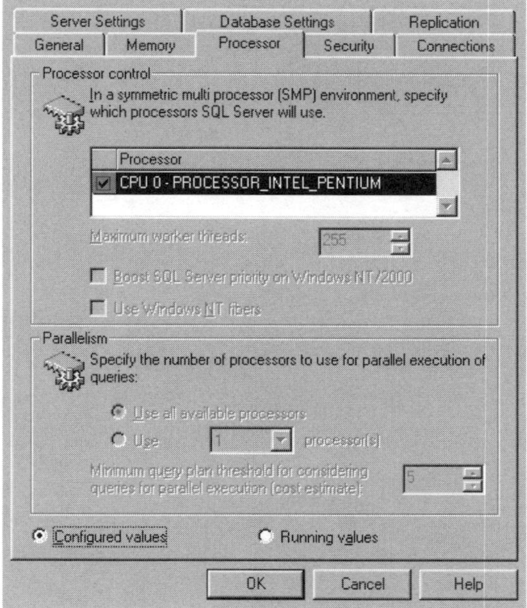


## Security Tab

Your authentication level was chosen at installation time. You should leave this alone unless your software vendor needs a different security scenario. Auditing is a way of identifying who is doing what on your system and will hinder performance a bit if enabled on a busy system.

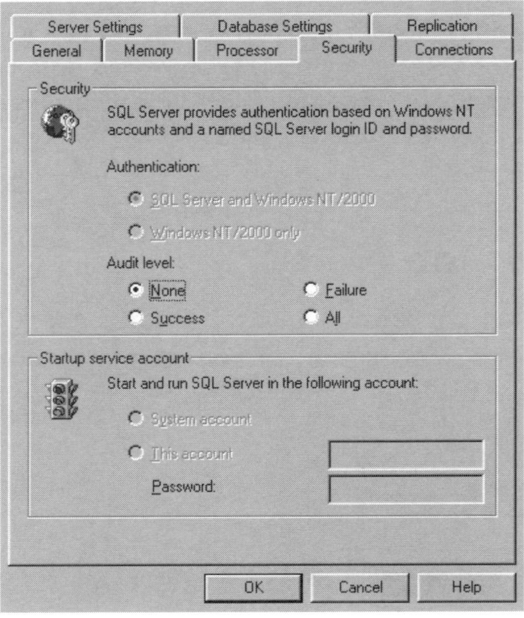

## Connections Tab

The Connections tab controls the behavior of the processes running on your system. This can occasionally be used to avoid arithmetic aborts, etc., but in general, this is another good tab to leave alone as it will affect the way your system processes queries.

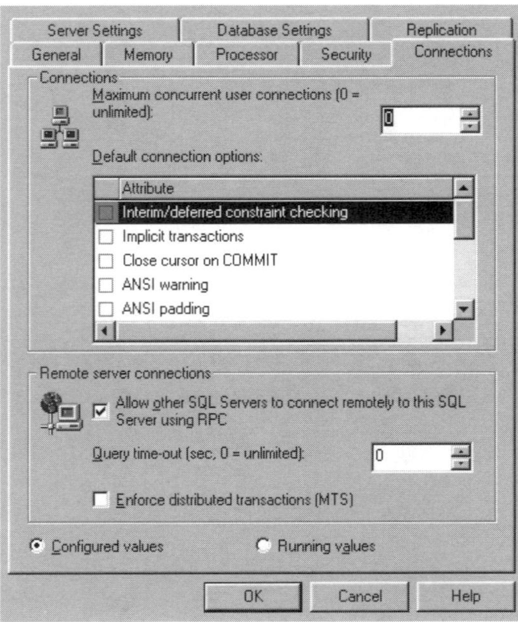

## Server Settings Tab

There are a few interesting options on this screen. The first is the Use query governor check box. It sets a time limit as to how long queries are allowed to run. If you have a user who is running queries that are running a long time and taking up large amounts of server resources, you can set this to a finite number of seconds and have that query terminate (it will abort) when it exceeds the permitted time. Note that the default (zero) removes any limit. The Year 2000 support option controls the treatment of the century rollover issue. For instance, if you store or query 1/1/00, is that January 1, 1900, or January 1, 2000?

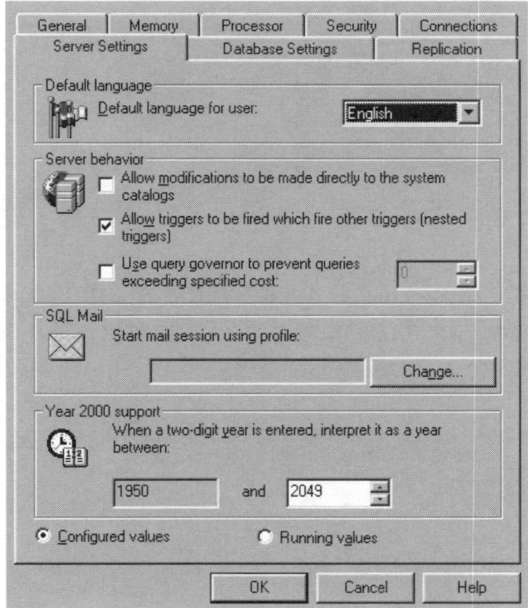

## Database Settings Tab

This is the server-wide default for intra-database processing behavior. Leave these at the defaults unless otherwise requested by your software vendor.

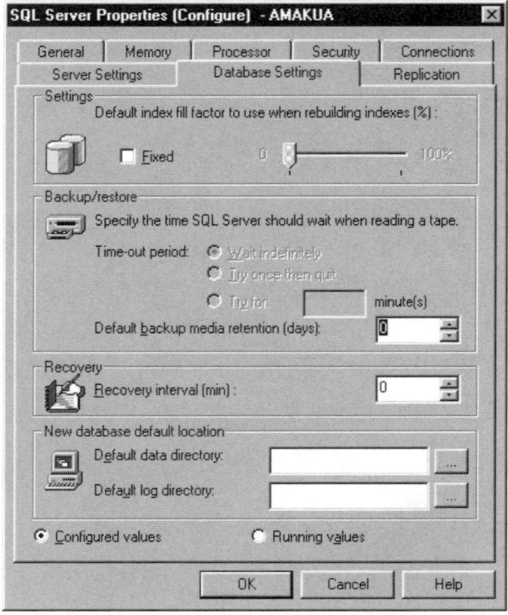

## Replication Tab

This is where you would configure replication if you are using it. Replication is the automatic transfer of data to or from another SQL Server. (See Appendix D for more information.)

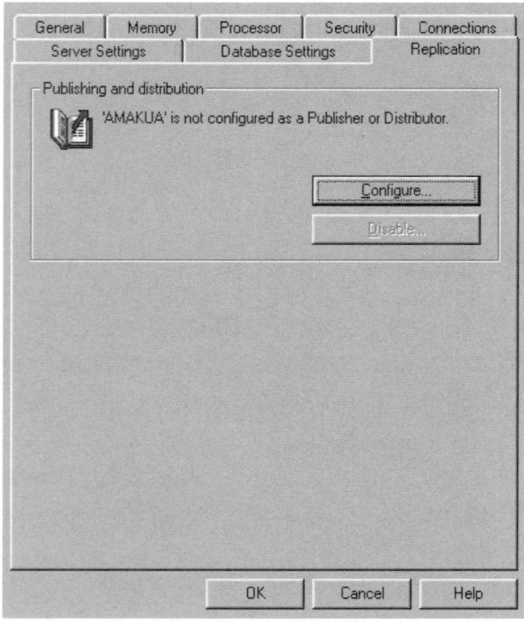

# Configuring Server Performance Using Windows NT Options

You can set Windows NT options on the server to maximize throughput or to configure server tasking or virtual memory.

## Maximize Throughput

When you install Microsoft SQL Server 2000, SQL Server setup automatically configures Microsoft Windows NT to maximize throughput for network applications. (Note that the network is a very likely bottleneck in a high-volume environment.) This helps the server accommodate more connections. Maximizing throughput for network applications is recommended for Microsoft SQL Server, but you can change this setting if you know enough about your NT server. As this is not recommended, it is beyond the scope of this book.

Note that if your application makes use of the full-text search feature (this is an enhanced ability to search for character strings quickly in a database), the Windows NT Server configuration must be set for maximizing throughput for network applications and must not be changed.

**Note:** The Windows NT Server configuration setting does not apply to computers running Windows NT Workstation. For more information, see your Windows NT documentation.

## Configure Server Tasking

If you plan to connect to SQL Server from a local client (the same computer as the server), you can improve processing time by setting up the server to run foreground and background applications with equal priority. SQL Server, which runs as a background application, then runs at equal priority to other applications running in the foreground.

**Note:** If your application uses an ODBC client connection to the same system that the server is on, set the ODBC Server name to (local), which does not use the network layer and will save a little time.

This means that no program will become starved for resources at the expense of another, which is a good reason for running Microsoft SQL Server 2000 on its own physical server. Note that when you run SQL Server setup, server tasking is set to none (the SQL Server default), which gives foreground and background programs equal processor time. You can set the server tasking setting to maximum (the Microsoft Windows NT default), which gives foreground applications the most processor time, but this is not recommended. (Again, this is an NT-tunable task, is not recommended, and is beyond the scope of this book.)

## Configure Virtual Memory

Windows NT virtual memory size should be configured based on the programs (services) concurrently running on the specific computer. Microsoft documentation on this is mixed; in one place, it recommends that you set virtual memory on the server to 1.5 times the amount of physical memory installed in the computer. In another, it suggests that this value be set to the amount of physical memory plus 12 MB. This author recommends that you set this to a flat 512 MB. Above this number, it takes more time for the system to manage the paging file than it helps, and we have even seen it cause problems. So, if your system has more than 512 MB of RAM, set your paging file to 512 and be done with it.

Additionally, if you are using the full-text search feature and will be running the Microsoft Search Service so that you can do full-text indexing and querying, consider configuring the virtual memory size to 3 times the amount of physical memory installed in the computer, and the SQL Server max server memory server configuration option to 1.5 times the physical memory (half the virtual memory size setting).

If you get the following Windows NT error, it means that virtual memory is configured too low:

```
Your system is running low on virtual memory. Please close some
applications. You can then start the System option in the Control Panel
and choose the Virtual Memory button to create an additional paging
file or increase the size of your current paging file.
```

**Note:** This can also be caused by using a program that was written for a
16-bit operating system (that is, an older application), which is still limited
to the high memory location between 640 KB and 1 MB. Nothing can be
done about this. Also, there is a desktop pool registry entry that needs to be
increased from 256 KB to 1 MB.

The memory configuration parameters can be modified by right-clicking
on the appropriate server in the Enterprise Manager, then selecting
Properties.

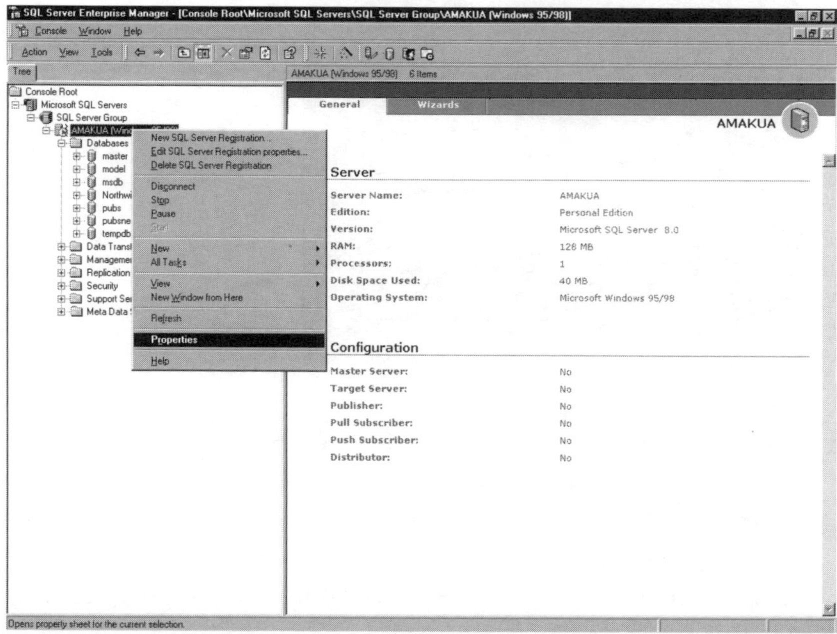

Click the Memory tab to display the memory configuration options.

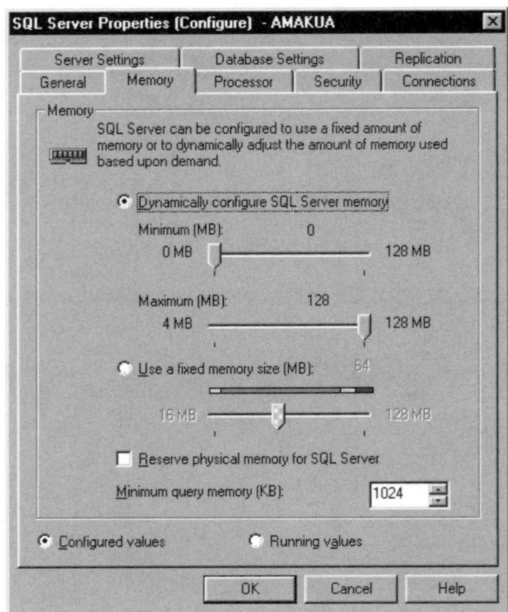


The maximum and minimum memory configuration options can be altered by dragging the appropriate bar. However, since memory is an autoconfiguring option, it is recommended that the defaults be kept. This means that SQL Server will dynamically configure memory. Remember, in the long run, we recommend that you do not change any of these options unless you are specifically required to by your application vendor.

# Chapter 4

# Activity Monitoring

Once a SQL Server is up and running, it is necessary to make sure that it is running well. The server should be operating at its best. While the SQL Server is pretty good at making sure it runs as efficiently as possible, there is one key factor that the SQL Server has minimal control over: how the users work with the databases. Since each user that connects to the server will require resources of some kind, it is necessary to keep an eye on how much the server is being used and when. Sometimes, these kinds of checks will illustrate that a server is running well and doesn't require much change. Other times, the server may be reaching the limits of its physical capabilities. In this case, an upgrade may be required for the server.

## Monitoring Tools

SQL Server provides tools for monitoring the activity on the server. They include the SQL Enterprise Manager and NT Performance Monitor.

### SQL Enterprise Manager

The SQL Enterprise Manager provides a quick and easy way to monitor the usage of the database server. It allows for the checking of the current activity of the system. Over time, this will allow an administrator to determine what is normal and what is abnormal usage of the server at any given time. For instance, an administrator may be aware that there are 100 people that access the server and during the late afternoon up to half of them may be connected to the server at once. This implies that having around 50 people connected to the server is a normal occurrence. However, if 200 connections were simultaneously made to the server, maybe suspicion is warranted.

Aside from just determining how many connections have been made to the SQL Server, information can also be obtained about what tasks those connections are performing. This can include what type of command was run, when the connection logged in, and when they executed their last commands. Also vital is the determination of whether one connection is blocking the work of another connection.

To check for existing processes on the SQL Server:

1.  In Enterprise Manager, expand the **Management** folder.

2.  Expand the **Current Activity** folder.

3.  Select **Process Info**.

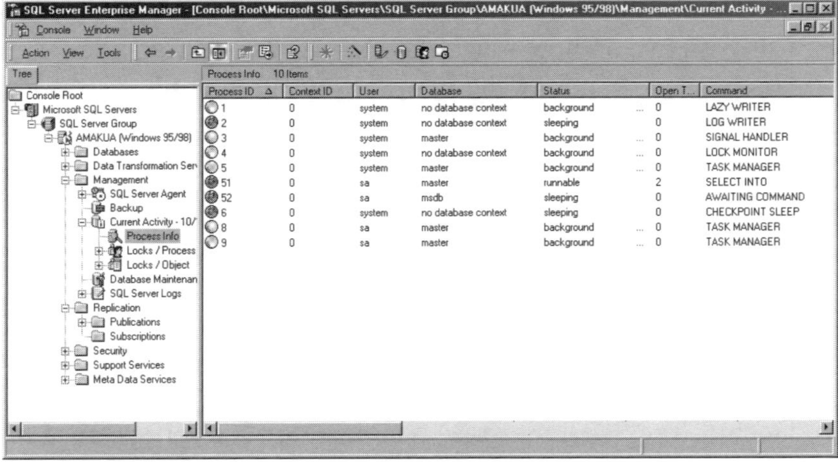

Note that each connection has a *spid*. The spid that you see here is the system process ID. This system process ID distinguishes one connection from another. The Blocked By column determines the connection that is preventing a task from completing. The Blocking column indicates the process being blocked by the current one.

Each one of the processes can also hold locks. When information is being read or written, a lock is held on the data. Depending on the kind of lock, this may allow only one user to be able to work with a specific piece of information. Or it may allow everyone to be able to read the same piece of information. Often locks are used to prevent two or more people from changing the exact same piece of information at the exact same time. Locks can also have different sizes. Some can be as large as a database, while others may only be as large as a single row of information. The type of lock is determined by the type of command executed. The size of the lock is determined by the SQL Server.

Locks can be viewed by expanding the Locks/Process ID folder or the Locks/Object folder under Current Activity. A list of the different locks owned by a particular process is provided:

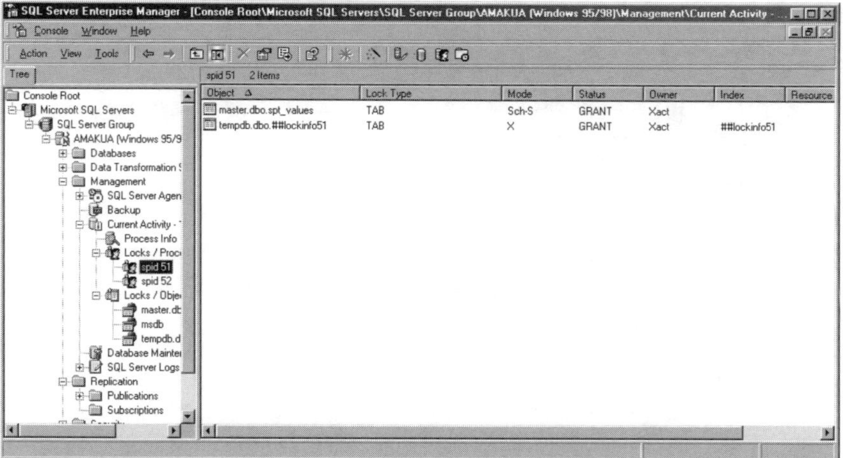

or a list of locks presently held on a particular object:

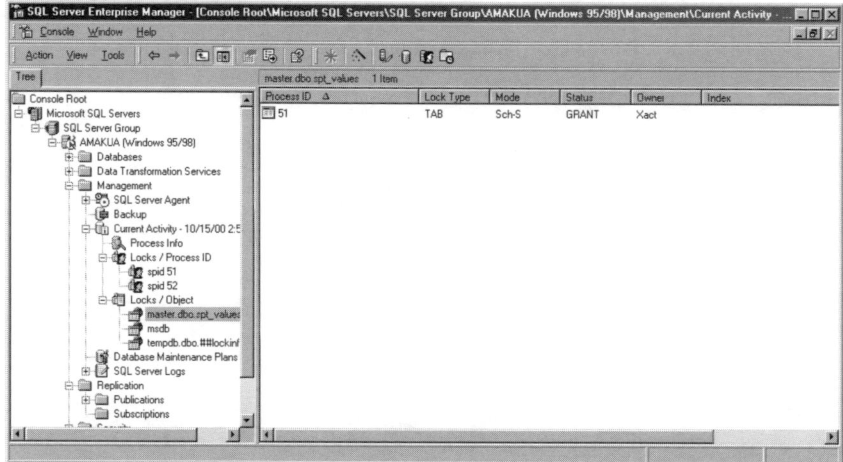

Sometimes if a process is blocking another, the system may seem to pause. This is normal. Often SQL Server will not allow newer users to work with data until the present user is done working with it. However, if the task is critical or if the original task is not running correctly, tasks can be killed to make way for other tasks.

To find blocking processes:

1.    Expand the **Management** folder.

2.    Expand the **Current Activity** folder.

3.    Expand the **Locks/Process ID** folder.

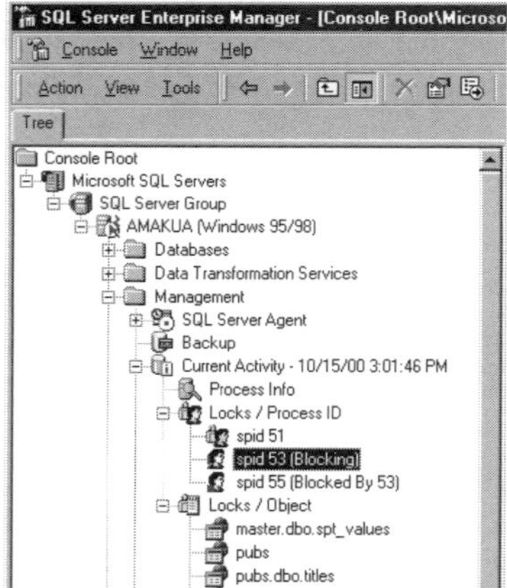

Note that spid 53 is labeled as Blocking and spid 55 is the process waiting for 53 to complete.

To eliminate blocking processes:

1.    Select **Process Info**.

2.    Select the blocking process (in this case spid 53).

3.    Click **Action,** then **Properties** on the menu bar. You will see this screen:

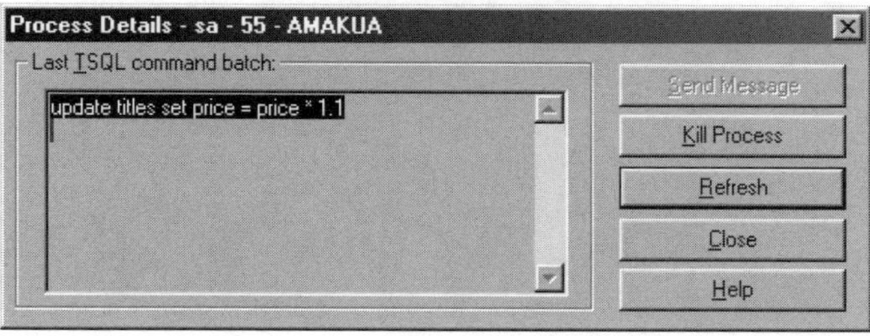

4.    Select **Kill Process**.

5.    You will see this screen:

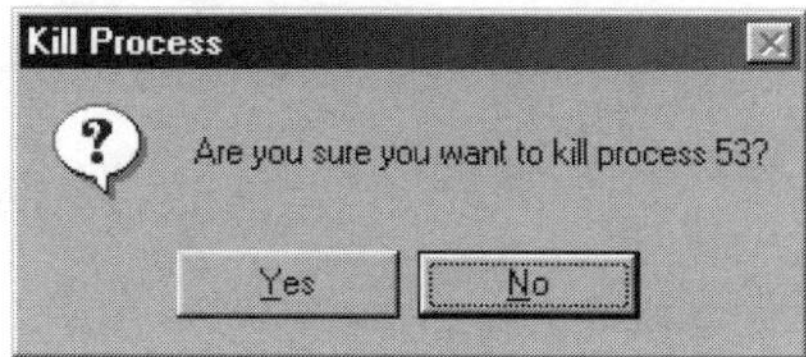


Click **Yes** to eliminate the process.

**Note:** Killing processes is a very dangerous business. The changes made by the removed processes can be lost. Sometimes the processes cannot be killed without shutting down and restarting the server. Do this only when absolutely necessary.

## NT Performance Monitor

Another way to monitor performance of the SQL Server is to monitor its performance on the NT Performance Monitor (NT systems only). The NT Performance Monitor is a tool provided by Windows NT and has connections to the SQL Server to monitor its performance. It produces a constant line graph that measures rises and drops in the server's activity.

To access the NT Performance Monitor:

1.    Click the **Start** button.

2.    Select **Programs**.

3.    Select **MS SQL Server**.

4.    Select **Performance Monitor**.

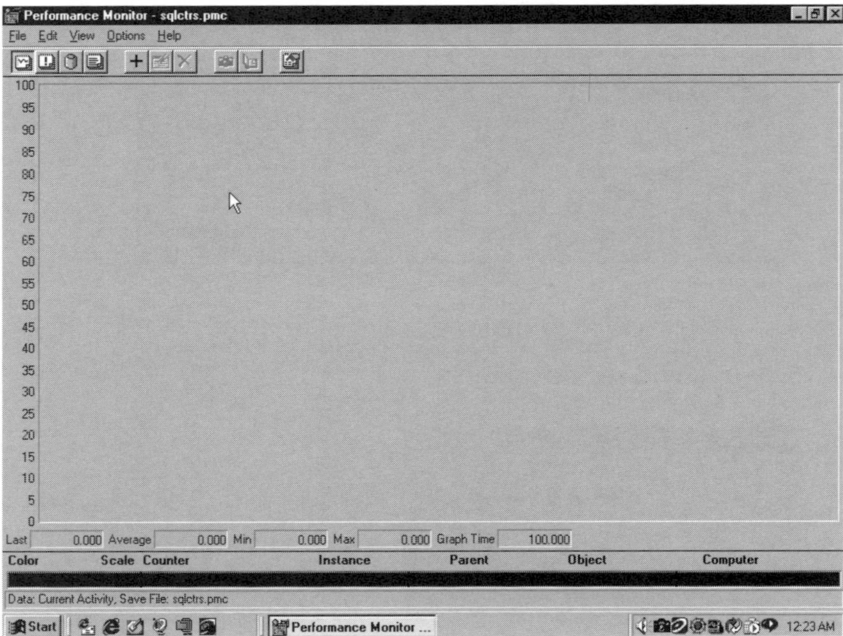

To add a counter:

1. Click the plus sign (+) on the toolbar.

2. Select a type of object from the Object box.

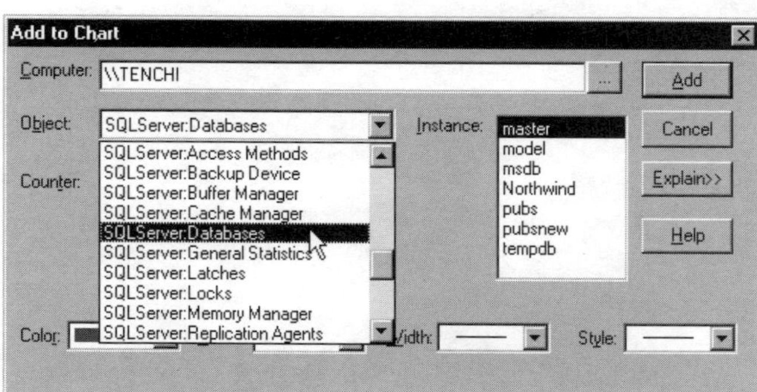

3. Select a counter from the Counter box.

4. Select a particular database for the counter to track.

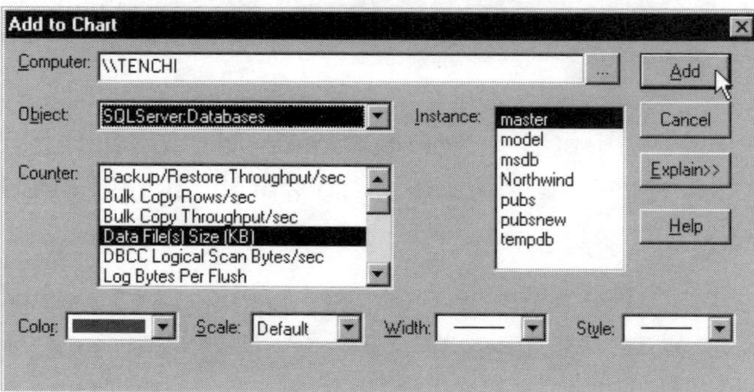

5. Click **Add** to add the graph.

6. Click **Done** when finished.

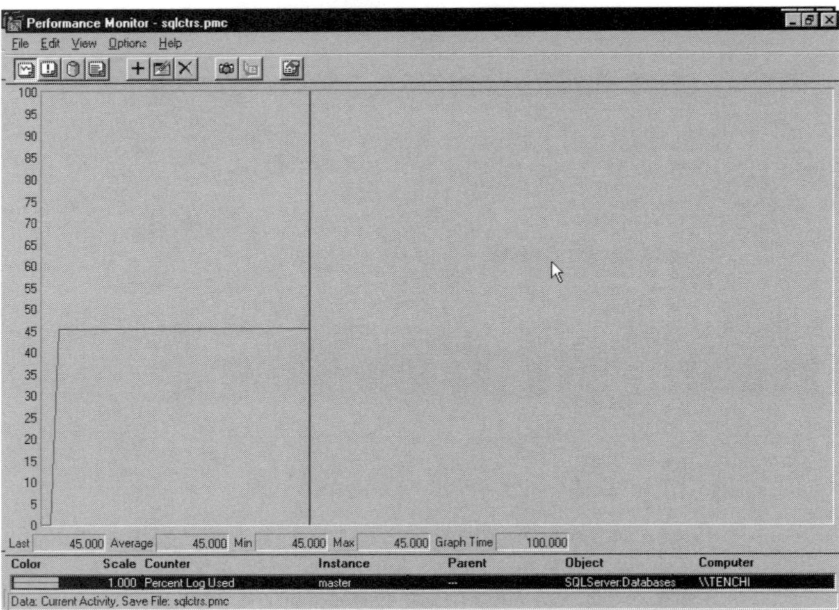

This graph will now display the percentage of the log that is full for the database. As the percentage increases, so will the height of the line in the graph.

Note that this tool is an NT-based tool, so it is not used exclusively for SQL Server. There are counters available for the NT system as well as any other programs that may be installed.

In order to make sure the server is performing at its best, it is a good idea to watch and see how the server performs at different times during the day. This also includes watching the usage of the server. Keeping track of the number of users, what they are doing, and when they are doing it will help determine the normal performance level for your server. This will help identify when the usage is out of the norm as well as how resources are being used. Keeping track of these measurements will help determine when the server needs to be changed to meet changing needs.

# Chapter 5

# Monitoring Your Error Log

Each time you start SQL Server it creates a record of all server-level information. This is called the error log. You need to become familiar with this log as it contains vital information that will tell you how SQL Server is running. This error log tells you whether vital processes have been completed successfully. Some of these operations include backups, restore operations, batch commands, scripts, and other processes.

## Accessing the Error Log

You can open the error log through any script editor or through SQL Server Enterprise Manager. This is the easiest route for you to view your error log. You open the log by performing the following steps:

1.  Click the **Start** button and select **Programs|Microsoft SQL Server|Enterprise Manager**.

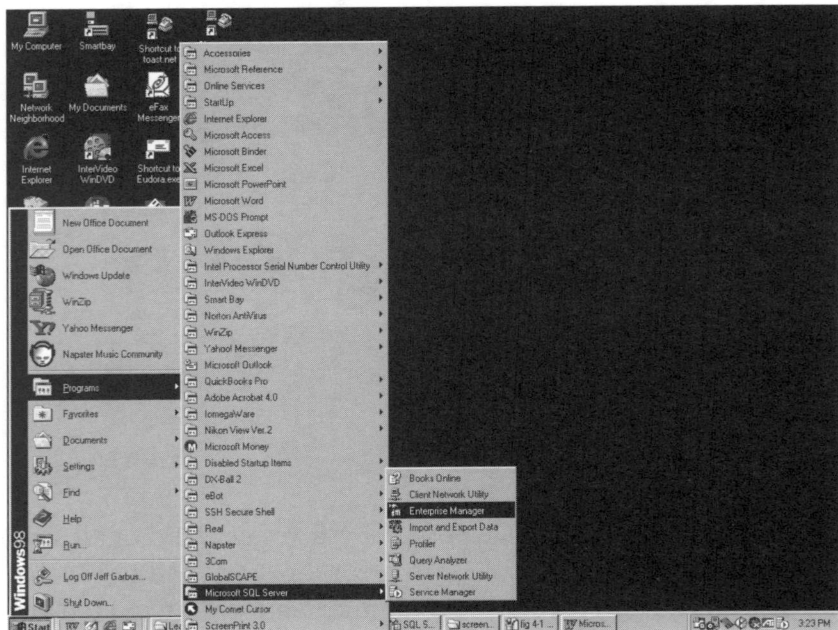

2. Select **Microsoft SQL Servers|SQL Server Group**. Choose the name of the server, then click on **SQL Server Logs**.

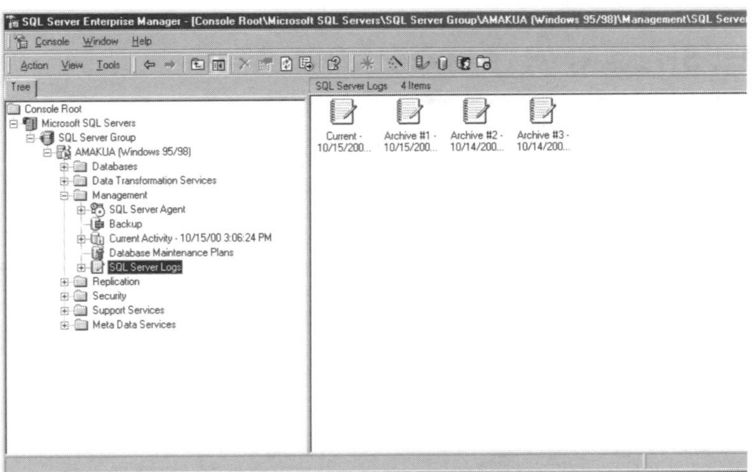

You will see icons to the right of the directory. The current log is the one that is running right now. The current log is started as soon as SQL Server is started. Each time SQL Server is stopped, the log is saved and becomes an archived log. SQL Server keeps six archived logs for you. It gives the most recent archived log a number 1 extension and the next archived log a number 2 extension. This continues with the succeeding logs. The current log has no numbered extension.

Click on the Current icon and look at the log. Try to familiarize yourself with the appearance and the language structure. (Please note this is a resizable window and you may have to stretch the window in order to read all of the information.)

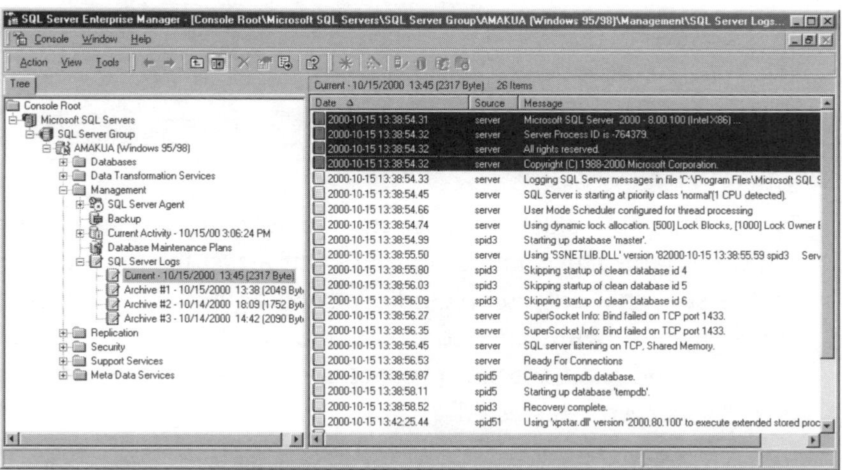

# Error Log Messages

The following are a few samples of items found in the error log that you should get used to reading and understanding what they mean to your system's running condition.

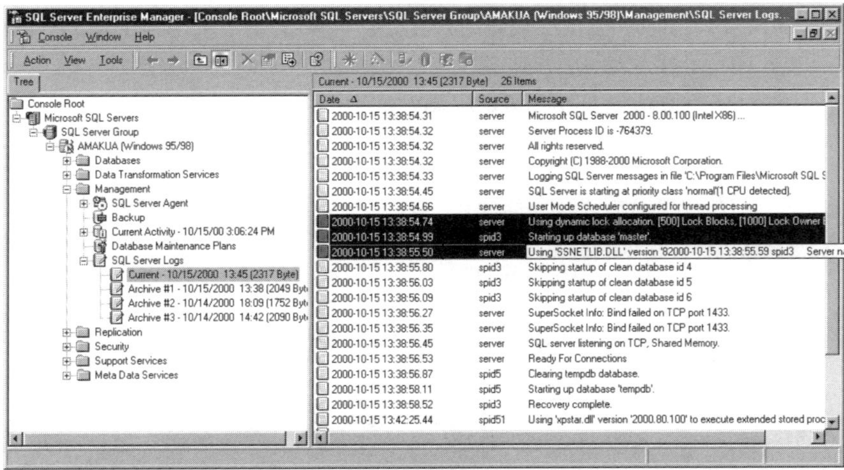

When the server starts, it takes time to synchronize the transaction log with the data. This sounds complex, but it just means that the server makes sure that any completed transaction in memory at the time the server went down is applied to the data on disk. This process is called recovery and is an automatic process that occurs on every database whenever the server is restarted.

There are some warnings that are necessary to see, but not to panic over. The "Skipping startup of clean database" message is an example of one of them. This warning just states that an autoexec procedure was skipped (see below) and has no major implications for the running of this SQL Server.

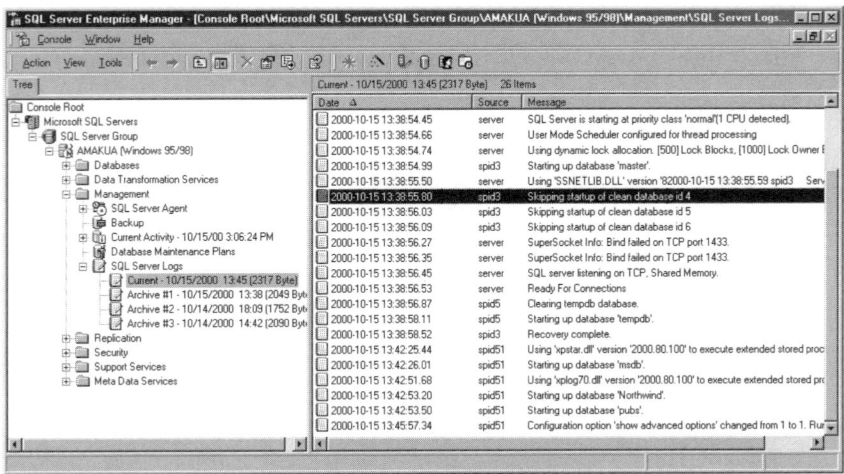

The "Recovery complete" message is an important message to look for. It means that the SQL Server was started and all startup procedures have been completed. This message gives you a level of comfort knowing that at this point in time your database system is running.

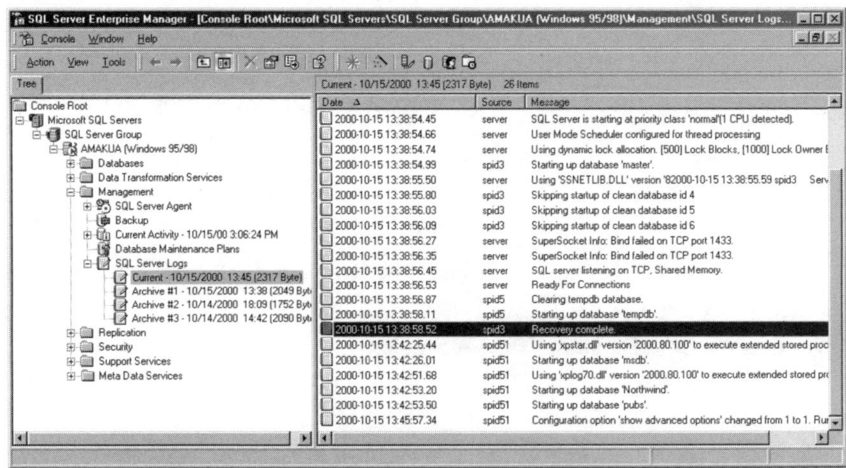

## Severity Level Error Messages

Severity level error messages provide a way of informing you as to the type and seriousness of the problem that your SQL Server has encountered. The following table lists the type and reason for each severity level.

| Severity Levels | Type | Explanation |
| --- | --- | --- |
| 0 | Not visible on SQL Server 2000 | |
| 1-10 | Information | Caused by mistakes in the information that you have entered. |
| 11-16 | User-generated errors | These messages can be caused and corrected by the user (anyone connected to the SQL Server at the time the message is sent, not limited to and including a data entry user). |
| 17 | Resource Error | SQL Server has run out of resources, disk space for the database, or locks, or has exceeded the limits set by the systems administrator. |

| Severity Levels | Type | Explanation |
| --- | --- | --- |
| 18 | Nonfatal Internal Error Detected | Internal software problem. |
| 19 | SQL Server Error in Resource | This means that an internal limit has been exceeded and must be corrected by your systems administrator or your system support provider. |
| 20-25 | System Problems; Fatal Errors | The processes (the set of programs that were written to complete a task) have failed. The program(s) are paused and a record of the error is kept, and then the program is terminated; SQL Server closes and may not reconnect (depending on the seriousness of the problem). |
| 20 | Fatal Error in Current Process | The problem has only affected the current process. |
| 21 | Fatal Error in Database (dbid) Process | A problem has affected all processes in the current database. This does not mean that the whole database has been corrupted. |
| 22 | Fatal Error Table Integrity Suspect | This message signifies that the table or index specified has been damaged by either a software or hardware problem. |
| | | Run DBCC CHECKDB to discover if other objects in the database are also damaged. If the problem is in cache only and not on the disk, then restarting SQL Server will correct the problem. You may have to restore the database. If restarting does not help, you may be able to solve the problem by destroying the object that is specified in the error message. |
| 23 | Fatal Error Database Integrity Suspect | The entire database is suspect due to damage caused by a hardware or software problem. |
| 24 | Fatal Hardware Error | Media failure. The database may have to be reloaded. Call your hardware vendor for support! |

This may be a good time to remind you that backing up your database and getting a copy off-site is vital. As you can see from just these few samples of what can go wrong, it is imperative to develop and maintain a database backup system.

# Accessing the Application Log

Although the SQL Server error log contains more complete information about the events of the processes occurring in SQL Server, you may also find the application log output essential in tracking down the root of the problems that are occurring on the Windows NT system.

To read the NT Event Viewer application log:

1.  Click the **Start** button.

2.  Select **Programs|Administrative Tools (Common)|Event Viewer**.

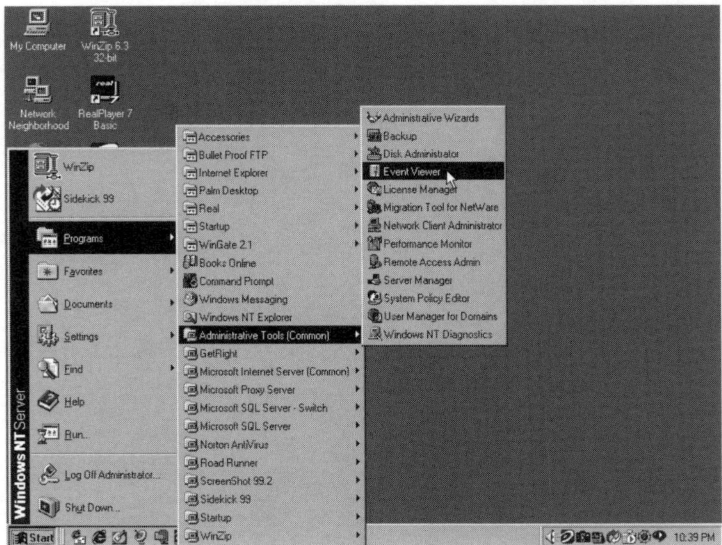

The Event Viewer allows you to filter the information that is shown in the application log. You can use filters for event types such as warnings, information, errors, success audits, and failure audits. Since both logs are time stamped for all recorded events, you can match process times and date messages to discover the root of your problems. Many of the common errors you will need to deal with are detailed in Appendix A.

# Chapter 6

# Disaster Recovery Plan

If you are really lucky, you will never have to open up your disaster recovery plan after you've thought it through and written it. In fact, this is a part of the job that you hope is a waste of your time. As a point of reference, here is Garbus' law of disaster preparedness:

> "The less you prepare for a disaster, the more likely it is to happen. Curiously, however, the more you prepare for a disaster, the more likely it is to happen."

Better to be prepared, don't you think? It's a good idea to have a written disaster recovery plan so that if there is trouble, panic does not need to set in; you can simply open the plan, and follow it.

If your transaction volume is low and you have the ability to duplicate a day's transactions easily, you may never need more disaster recovery than to reload the database. However, this is a decision to make after you take into account all types of disasters you might have to deal with and accept the risks accordingly.

## What Can Go Wrong?

There are actually a limited number of things you can do if there is a disaster. What you need to do is to make a plan that categorizes the types of disasters and the appropriate responses to those disasters. First, for convenience, here is a relatively complete list of potential disasters (talk to the practical joker in your office for others):

## Loss of Hardware

The physical machine is:

- Stolen
- Dysfunctional (chip/board failure)
- In disk failure

**Note:** Disk failure can be mitigated by utilizing disk mirroring, which is highly recommended. Disk mirroring is performed at the NT level, by telling the NT operating system that you want a pair of disks tied together at the operating system level and used for *fail-over*. This means that if one disk fails, you want the other one to take over for it immediately.

- Burned in a fire
- Drowned in a flood (or by a sprinkler system, activated environmentally or otherwise)
- Shaken (not stirred) by an earthquake

If you lose your hardware, it is decision time, and you should be ready in advance to make this call. Do you try to fix the hardware or do you go with new hardware? Based on your agreement with your hardware vendor, decide when you try to fix versus replace, based on how long it will take to replace the hardware and how long you can wait for it to be repaired. Plan ahead for how you will act in specific situations.

## Loss of SQL Server

- The operating system *blue screens*. This means that the operating system had an unrecoverable error, which led to a blue screen describing the problem, which forces you to restart NT.

**Note:** Observation has shown a very high percentage (upwards of 90%) of NT blue screens seem to be caused by a faulty piece of equipment, one that's not on NT's compatibility list, or a faulty driver for a piece of hardware.

- The Microsoft SQL Server crashes. Sometimes an error is severe enough to cause a server to simply shut itself down or system files or tables become corrupt.

Every once in a while, the server will crash. This may never happen to you, but in a high-volume environment, I know places that never have this problem and others that need to restart their operating systems a few times per week.

If the server shuts itself down, simply restart it, whether it is at the NT level or the SQL Server level. After the server restarts (it will restart after NT restarts if you restart NT) you should look at the error log and verify that all databases started normally. Note that a sudden shutdown of the server can cause damage to the databases, and you should verify that it has not.

## Loss of Power

- Somebody forgets to pay the bill
- There is a problem at the power plant
- Lightning strikes the power line
- A squirrel chews through a transformer

In case of loss of power, hopefully you have been notified by the sharp beeping of your UPS, and have shut down first the SQL Server, then the NT box. A UPS (uninterruptible power supply) is essential; in case of a loss of power, you do not want your server to suddenly shut down. This can cause data loss or database corruption. You can get a UPS from any computer supply shop or, these days, office supply store. If you spend a bit more on your UPS, you can get one that automatically shuts down the box when there is a power failure. Then, when the power comes back on, simply turn the box back on.

## Loss of Data

- Database corruption
- A user deletes something that shouldn't have been deleted
- Sabotage

# Let's Fix the Problem!

Now, here is a list of remedies, in decreasing order of effort and aggravation:

- Build a new physical server

  This means you buy new hardware, because you've given up on the old box.

- Build a new database server

  This means that you need to reinstall Microsoft SQL Server, as you did the first time. This is typically the result of losing the physical disks upon which the server is installed.

- Restore the database

  Refer to Chapter 8 for the restore technique.

- Run DBCC with the fix option

Of all the above options, it is most likely that you will have to restore the database.

## Disaster/Remedy Grid

What we have, then, is a list of potential problems along with a list of potential solutions. Remember to try the least-invasive solution first. You may want to start with the following chart and modify it to suit your own needs.

| | Rebuild Physical Server | Rebuild SQL Server | Restore Database | Run DBCC with "Fix" Option |
|---|---|---|---|---|
| Loss of Hardware Disk | | | (After replacing the damaged disk) | |
| Anything other than disk | ● | ● | ● | |
| Loss of SQL Server (If the server error log reports an error) | | | 2nd (if DBCC fails) | 1st |

| | Rebuild Physical Server | Rebuild SQL Server | Restore Database | Run DBCC with "Fix" Option |
|---|---|---|---|---|
| Loss of Power<br>　The server<br>　shuts down<br>　suddenly | | | 2nd (if DBCC fails)<br>2nd (if DBCC fails) | 1st<br>1st |
| Loss of Data<br>　Preventive<br>　DBCC shows<br>　an error | | | ●<br>2nd (if DBCC fails) | 1st |

## Recommended Approach

More generally, here are the four basic types of problems and instructions for how you should proceed if they are encountered. You should look at this list when everything is functioning normally and decide whether these solutions will be the best for your site or if you need to rewrite them to suit your specific needs.

| | |
|---|---|
| Damage to hardware | Diagnose, contacting your hardware vendor if possible, and then replace the damaged part. |
| Hardware catastrophe | Replace hardware, reload all necessary software, and restore from backup (very important to ensure backup media are compatible between old and new system). |
| Data corruption | Your only option here is to determine the last known point in time you were able to trust your data, and then restore from tape. |
| Software catastrophe | Reinstall the server; restore the database from tape. Discuss expectations with management prior to this occurrence. |

Though there are ways to repair your system after disaster strikes, the best disaster recovery plan is to avoid disaster as much as possible by following your preventive maintenance regimen.

# The Database Consistency Checker (DBCC)

The Database Consistency Checker (DBCC) is a tool that verifies the internal consistency of your database. This is probably the single most technical part of the book, because this is where we talk about the specific tasks that check the physical storage structures. Like disaster recovery, you hope that the DBCC never catches a problem, but on the off chance that it does, you want to repair the problem sooner rather than later. Problems caught early can often be fixed; problems caught late often snowball into complete disasters. Chapter 2 showed you how to run DBCCs quickly and easily, so here we talk about the options, what you are doing, and why.

## DBCC Commands

For each database, you have to run the following:

| | |
|---|---|
| DBCC CHECKALLOC | The data on the SQL Server are broken up into units called pages, which are 8,196 bytes in size (think of a byte as one character of information, like the period at the end of this sentence). Each page is a part of the database, but is also part of a data structure like a table or index. This DBCC task checks the allocation pages (which helps the server determine which pages are free), as well as the usage of each individual page in each database. This does not need to be run if you run DBCC CHECKDB, as it is now a subset of that command. |
| DBCC CHECKCATALOG | Information about how the data is stored is contained inside the database in special tables called system tables. This DBCC function checks for consistency in and between the system tables in each database. Run this for every database, not just your production database. It catches a wide variety of possible errors and repairs them. In fact, go ahead and run it with the repair option; it should not hurt anything, and will fix the database automatically. |
| DBCC CHECKDB | This option checks the allocation (see DBCC CHECKALLOC) and structural integrity of all the objects (tables and indexes) in the specified database. Run this for every database, not just your production database. |
| DBCC CHECKFILEGROUP | Sometimes databases are divided up into filegroups for the purpose of controlling data placement or growth. This option is a subset of DBCC CHECKDB, which checks the allocation and structural integrity of all tables in the specified filegroup in the current database. If you run DBCC CHECKDB, you do not need to run this. |

# DBCC CHECKALLOC

### Syntax

```
DBCC CHECKALLOC
( 'database_name'
[, NOINDEX
|
{ REPAIR_ALLOW_DATA_LOSS
| REPAIR_FAST
| REPAIR_REBUILD
```

```
}]
) [WITH {ALL_ERRORMSGS | NO_INFOMSGS}]
```

## Arguments

'database_name'
> The name of the database you want to check. Defaults to the current database. You should specify this to be sure you're checking the right database.

NOINDEX
> This option is ignored, so don't use it.

REPAIR_ALLOW_DATA_LOSS | REPAIR_FAST | REPAIR_REBUILD
> Instructs the server to repair the errors it finds. You should use the REPAIR_REBUILD option as it is the most complete option.

WITH ALL_ERRORMSGS | NO_INFOMSGS
> Specifies an option for error messages. ALL_ERRORMESSAGES shows all error messages (if you don't specify this, SQL Server displays a maximum of 200 error messages per object, which is recommended). NO_INFOMSGS hides all output.

If you do not suppress output, your output will look something like this. Note that you do not need to do anything unless the output reports errors.

```
DBCC checkalloc (pubs)
DBCC results for 'pubs'.
******************************************************************
Table sysobjects                Object ID 1.
Index ID 1          FirstIAM (1:10)   Root (1:11)     Dpages 1.
Index ID 1. 3 pages used in 0 dedicated extents.
Index ID 2          FirstIAM (1:25)   Root (1:15)     Dpages 1.
Index ID 2. 2 pages used in 0 dedicated extents.
Index ID 3          FirstIAM (1:33)   Root (1:31)     Dpages 1.
Index ID 3. 2 pages used in 0 dedicated extents.
Total number of extents is 0.
******************************************************************
Table sysindexes                Object ID 2.
Index ID 1          FirstIAM (1:13)   Root (1:14)     Dpages 3.
Index ID 1. 5 pages used in 0 dedicated extents.
Index ID 255        FirstIAM (1:27)   Root (1:64)     Dpages 0.
Index ID 255. 5 pages used in 1 dedicated extents.
```

```
Total number of extents is 1.
*****************************************************************
Table syscolumns                  Object ID 3.
Index ID 1          FirstIAM (1:26)    Root (1:17)    Dpages 5.
Index ID 1. 7 pages used in 1 dedicated extents.
Index ID 2          FirstIAM (1:35)    Root (1:34)    Dpages 2.
Index ID 2. 4 pages used in 0 dedicated extents.
Total number of extents is 1.
*****************************************************************
Table systypes                    Object ID 4.
Index ID 1          FirstIAM (1:29)    Root (1:30)    Dpages 1.
Index ID 1. 3 pages used in 0 dedicated extents.
Index ID 2          FirstIAM (1:37)    Root (1:36)    Dpages 1.
Index ID 2. 2 pages used in 0 dedicated extents.
Total number of extents is 0.
*****************************************************************
Table syscomments                 Object ID 6.
Index ID 1          FirstIAM (1:52)    Root (1:51)    Dpages 5.
Index ID 1. 7 pages used in 0 dedicated extents.
Total number of extents is 0.
*****************************************************************
Table sysfiles1                   Object ID 8.
Index ID 0          FirstIAM (1:12)    Root (1:32)    Dpages 1.
Index ID 0. 2 pages used in 0 dedicated extents.
Total number of extents is 0.
*****************************************************************
Table syspermissions              Object ID 9.
Index ID 1          FirstIAM (1:72)    Root (1:63)    Dpages 1.
Index ID 1. 3 pages used in 0 dedicated extents.
Total number of extents is 0.
*****************************************************************
Table sysusers                    Object ID 10.
Index ID 1          FirstIAM (1:39)    Root (1:38)    Dpages 1.
Index ID 1. 3 pages used in 0 dedicated extents.
Index ID 2          FirstIAM (1:42)    Root (1:41)    Dpages 1.
Index ID 2. 2 pages used in 0 dedicated extents.
Index ID 3          FirstIAM (1:44)    Root (1:43)    Dpages 1.
Index ID 3. 2 pages used in 0 dedicated extents.
Total number of extents is 0.
*****************************************************************
```

```
Table sysproperties                Object ID 11.
Index ID 1          FirstIAM (0:0)   Root (0:0)     Dpages 0.
Index ID 1. 0 pages used in 0 dedicated extents.
Total number of extents is 0.
*******************************************************************
Table sysdepends                Object ID 12.
Index ID 1          FirstIAM (1:55)   Root (1:54)    Dpages 1.
Index ID 1. 3 pages used in 0 dedicated extents.
Index ID 2          FirstIAM (1:58)   Root (1:57)    Dpages 1.
Index ID 2. 2 pages used in 0 dedicated extents.
Total number of extents is 0.
*******************************************************************
Table sysreferences                Object ID 14.
Index ID 1          FirstIAM (1:78)   Root (1:77)    Dpages 1.
Index ID 1. 3 pages used in 0 dedicated extents.
Index ID 2          FirstIAM (1:81)   Root (1:80)    Dpages 1.
Index ID 2. 2 pages used in 0 dedicated extents.
Index ID 3          FirstIAM (1:83)   Root (1:82)    Dpages 1.
Index ID 3. 2 pages used in 0 dedicated extents.
Total number of extents is 0.
*******************************************************************
Table sysfulltextcatalogs            Object ID 19.
Index ID 1          FirstIAM (0:0)   Root (0:0)     Dpages 0.
Index ID 1. 0 pages used in 0 dedicated extents.
Index ID 2          FirstIAM (0:0)   Root (0:0)     Dpages 0.
Index ID 2. 0 pages used in 0 dedicated extents.
Total number of extents is 0.
*******************************************************************
Table sysfulltextnotify            Object ID 24.
Index ID 1          FirstIAM (0:0)   Root (0:0)     Dpages 0.
Index ID 1. 0 pages used in 0 dedicated extents.
Total number of extents is 0.
*******************************************************************
Table sysfilegroups                Object ID 96.
Index ID 1          FirstIAM (1:47)   Root (1:46)    Dpages 1.
Index ID 1. 3 pages used in 0 dedicated extents.
Index ID 2          FirstIAM (1:50)   Root (1:49)    Dpages 1.
Index ID 2. 2 pages used in 0 dedicated extents.
Total number of extents is 0.
*******************************************************************
```

```
Table titleauthor                    Object ID 53575229.
Index ID 1          FirstIAM (1:101)    Root (1:100)    Dpages 1.
Index ID 1. 3 pages used in 0 dedicated extents.
Index ID 2          FirstIAM (1:129)    Root (1:128)    Dpages 1.
Index ID 2. 2 pages used in 0 dedicated extents.
Index ID 3          FirstIAM (1:132)    Root (1:131)    Dpages 1.
Index ID 3. 2 pages used in 0 dedicated extents.
Total number of extents is 0.
*******************************************************************
Table stores                 Object ID 117575457.
Index ID 1          FirstIAM (1:104)    Root (1:103)    Dpages 1.
Index ID 1. 3 pages used in 0 dedicated extents.
Total number of extents is 0.
*******************************************************************
Table sales                  Object ID 149575571.
Index ID 1          FirstIAM (1:107)    Root (1:106)    Dpages 1.
Index ID 1. 3 pages used in 0 dedicated extents.
Index ID 2          FirstIAM (1:119)    Root (1:118)    Dpages 1.
Index ID 2. 2 pages used in 0 dedicated extents.
Total number of extents is 0.
*******************************************************************
Table roysched               Object ID 213575799.
Index ID 0          FirstIAM (1:110)    Root (1:109)    Dpages 1.
Index ID 0. 2 pages used in 0 dedicated extents.
Index ID 2          FirstIAM (1:134)    Root (1:133)    Dpages 1.
Index ID 2. 2 pages used in 0 dedicated extents.
Total number of extents is 0.
*******************************************************************
Table discounts              Object ID 245575913.
Index ID 0          FirstIAM (1:112)    Root (1:111)    Dpages 1.
Index ID 0. 2 pages used in 0 dedicated extents.
Total number of extents is 0.
*******************************************************************
Table jobs               Object ID 277576027.
Index ID 1          FirstIAM (1:114)    Root (1:113)    Dpages 1.
Index ID 1. 3 pages used in 0 dedicated extents.
Total number of extents is 0.
*******************************************************************
Table pub_info               Object ID 357576312.
Index ID 1          FirstIAM (1:95)     Root (1:94)     Dpages 1.
```

```
Index ID 1. 3 pages used in 0 dedicated extents.
Index ID 255          FirstIAM (1:93)    Root (1:92)     Dpages 0.
Index ID 255. 14 pages used in 1 dedicated extents.
Total number of extents is 1.
****************************************************************
Table employee                  Object ID 405576483.
Index ID 1          FirstIAM (1:121)   Root (1:122)    Dpages 1.
Index ID 1. 3 pages used in 0 dedicated extents.
Index ID 2          FirstIAM (1:125)   Root (1:124)    Dpages 1.
Index ID 2. 2 pages used in 0 dedicated extents.
Total number of extents is 0.
****************************************************************
Table authors                   Object ID 1977058079.
Index ID 1          FirstIAM (1:87)    Root (1:86)     Dpages 1.
Index ID 1. 3 pages used in 0 dedicated extents.
Index ID 2          FirstIAM (1:117)   Root (1:116)    Dpages 1.
Index ID 2. 2 pages used in 0 dedicated extents.
Total number of extents is 0.
****************************************************************
Table publishers                Object ID 2057058364.
Index ID 1          FirstIAM (1:90)    Root (1:89)     Dpages 1.
Index ID 1. 3 pages used in 0 dedicated extents.
Total number of extents is 0.
****************************************************************
Table titles             Object ID 2121058592.
Index ID 1          FirstIAM (1:98)    Root (1:97)     Dpages 1.
Index ID 1. 3 pages used in 0 dedicated extents.
Index ID 2          FirstIAM (1:127)   Root (1:126)    Dpages 1.
Index ID 2. 2 pages used in 0 dedicated extents.
Total number of extents is 0.
****************************************************************
Processed 45 entries in sysindexes for database ID 5.
File 1. Number of extents = 20, used pages = 135, reserved pages = 153.
        File 1 (number of mixed extents = 16, mixed pages = 121).
   Object ID 1, Index ID 0, data extents 0, pages 3, mixed extent
pages 3.
   Object ID 1, Index ID 2, index extents 0, pages 2, mixed extent
pages 2.
   Object ID 1, Index ID 3, index extents 0, pages 2, mixed extent
pages 2.
```

```
     Object ID 2, Index ID 0, data extents 0, pages 5, mixed extent
pages 5.
     Object ID 2, Index ID 255, index extents 1, pages 5, mixed extent
pages 4.
     Object ID 3, Index ID 0, data extents 1, pages 7, mixed extent
pages 5.
     Object ID 3, Index ID 2, index extents 0, pages 4, mixed extent
pages 4.
     Object ID 4, Index ID 0, data extents 0, pages 3, mixed extent
pages 3.
     Object ID 4, Index ID 2, index extents 0, pages 2, mixed extent
pages 2.
     Object ID 6, Index ID 0, data extents 0, pages 7, mixed extent
pages 7.
     Object ID 8, Index ID 0, data extents 0, pages 2, mixed extent
pages 2.
     Object ID 9, Index ID 0, data extents 0, pages 3, mixed extent
pages 3.
     Object ID 10, Index ID 0, data extents 0, pages 3, mixed extent
pages 3.
     Object ID 10, Index ID 2, index extents 0, pages 2, mixed extent
pages 2.
     Object ID 10, Index ID 3, index extents 0, pages 2, mixed extent
pages 2.
     Object ID 12, Index ID 0, data extents 0, pages 3, mixed extent
pages 3.
     Object ID 12, Index ID 2, index extents 0, pages 2, mixed extent
pages 2.
     Object ID 14, Index ID 0, data extents 0, pages 3, mixed extent
pages 3.
     Object ID 14, Index ID 2, index extents 0, pages 2, mixed extent
pages 2.
     Object ID 14, Index ID 3, index extents 0, pages 2, mixed extent
pages 2.
     Object ID 96, Index ID 0, data extents 0, pages 3, mixed extent
pages 3.
     Object ID 96, Index ID 2, index extents 0, pages 2, mixed extent
pages 2.
     Object ID 99, Index ID 0, data extents 1, pages 7, mixed extent
pages 1.
```

```
        Object ID 53575229, Index ID 0, data extents 0, pages 3, mixed
extent pages 3.
        Object ID 53575229, Index ID 2, index extents 0, pages 2, mixed
extent pages 2.
        Object ID 53575229, Index ID 3, index extents 0, pages 2, mixed
extent pages 2.
        Object ID 117575457, Index ID 0, data extents 0, pages 3, mixed
extent pages 3.
        Object ID 149575571, Index ID 0, data extents 0, pages 3, mixed
extent pages 3.
        Object ID 149575571, Index ID 2, index extents 0, pages 2, mixed
extent pages 2.
        Object ID 213575799, Index ID 0, data extents 0, pages 2, mixed
extent pages 2.
        Object ID 213575799, Index ID 2, index extents 0, pages 2, mixed
extent pages 2.
        Object ID 245575913, Index ID 0, data extents 0, pages 2, mixed
extent pages 2.
        Object ID 277576027, Index ID 0, data extents 0, pages 3, mixed
extent pages 3.
        Object ID 357576312, Index ID 0, data extents 0, pages 3, mixed
extent pages 3.
        Object ID 357576312, Index ID 255, index extents 1, pages 14, mixed
extent pages 9.
        Object ID 405576483, Index ID 0, data extents 0, pages 3, mixed
extent pages 3.
        Object ID 405576483, Index ID 2, index extents 0, pages 2, mixed
extent pages 2.
        Object ID 1977058079, Index ID 0, data extents 0, pages 3, mixed
extent pages 3.
        Object ID 1977058079, Index ID 2, index extents 0, pages 2, mixed
extent pages 2.
        Object ID 2057058364, Index ID 0, data extents 0, pages 3, mixed
extent pages 3.
        Object ID 2121058592, Index ID 0, data extents 0, pages 3, mixed
extent pages 3.
        Object ID 2121058592, Index ID 2, index extents 0, pages 2, mixed
extent pages 2.
Total number of extents = 20, used pages = 135, reserved pages = 153 in
this database.
```

```
       (number of mixed extents = 16, mixed pages = 121) in this
database.
CHECKALLOC found 0 allocation errors and 0 consistency errors in
database 'pubs'.
DBCC execution completed. If DBCC printed error messages, contact your
system administrator.
```

## DBCC CHECKCATALOG

### Syntax

```
DBCC CHECKCATALOG
( 'database_name'
) [WITH NO_INFOMSGS]
```

### Arguments

'database_name'
> The name of the database you want to check. Defaults to the current
> database. You should specify this to be sure you're checking the
> right database.

WITH NO_INFOMSGS
> Hides all the output.

If you do not suppress output, your output will look something like this.
Note that you do not need to do anything unless the output reports
errors. Also note there is not much output from CHECKCATALOG.

```
DBCC checkcatalog (pubs)
DBCC results for 'pubs'.
DBCC execution completed. If DBCC printed error messages, contact your
system administrator.
```

## DBCC CHECKDB

### Syntax

```
DBCC CHECKDB
( 'database_name'
[, NOINDEX
| { REPAIR_ALLOW_DATA_LOSS
| REPAIR_FAST
| REPAIR_REBUILD
```

```
}]
) [WITH {ALL_ERRORMSGS | NO_INFOMSGS}]
```

**Arguments**

'database_name'
> The name of the database you want to check. Defaults to the current database. You should specify this to be sure you're checking the right database.

NOINDEX
> Specifies that non-clustered indexes for non-system tables should not be checked.

> Don't do this. It's for folks with databases so big they do not have the time to run a full CHECKDB every night.

REPAIR_ALLOW_DATA_LOSS | REPAIR_FAST | REPAIR_REBUILD
> Instructs the server to repair the errors it finds. You should use the REPAIR_REBUILD option as it is the most complete option.

WITH ALL_ERRORMSGS | NO_INFOMSGS
> Specifies an option for error messages. ALL_ERRORMESSAGES shows all error messages (if you don't specify this, SQL Server displays a maximum of 200 error messages per object, which is recommended). NO_INFOMSGS hides all output.

If you do not suppress output, your output will look something like this. Note that you do not need to do anything unless the output reports errors.

```
DBCC checkdb (pubs)
DBCC results for 'pubs'.
        DBCC results for 'pubs'.
        DBCC results for 'sysobjects'.
        There are 72 rows in 1 pages for object 'sysobjects'.
        DBCC results for 'sysindexes'.
        There are 50 rows in 3 pages for object 'sysindexes'.
        DBCC results for 'syscolumns'.
        There are 330 rows in 5 pages for object 'syscolumns'.
        DBCC results for 'systypes'.
        There are 29 rows in 1 pages for object 'systypes'.
        DBCC results for 'syscomments'.
        There are 113 rows in 5 pages for object 'syscomments'.
        DBCC results for 'sysfiles1'.
```

```
There are 2 rows in 1 pages for object 'sysfiles1'.
DBCC results for 'syspermissions'.
There are 37 rows in 1 pages for object 'syspermissions'.
DBCC results for 'sysusers'.
There are 12 rows in 1 pages for object 'sysusers'.
DBCC results for 'sysproperties'.
There are 0 rows in 0 pages for object 'sysproperties'.
DBCC results for 'sysdepends'.
There are 241 rows in 1 pages for object 'sysdepends'.
DBCC results for 'sysreferences'.
There are 10 rows in 1 pages for object 'sysreferences'.
DBCC results for 'sysfulltextcatalogs'.
There are 0 rows in 0 pages for object 'sysfulltextcatalogs'.
DBCC results for 'sysfulltextnotify'.
There are 0 rows in 0 pages for object 'sysfulltextnotify'.
DBCC results for 'sysfilegroups'.
There are 1 rows in 1 pages for object 'sysfilegroups'.
DBCC results for 'titleauthor'.
There are 25 rows in 1 pages for object 'titleauthor'.
DBCC results for 'stores'.
There are 6 rows in 1 pages for object 'stores'.
DBCC results for 'sales'.
There are 21 rows in 1 pages for object 'sales'.
DBCC results for 'roysched'.
There are 86 rows in 1 pages for object 'roysched'.
DBCC results for 'discounts'.
There are 3 rows in 1 pages for object 'discounts'.
DBCC results for 'jobs'.
There are 14 rows in 1 pages for object 'jobs'.
DBCC results for 'pub_info'.
There are 8 rows in 1 pages for object 'pub_info'.
DBCC results for 'employee'.
There are 43 rows in 1 pages for object 'employee'.
DBCC results for 'authors'.
There are 23 rows in 1 pages for object 'authors'.
DBCC results for 'publishers'.
There are 8 rows in 1 pages for object 'publishers'.
DBCC results for 'titles'.
There are 18 rows in 1 pages for object 'titles'.
```

```
        CHECKDB found 0 allocation errors and 0 consistency errors
        in database 'pubs'.
DBCC execution completed. If DBCC printed error messages, contact your
system administrator.
```

You will occasionally see messages here that indicate system tables being corrected, or problems caused by people accessing the database while the command is being run. In general, you do not need to take action unless the severity is over 19, and at that point you should check your systems administration guide for instructions as to how to proceed.

# DBCC CHECKFILEGROUP

### Syntax

```
DBCC CHECKFILEGROUP
( [{'filegroup' | filegroup_id}] [, NOINDEX]
) [WITH {ALL_ERRORMSGS | NO_INFOMSGS}]
```

### Arguments

'filegroup'
>    The name of the filegroup you want to check. Note that filegroups are database-specific.

filegroup_id
>    This is the filegroup identification number (ID) for the filegroup we are going to check. You can obtain filegroup_id from either the FILEGROUP_ID function or the sysfilegroups system table in the database containing the filegroup.

NOINDEX
>    Specifies that non-clustered indexes for non-system tables should not be checked.

>    Don't do this. It is for folks with databases so big they do not have the time to run a full CHECKDB every night.

WITH ALL_ERRORMSGS | NO_INFOMSGS
>    Specifies an option for error messages. ALL_ERRORMESSAGES shows all error messages (if you don't specify this, SQL Server displays a maximum of 200 error messages per object, which is recommended). NO_INFOMSGS hides all output.

If you do not suppress output, your output will look something like this. Note that you do not need to do anything unless the output reports errors.

```
DBCC checkfilegroup ('PRIMARY')
        DBCC results for 'pubs'.
        DBCC results for 'sysobjects'.
        There are 72 rows in 1 pages for object 'sysobjects'.
        DBCC results for 'sysindexes'.
        There are 50 rows in 3 pages for object 'sysindexes'.
        DBCC results for 'syscolumns'.
        There are 330 rows in 5 pages for object 'syscolumns'.
        DBCC results for 'systypes'.
        There are 29 rows in 1 pages for object 'systypes'.
        DBCC results for 'syscomments'.
        There are 113 rows in 5 pages for object 'syscomments'.
        DBCC results for 'sysfiles1'.
        There are 2 rows in 1 pages for object 'sysfiles1'.
        DBCC results for 'syspermissions'.
        There are 37 rows in 1 pages for object 'syspermissions'.
        DBCC results for 'sysusers'.
        There are 12 rows in 1 pages for object 'sysusers'.
        DBCC results for 'sysproperties'.
        There are 0 rows in 0 pages for object 'sysproperties'.
        DBCC results for 'sysdepends'.
        There are 241 rows in 1 pages for object 'sysdepends'.
        DBCC results for 'sysreferences'.
        There are 10 rows in 1 pages for object 'sysreferences'.
        DBCC results for 'sysfulltextcatalogs'.
        There are 0 rows in 0 pages for object 'sysfulltextcatalogs'.
        DBCC results for 'sysfulltextnotify'.
        There are 0 rows in 0 pages for object 'sysfulltextnotify'.
        DBCC results for 'sysfilegroups'.
        There are 1 rows in 1 pages for object 'sysfilegroups'.
        DBCC results for 'titleauthor'.
        There are 25 rows in 1 pages for object 'titleauthor'.
        DBCC results for 'stores'.
        There are 6 rows in 1 pages for object 'stores'.
        DBCC results for 'sales'.
        There are 21 rows in 1 pages for object 'sales'.
```

```
DBCC results for 'roysched'.
There are 86 rows in 1 pages for object 'roysched'.
DBCC results for 'discounts'.
There are 3 rows in 1 pages for object 'discounts'.
DBCC results for 'jobs'.
There are 14 rows in 1 pages for object 'jobs'.
DBCC results for 'pub_info'.
There are 8 rows in 1 pages for object 'pub_info'.
DBCC results for 'employee'.
There are 43 rows in 1 pages for object 'employee'.
DBCC results for 'authors'.
There are 23 rows in 1 pages for object 'authors'.
DBCC results for 'publishers'.
There are 8 rows in 1 pages for object 'publishers'.
DBCC results for 'titles'.
There are 18 rows in 1 pages for object 'titles'.
CHECKFILEGROUP found 0 allocation errors and 0 consistency
errors in database 'pubs'.
```
DBCC execution completed. If DBCC printed error messages, contact your
system administrator.

# Chapter 8

# Backing Up and Restoring Your Database

"Be prepared," the adage that you heard from your grandmother years ago, definitely applies here. Disasters tend to happen at the worst possible time (like just a few hours before your long-dreamed-of vacation or an important holiday or family event). This will be the moment your database system will fail and ruin all of your plans. Often corporations (of all sizes) do not create effective backup procedures.

## Database Backups

A database backup is a full copy of all of the data in the database. This is typically performed at the end of the business day in order to capture data that reflects an entire day's work. You may want to back up more or less often based upon your own business needs. After the backups (one for each database) have been completed and the integrity of the backup has been verified, get the backups off-site (home, safety deposit box, anywhere it will not be affected by a disaster at work). Note that you do not want all copies of your most recent backup off-site. A disaster during the day should not send you home looking for the prior evening's backup. It is also important to be able to replace the tape drive, if it goes bad, as well as whatever software you use for backup.

There are many different media to choose from, including writeable CD-ROMs, floppy disks, tapes, Zip drives, and Jaz drives. You may pick a particular media dependent on hardware you have already purchased, or you may choose based on price, amount of data that can be held on the media, or other personal factors. You may back up your database to one or as many tapes as needed, based upon the size of your database.

| Drive Type/Cost* | Storage Medium/Cost* | Capacity* |
| --- | --- | --- |
| Floppy disk/$100 | Floppy disks/10 for $6 | 1.44 megabytes |
| CD-ROM drive/ $300-$400 | CD/$1-$1.50 | 600 megabytes |
| Tape drive/$300-$3000 (price varies for storage capacity and vendor) | Tape cartridge/$2-$20 | 8-40 gigabytes |
| Jaz drive/$300 | Jaz cartridge/$90 | 1 gigabyte |
| Zip drive/$150 | Zip cartridge/$10-$15 | 100 megabytes |

** This table shows pricing and capacity for a variety of backup media. The information was current in December 2000. Note that prices drop seemingly daily.*

As you can see, for a small investment you can purchase a great insurance policy against data loss.

## Backup Types

There are two backup types:

- **Complete Backup**—This is the most important. To run a full database backup you must use the BACKUP DATABASE command. It is used to make a full copy of the entire database. It backs up all of the tables including your transaction log (note that this does not clean out your transaction log—see Chapter 9 for more information). This backup must be performed prior to a differential backup because the differential backup only copies changes that have been made since this backup.

- **Differential Backup**—To do this you run the BACKUP TRANS-ACTION command (or choose differential backup in Enterprise Manager). It will make a copy of your transaction log, which contains all modifications to the database. After copying the log to the backup media, this command clears the transaction log of any information no longer needed (permanent changes to the database), unless the database option Truncate log on checkpoint is selected. This option must be selected to keep the transaction log from filling up, which will cause all data modification statements to stop executing until you clear the log. You can use the SP_DBOPTION command from the Query Analyzer to see what database options are turned on.

## Backup Strategy

Now that we have covered the basics of backups, we will develop a comprehensive backup strategy.

First, we create a list of all of the logs, tables, and databases that should be backed up daily. These include:

- All user databases
- The master database
- Transaction log (remember—the transaction log fills up and must be cleaned out)

**Note:** Be sure to date/time stamp your backup media before you start your backup. It's stressful to need to restore from backup and not know which tape is the right one.

You should verify the success of the backup before you can be assured that the backup is complete. To be sure that your backup media is healthy, restore your database to a test area. A successful restore equals a good media backup. Remember, tapes and storage devices can be faulty, and you do not always know this until you try to read the device.

SQL Server (depending on your database size) will allow you to store more than one backup on a backup device. However, for simplicity, we suggest you use a one-to-one system (one database, one disk). If you really want multiple database backups on a single backup media, here is the procedure you need to follow:

1.  For the first backup, initialize the tape but do not rewind (this gets the tape ready).

2.  Back up the second database.

3.  Back up the third database.

4.    Rewind or record over the original backup.

Syntax (if you are not using Enterprise Manager):

```
backup database CustomerDB "Tape 1" volume = CustVol1 with init
backup database ProductionDB to Tape 1 volume = ProdVol1/* nounload is
the default */backup database SecurityDB to tape 1 volume = SecVol1
with unload
```

SQL Server Enterprise Manager allows you to choose Append to media, thus allowing you to do graphically the same work that we just went through one step at a time. This is a great option to use for something like the differential backups, but when you are performing a complete backup, use one media per backup.

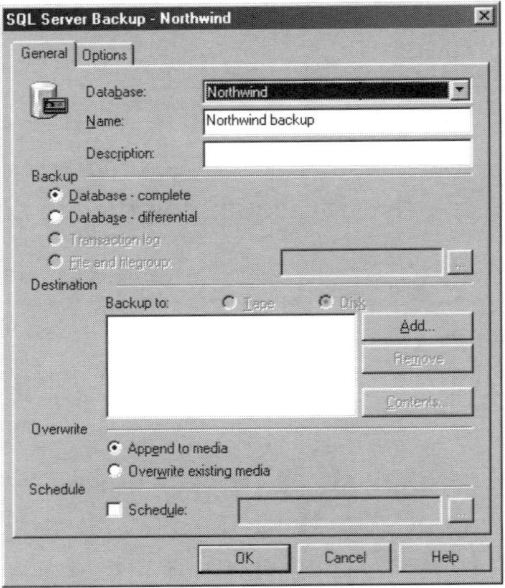



Another nice feature of SQL Server is that it automatically detects the media capacity of your backup device. This makes it harder to make a mistake. There was a time you specified the size, and you wrote that much to the tape whether the tape would hold the data or not.

## Backup Approach

Backing up the individual databases is only one step of the complete backup procedure. The process should include all of the following steps to ensure a functional, thorough backup.

1.    Standardize your backup procedures.

2.  Back up your database.

    a.  Back up the transaction log (only needs to be done if syslogs is located on a different device).

    b.  Check your tape by restoring the database.

3.  Back up the master database.

    a.  Check the media (tape or disk) by restoring the database.

## Standardizing Your Backup Procedures

There are some things to consider that are just from a pure business process perspective. Share your strategy so that someone else in your office understands it and knows how to complete the backups. They also should be able to follow the same procedure for labeling and getting the backups off-site. Make sure that the location of the backups is known. This assures your ability to have an uninterrupted vacation some day. You may want to post a schedule (see the following table) that works for your office. The schedule should describe the frequency with which you need to back up your logs and the databases.

| Who | When | Frequency of Backups | Naming Standards | Which Databases | Types of Backups | How | Location |
| --- | --- | --- | --- | --- | --- | --- | --- |
| Identify responsible party | Date/time | Schedule backups | Define standards for:<br><br>● Media labeling<br><br>● Database naming<br><br>● Device naming | List all databases | Database and transaction log backups | Disk or file devices | Where are the physical media copies? |

You may want to include a rotation schedule for reusing your backup media. You will have to decide how far you need to track backups. In most shops, a one-week rotation should work well. However, you have to decide on the volatility of your site and what works for you.

| Who | When | Backups | How | Device |
|---|---|---|---|---|
| Barney | M_W_F 4:00 | customer | Striped multi tape | cd |
| | M_W_F 4:00 | master | Not striped, single tape | tape |
| | Every 4 hours | transaction log | Appended single tape in one-day intervals | files |

Create a naming convention for your media backups. For example, you will want to include the name of the database, date, time, and possibly a notation of who created the backup (Customer Database/December 15, 2000/5:05 pm—Joe) or use the volume naming convention especially for tapes that you plan on appending (CustomerDB December 15 Dec 20). Then name your database backups so that they can easily be found on the tape CustomerDB December 17. Consistency in your naming conventions helps other people remember what to do and gets the tasks done faster. It also helps the recovery process along when/if a disaster strikes and you have to restore your database.

## Backing Up the Databases

You can use SQL Enterprise Manager to back up your database.

1. Click the **Start** button.

2. Select **Programs**.

3. Select **Microsoft SQL Server**.

4. Select **Enterprise Manager**.

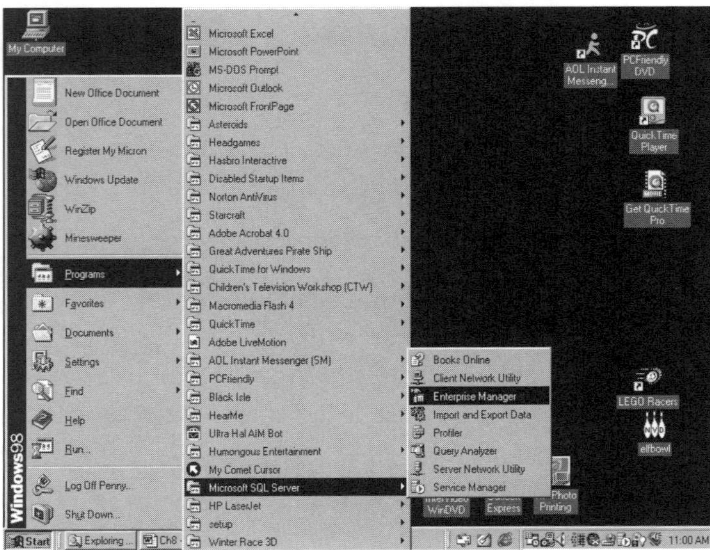

5.    Open your server folder and then the **Databases** file. You will see
      your databases come up on the right side.

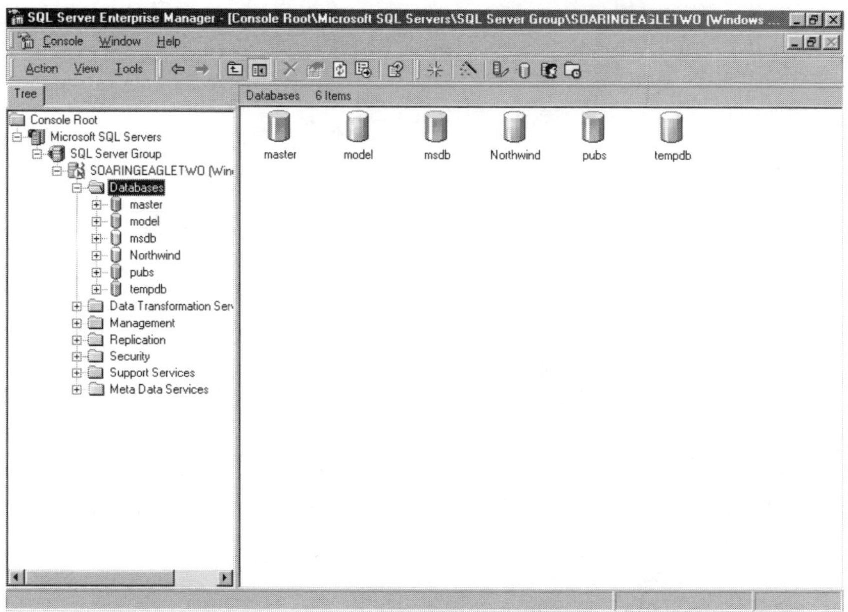

6.    Right-click the database you want to back up. Select **Tools|All
      Tasks|Backup Database**.

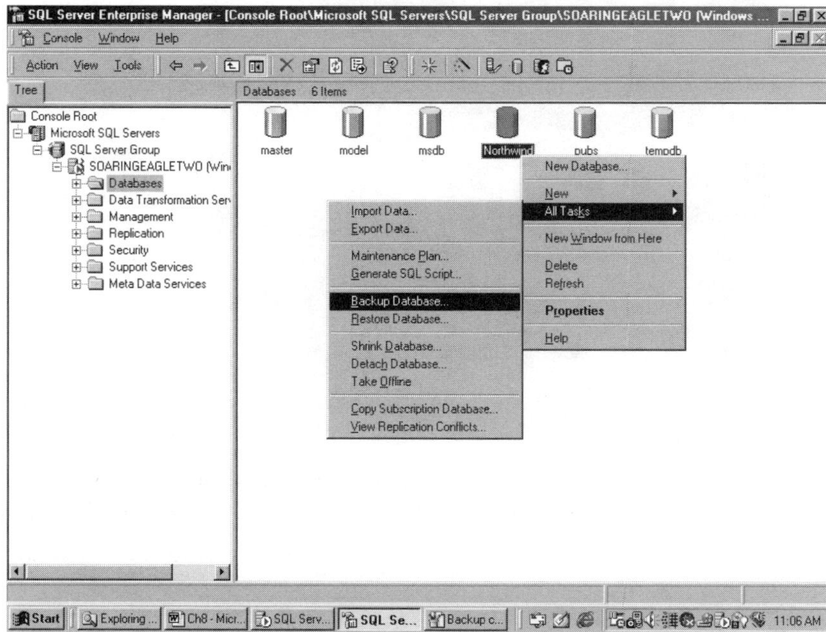

Notice on the SQL Server Backup dialog that the name of your database automatically appears, along with any description you may have entered at the time you built your database. Enterprise Manager gives you two choices of backups: complete (full backup of your database and logs) and differential (only a backup of the transaction log). At this time, we will choose the Complete backup option.

### Overwrite Option

Append to media means that you would like SQL Server to search for the end of the old database backup and add the new backup onto the same media.

Overwrite means that you would like to use the whole media space again. This will cause an error if you have set an expiration date or time period on that media and the date or time period has not elapsed. This is a good thing; it helps us with our human flaws that come with overwork and fatigue. We recommend that you overwrite each time, and age out your backups manually.

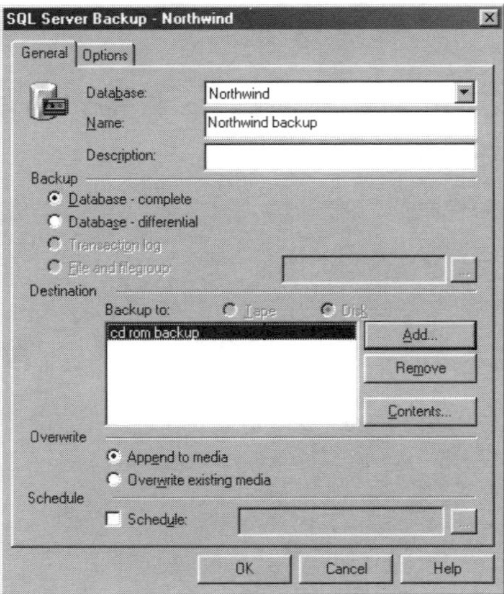


### Schedule Option

This option will allow you to schedule your backups and automate this process. Don't forget to install new media and label it. However, the rest can be automated for you. This is a nice way to perform your backups overnight. Check the Schedule box, then click the button with the ellipsis (next to the Schedule text box) to see more detailed options.

Under Schedule Type, you will see many options:

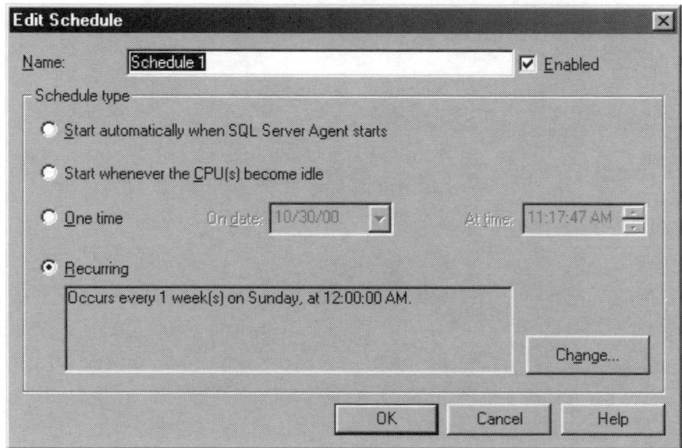


*Start automatically when SQL Server Agent starts*
> The full use of Server Agent is covered in Chapter 13. It is a tool which can be directed to watch certain occurrences in your database and sends alarms to you to notify you of a pending problem or occurrence.

*Start whenever the CPU(s) become idle*
> You may want to use this option to back up the transaction log at several points in a day. If you use this option, though, you will still have to watch the transaction log as it fills throughout the day.

*One time*
> This option is just what it sounds like.

*Recurring*
> Under the Recurring option is a text box. Next to the text box is a button labeled Change. If you want to select a backup to occur daily, weekly, or monthly, you click on the Change button and set those backup intervals for yourself.

## Daily screen

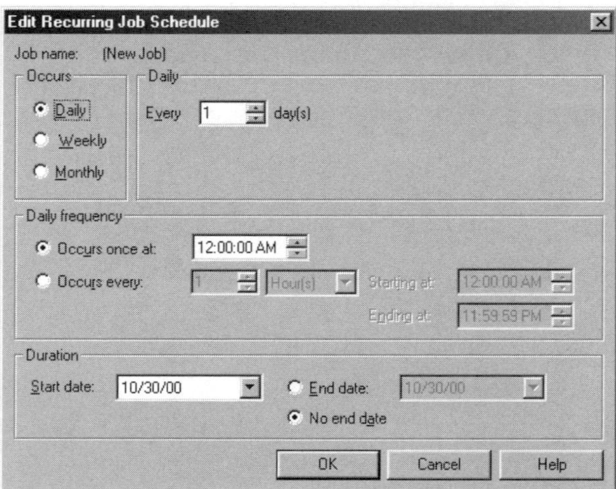

## Weekly screen

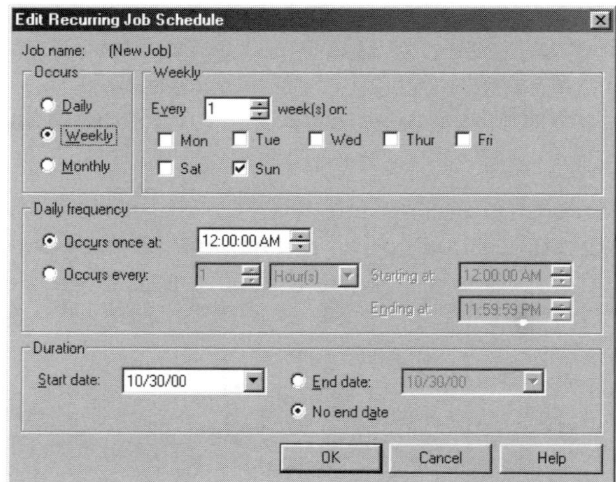

## Monthly screen

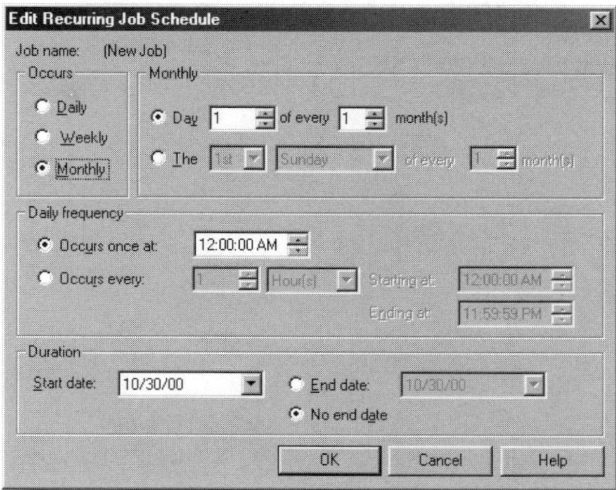

For all of the interval choices, you are able to enter the hour and duration start and end dates. Select a backup plan that fits your needs.

## Adding Your Backup Device

In the SQL Server Backup dialog you will be able to add your backup device (if you have not done this previously). To do this:

1.  Click the **Add** button under Destination. The Select Backup Destination dialog box appears.

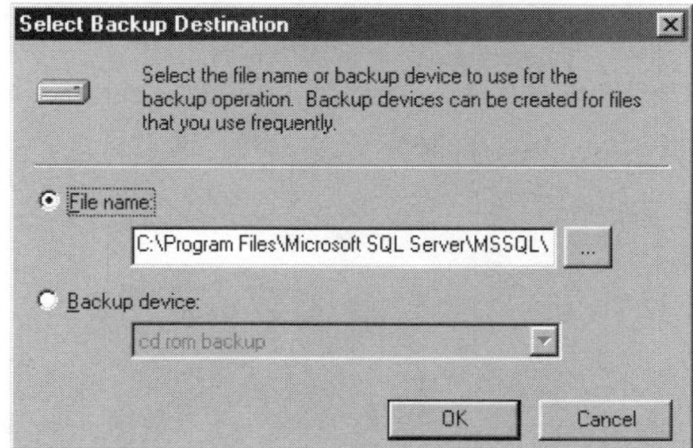

2. Click **Backup device**, then click on the down arrow in the drop-down list, and select **new backup device**.

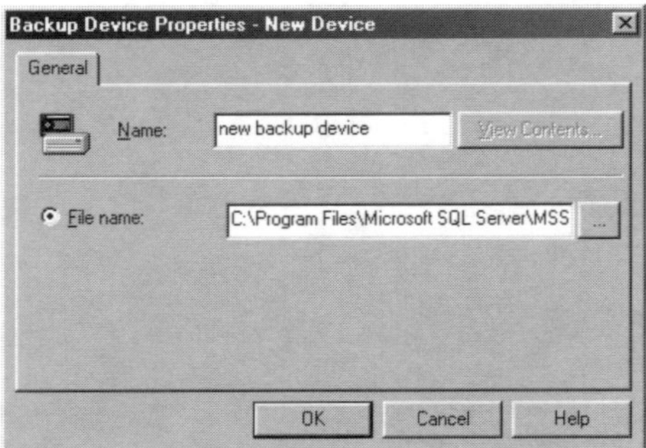

The next screen that pops up is the Backup Device Properties—New Device screen.

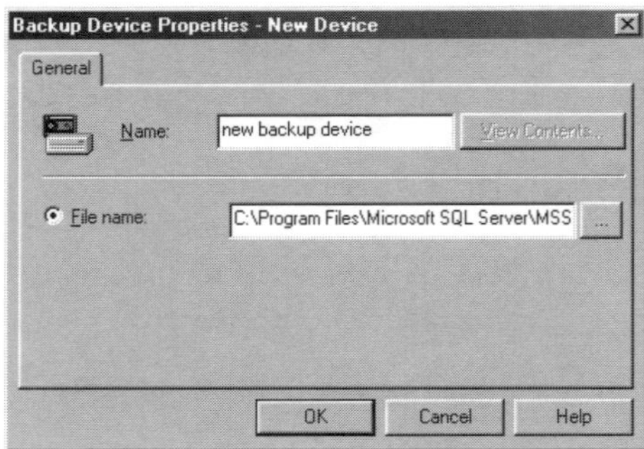

3. Enter the name of your device and file location in the Name and File name fields. Click **OK**. You should get a message that says, "Your new device has been created successfully." Now click **OK** on the next screen.

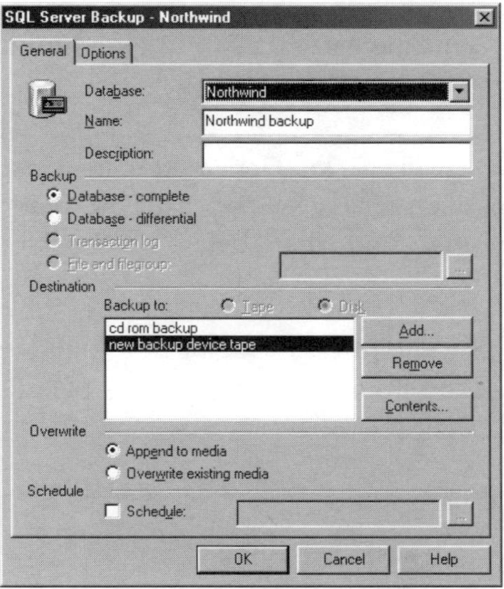

## The Options Tab

You should see your new device in the Backup to list. At the top of the screen you will see an Options tab. Click on that tab.

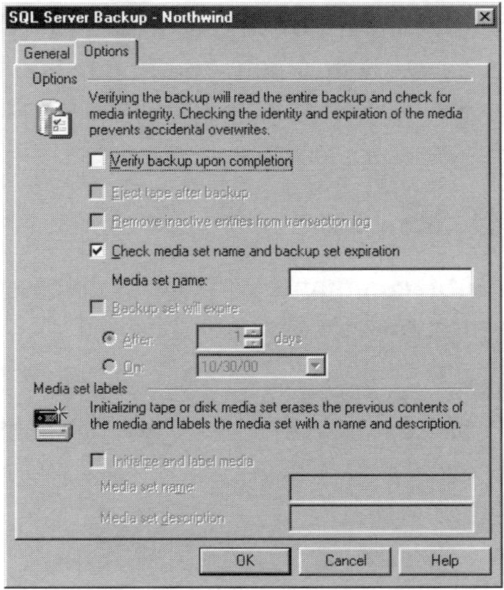

This is a very useful dialog. Here you can do many things to make restoring easier. Check Verify backup upon completion to give you that comfortable feeling of a job successfully completed. Then be sure to use the Check media set name and backup set expiration option so that SQL

Server will help you with your tape rotations and help eliminate human error.

---

**Note:** If you select Append to media on the General tab, the Check media set name and backup set expiration option will be turned off. Therefore, you should double-check your media name tag before you overwrite your media.

When you click OK at this point your database backup will begin. Then if you have selected Verify backup upon completion your SQL Server will notify you of a successful backup.

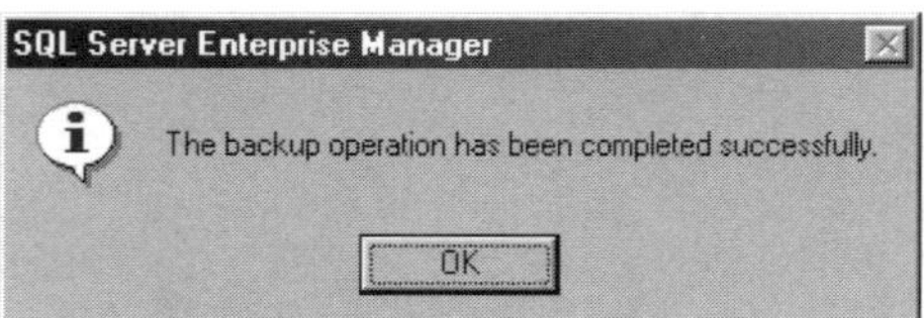


# A Behind-the-Scenes Look: Database Backups

SQL Server Enterprise Manager is actually performing some programming functions for you automatically. The following information will give you a little insight as to what is happening and help you to develop as a systems administrator by learning methods you should follow to get more information from your database.

## Step 1: Back Up the Database

You use the BACKUP DATABASE command to make a full copy of your database. The simplified syntax for this command is:

```
Backup database {dbname | @dbname_var}
      TO backup_device [, backup_device[. . . , backup_device32]]
[WITH options
[[,] STATS [ = percentage]]]
where
backup_device =
{backup_device_name \ @backup_device_namevar}
\ {DISK | TAPE \ FLOPPY |PIPE} =
{temp_backup_device' | @tempp_backup_+device_var}}
[VOLUME == {volid | @volid_var}]
options =
```

```
[[,] {UNLOAD | NOUNLOAD}]
[[,] {INIT | NOINIT}]
[[,] {SKIP | NOSKIP}]
[[,] {{EXPIREDATE =  {date | @date_var}}
| {RETAINDAYS = {days | @days_var}}]
```

The following table describes the parameters used in the full database backup syntax.

| Parameter | Description |
| --- | --- |
| dbname | The name of the database you are attempting to back up. |
| backup_device | The backup device that is defined with sp_addbackupdevice or you can directly specify a disk or tape device when you are striping them. |
| RETAINDAYS = days | An option used for any backup device. It keeps the backup from being overwritten until a specific amount of time has passed. |
| EXPIREDATE  date | Actually, this option is a toggle button in SQL Enterprise Manager which does not allow a backup to be overwritten until the date has passed. |
| STATS = percentage | Returns the percentage of pages backed up in increments specified by the value of the percentage. If the percentage is not specified, SQL Server automatically shows the statistics in 10% increments. |

Listed below are the options used in the full database backup syntax and their descriptions.

| | |
| --- | --- |
| VOLUME | Labels your backup, which can be specified during a load onto your media; for example, a value for volume as a concatenation of your database name and the date (CustomerDB_Mar02). If your backup media contains backups from Mar 01–05, then by using VOLUME you will be able to find the backup that you want. |
| UNLOAD \| NOUNLOAD | Controls the rewinding of the tape. NOUNLOAD should be used unless this is the last backup you want on the tape. |
| INIT \| NOINIT | Determines whether the backup will be appended to the tape or the entire tape volume will be reinitialized. You use INIT when backing up the first time to a tape; you use NOINIT to allow for multiple backups to a single tape. |

| SKIP \| NOSKIP | Indicates whether ANSI tape labels are read (NOSKIP) or ignored (SKIP). When SKIP is specified and the ANSI label of a tape warns that it has expired or that you don't have permission to write to it, SQL Server will ignore the warning. If the tape on which you are writing is new, then SQL Server writes a new label on the first try. NOSKIP tells the SQL Server to read the warnings. The default is NOSKIP. |
| --- | --- |

## Step 2: Back Up the Transaction Log

You may want to back up the transaction log more often than executing a full database backup. Backing up the transaction log in Enterprise Manager is called a differential backup. This option is given to you on your Backup Database tool in SQL Enterprise Manager. Because the log will grow until it is truncated, backing up the transaction log (to truncate unused transactions) is very important to remember.

To perform a differential backup, right-click the database you want to back up and select All Tasks|Backup Database from the pop-up menu.

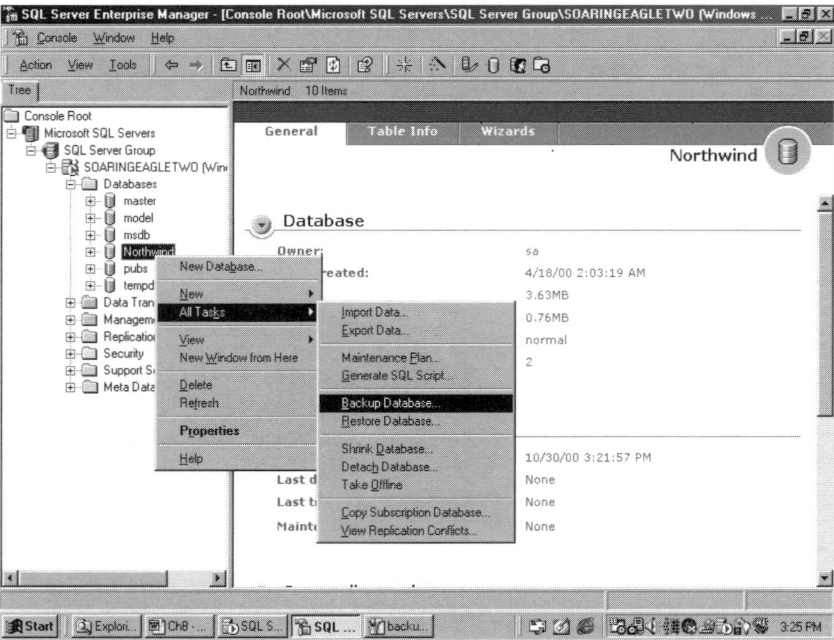

In the SQL Server Backup window, choose Database-differential under Backup instead of Database-complete like we did earlier in this chapter.

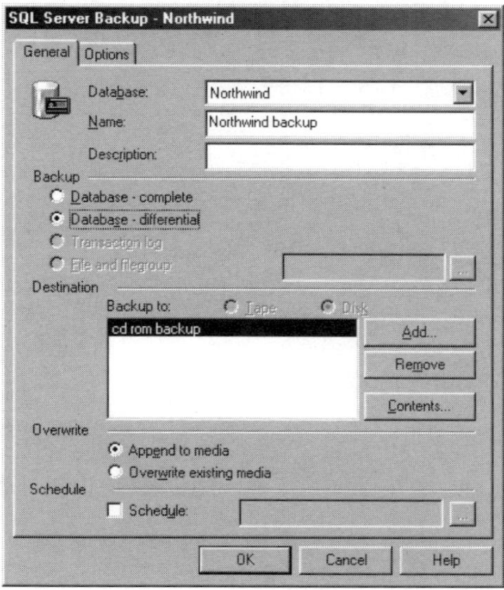

Just as when performing a complete backup, you will not have the ability to set the same options on all of the tabs. You only need to keep your differential backups until your next complete backup. For example, if you back up the transaction log three times a day, you need only keep those three differential backups.

We recommend that you track your transaction log to be sure that it has not filled. Remember that SQL Server will pause when the transaction log is full. SQL Server Enterprise Manager will find the transaction log that coincides with the database that you are in. If the log fills, all transactions will stop until space is made for the log. To track the transaction log and to understand more details about the transaction log, please refer to Chapter 9.

## A Behind-the-Scenes Look: Transaction Log Backups

The transaction log backup copies to your backup media all changes that have been logged to the database. Along the way, it also cleans out all of these completed transactions from the log. This is the normal way that you empty out a transaction log in a production database (see Chapter 9 for a more detailed discussion). To back up the transaction database name to devicename, use the following code:

```
BACKUP TRANSACTION {dbname | @dbname_var}
        [To dump_device [, dump_device2 [..., dump_device32]]]
   [WITH [TRUNCATE_ONLY | NO_LOG | NO_TRUNCATE}
        {options}]
where
dump_device =
{dump_device_name | @dump_device_name_var}
| {DISK | TAPE | FLOPPY | PIPE} =
        {'temp_dump_device' }}
[VOLUME = {volid | @volid_var}]
options=
[[, ] {UNLOAD | NOUNLOAD}]
[[,] {INIT | NOINIT}]
[[,] {SKIP | NOSKIP}]
[[,] {EXPIREDATE == {date | @date_var}}
        | {RETAINDAYS = {days | @days_Var}}]
```

## The Master Database

The master database is small. In fact, the default space allocation is only 17 megabytes. It is also not a very active database. However, if there is a master device failure, then not having a current backup of the master database can be traumatic; you will have to rebuild the entire server.

You need to back up this database whenever you are inserting or deleting rows in the system tables—in other words, any server activities like database creation or growth, option changes, adding users, defining new disks, etc. The master database does not have a separate log, so all backups are complete database backups.

---

**Note:** As a precaution, you should back up your master database as often as you back up your other databases. Place the master database on a single tape/disk alone. Do not stripe (putting a database backup on more than one device SQL Server can break up the database in equal portions and spread the data over 32 devices) the master database if at all possible. For most systems, the master database will fit on one backup medium so this should not be a problem.

# Restoring Your Database

It is important to keep your cool when something goes wrong. Remember, you can't fall off the floor! (If you can, your problems are too severe for this book.) Focus on the steps required to solve the problem, and later decide if it was avoidable, to improve for the next time. Once something happens, the most important thing to do is to think, take a deep breath, and get your system up and running. It can happen to anybody. Just get started, restore your database, and get everyone back to work. You can restore your database by right-clicking on your database and choosing All Tasks|Restore Database.

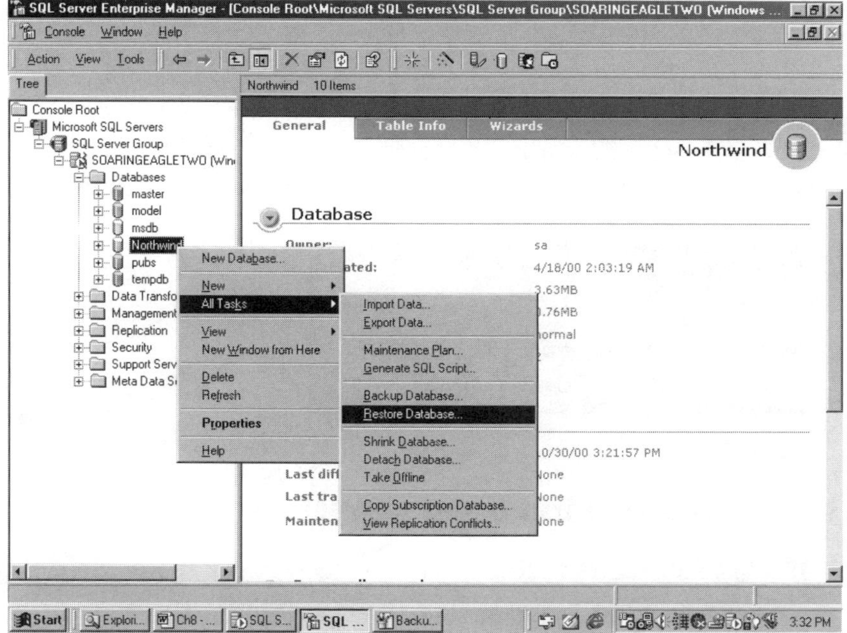

Since you have already selected your database, SQL Server Enterprise Manager can detect the database that you want to restore and determines whether you can apply a transaction log backup as well.

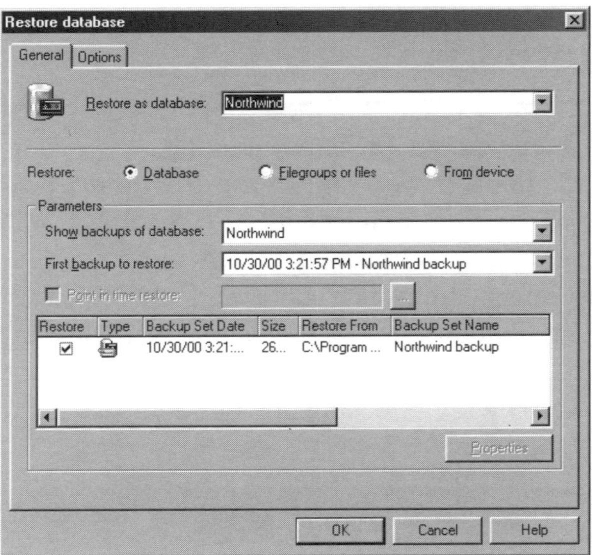

The SQL Server Enterprise Manager also automatically tells you when your restore has been successfully completed.

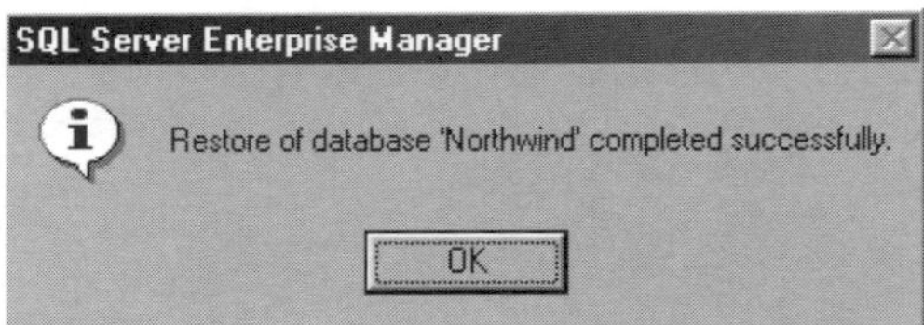

## If a Disaster Has Struck

If a disaster has occurred, you may need to re-create the database. First, you will have to drop the corrupt database. Try this first by right-clicking on the database in the SQL Server Enterprise Manager, and highlighting Delete.

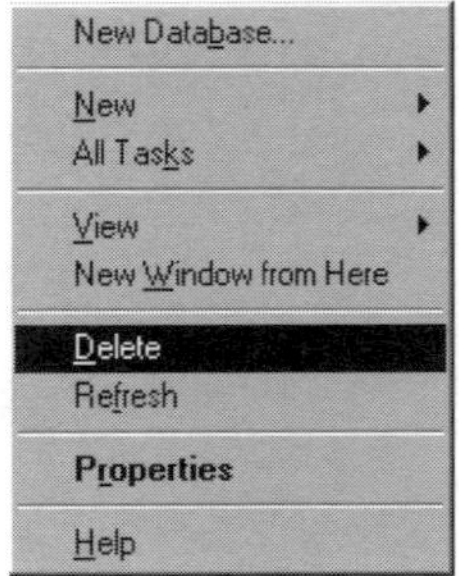

If, for any reason, this does not work (sometimes, if a database is in an odd state, the server will not remove it normally), you can use the following syntax from SQL Profiler:

```
sp_dbremove database [ , dropdev]
```

Second, you must create a new database structure. To check to see if you have space available on your disk, click once on the drive, and you'll see disk information on the left:

Access the Enterprise Manager, right-click on Databases, and select New Database from the pop-up menu.

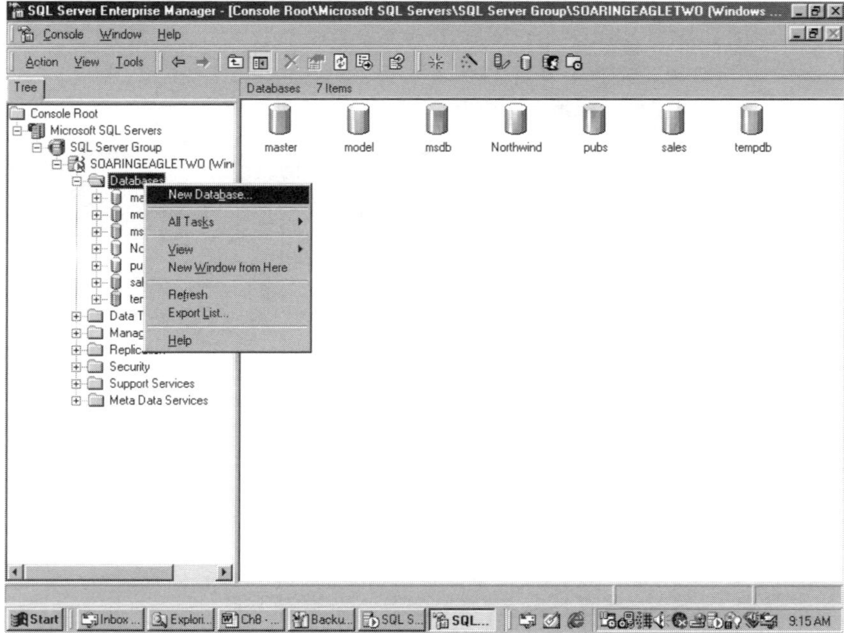

You'll need to enter your database name, where you'd like it to go, and an initial size. We recommend you check the Automatically grow file option. You can choose whether to do this in megabytes or by percent.

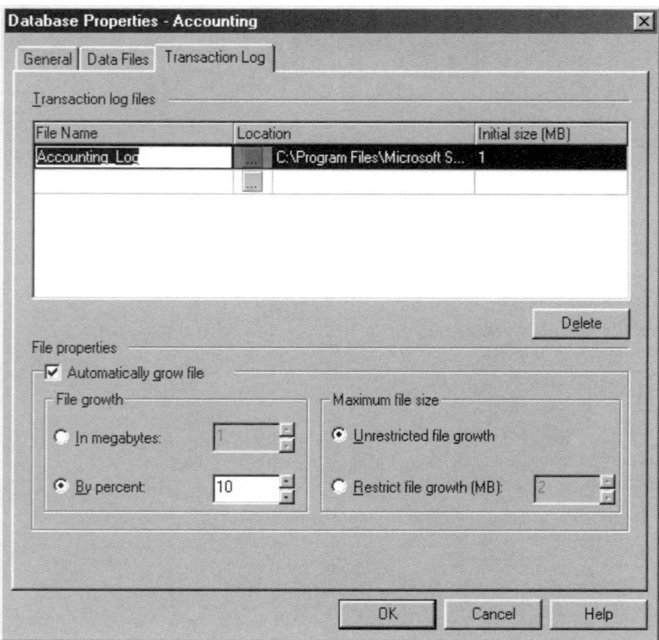

That is really all there is to it. You now have a database. Note that if the database is very large, this step may take a while.

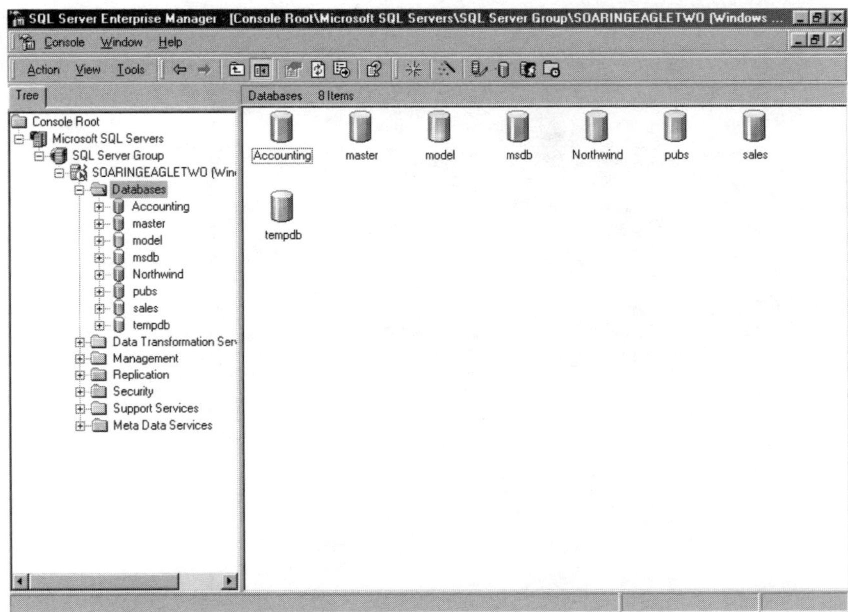

Microsoft SQL Server 2000 has added a new tool, the Backup Restore GUI tool, so you no longer have to do the above restore unless you have deleted the corrupted database.

Use Enterprise Manager and drill down until you get to the database that you need to restore. Right-click on the database, select All Tasks, then Restore Database.

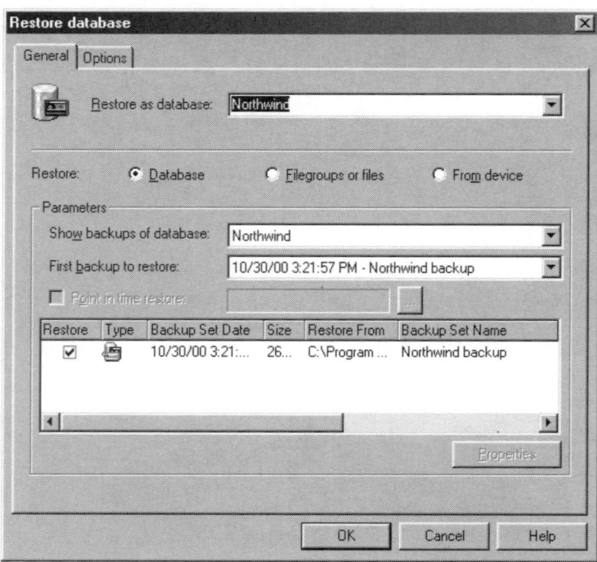

Click the Options tab.

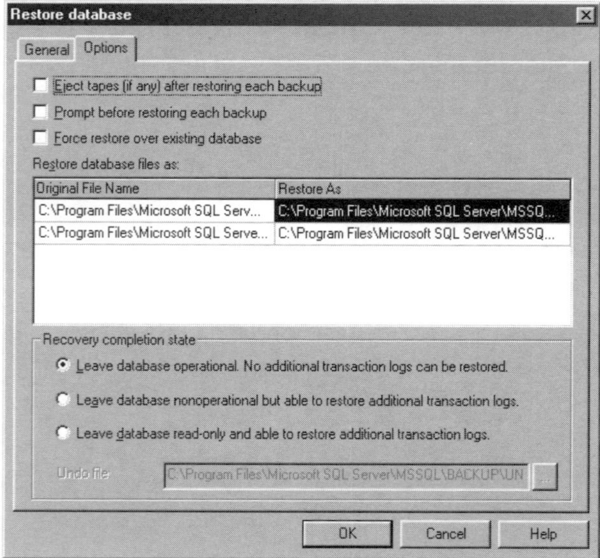

Use as many check boxes here as are necessary. Ejecting after backup or prompting before restore are optional; if you have an existing database, you will have to force the restore. If this is your only backup, leave the first radio button selected. If you will be restoring transaction logs, pick one of the last two.

Now click OK.

When your database has been restored, you will see this message:

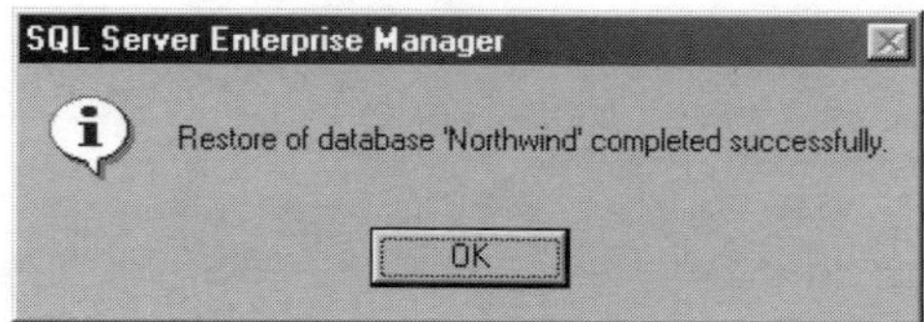

# Chapter 9

# Transaction Log Management

A transaction is defined among "techies" simply as a unit of work. More specifically, it is some amount of data processing that you want to have complete as a group or fail as a group. For example, you are at your ATM machine trying to get cash out. The machine will verify that you have money in your account to cover the cash withdrawal, subtract that amount from your account balance, and give you your money. But what happens if in between steps two and three, a squirrel chews through a transformer cable, and the power to the ATM goes out? Is your bank account still debited? When the power comes back on, do you suddenly get your cash? Or does it go to the fortunate person who was waiting for the power to come on, way after you left? In real life, you do not want steps two and three to be independent; you want them to be completely dependent. This is called a unit of work, or a *transaction*. The Microsoft SQL Server transaction log exists for the purpose of making sure that not only does your transaction complete or fail as a unit, but everybody else's transactions, potentially running at the same time, also complete or fail as a unit.

## Truncating the Transaction Log

The transaction log, as you can imagine, will get large over time, because it records every change that is made to the data, so that nothing is ever partially completed. You, as a DBA, must make sure that the transaction log does not fill up. If it does, all data modification on your server will simply stop.

Remember that this section of the book is on database-specific maintenance, and that a transaction log is specific to a database. This means that if you are managing multiple databases on a server, you must do this for each. There are two basic ways of accomplishing this.

First, you can turn on the database option Truncate log on checkpoint. This will truncate all the inactive (completed and recorded on disk) transactions in your database transaction log. You can turn the option on like this:

1.   Right-click the database and choose **Properties**.

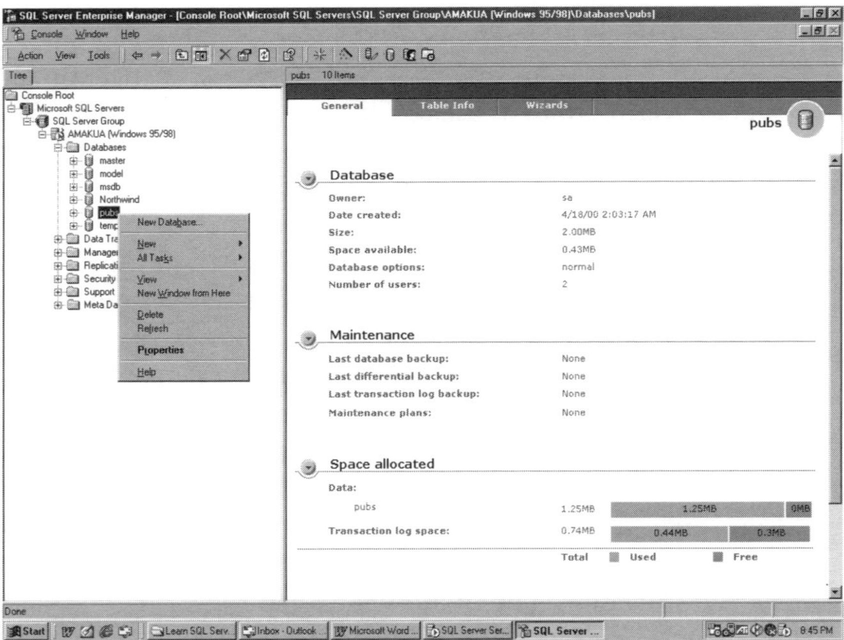

2.   Select the **Options** tab in the Properties dialog.

3.   Check **Truncate log on checkpoint**.

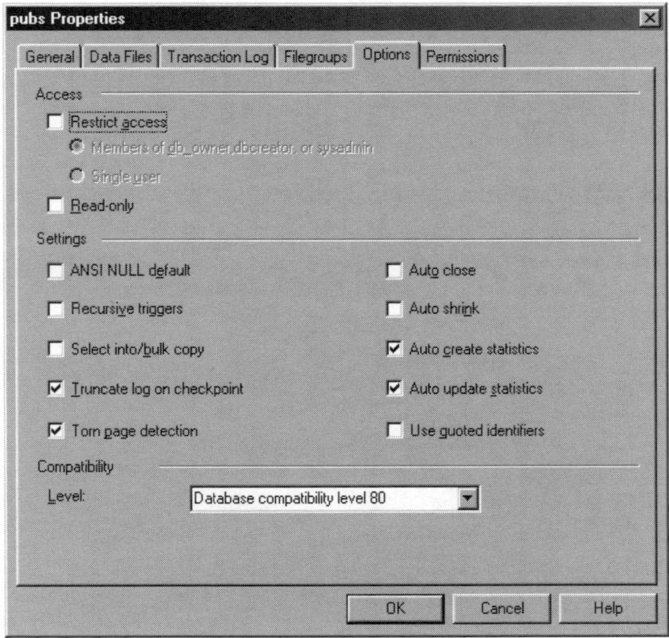

4.    Click **OK**.

There is a downside to turning this on. Picture the following scenario: You backed up your database overnight. Everything has been going great all morning. Suddenly, mid-afternoon, you have a data corruption. What happens to all the work that was entered into the system all morning?

If you restore the database from a backup, you will overlay/replace/destroy/etc. your current database. A database restore is destructive to the old database. This means that you will have lost all the work from that morning. Your solution, then, before you load, is to do a differential backup. This stores all the changes from the database, and when you load the differential backup, those changes will be applied. If luck is with you, this differential backup may allow you to retain all the work you have done that morning. If you are truncating the log, however, there will be nothing there. So, if you want to be able to preserve the day's work (transactions) you do not want to turn that option on. Instead, you will go with option two, which is to maintain your transaction log.

You can find out how big your transaction log is like this:

1. Click on the appropriate database in the Enterprise Manager.

2. Look at the bottom of the General tab:

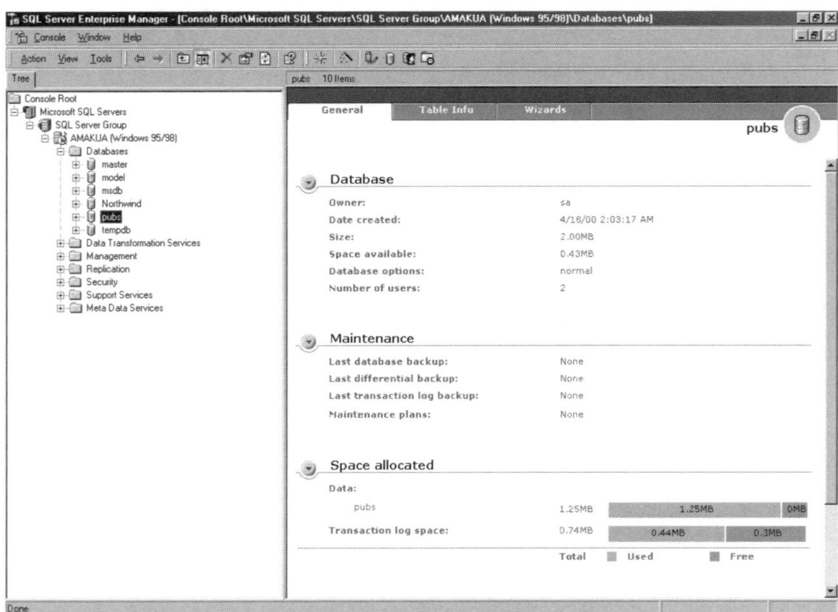

If your log is filling up, you have two options. The first is to perform a differential backup (see Chapter 8). This will empty out the log. As each log grows and fills, you can make additional incremental backups. The second option, preferred for small systems, is to simply make the log big enough to accommodate all the day's transactions, and then some. This way, if there is a corruption, you only have to take a current differential backup, restore the backup, and apply the differential backup. There is one catch: If you are not automatically truncating the log, you must do it manually. The database backup does not automatically truncate it. If the log does fill up, you need to truncate it to allow additional transactions to take place in the log. We suggest truncating the transaction log (perform a differential backup) right before you back up the database. So, initially, check the size of the transaction log during the day to make sure it does not fill. At the end of the day, note how full it is, and make sure it has room to accommodate twice as many transactions. Once a month or so, check again at the end of the day to make sure it's not nearing the point where it might fill up.

If you need to make the transaction log bigger, you can do it like this:

1.  In the Enterprise Manager, right-click on the appropriate database and select **Properties**.

2.  Select the **General** tab in the Properties dialog.

3.  Click the **Database Properties** option.

4.  Select the **Transaction Log** tab.

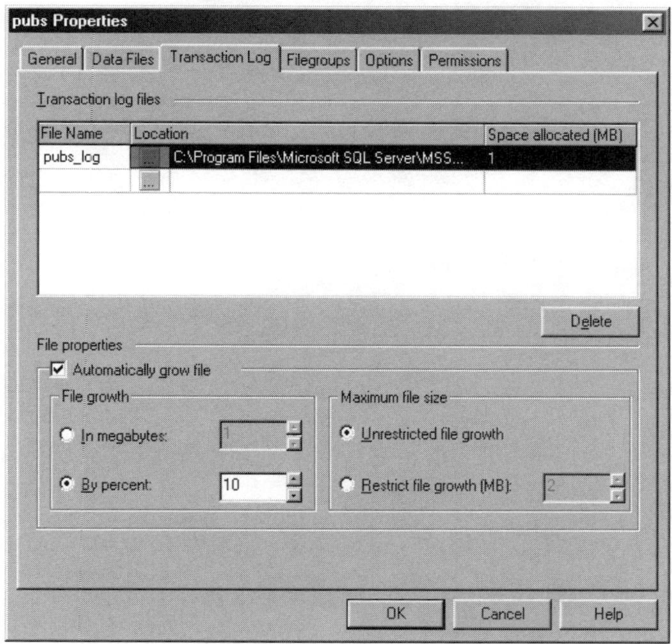


5.  Click inside the Space Allocated (MB) box of a transaction log file and enter a larger number.

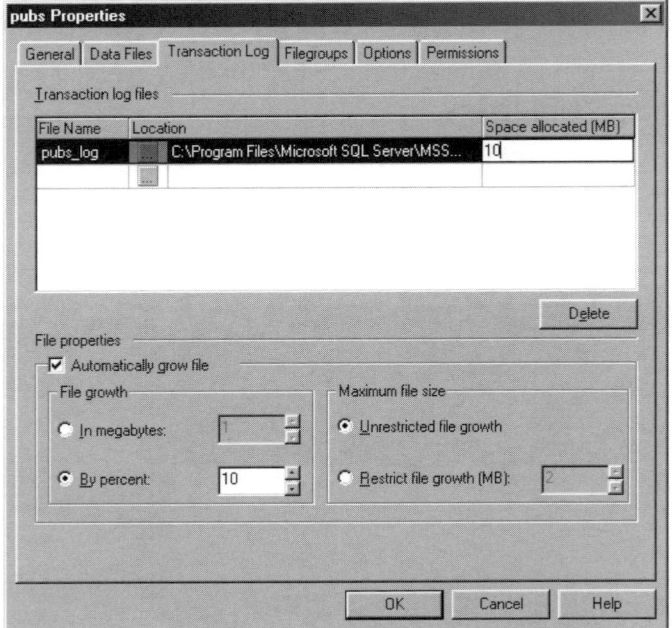

6.   Click **OK**.

If you would like to get fancier, you can tell the log to automatically get bigger rather than fill up, like this:

1.   In the Properties window, click on the **Transaction Log** tab.

2.   Check the **Automatically grow file** option.

There are two options you can use to set automatic growth:

- **In megabytes** The transaction log file will increase by exactly the number of megabytes specified.

- **By percent** The transaction log file will increase by the percentage specified.

3.   Click **OK**.

The basic things to remember here are to monitor the growth of your transaction log, make sure it doesn't fill, and decide how to manage it based on the needs of your business.

# Chapter 10

# Database Space Management

A database is not a physical thing that you can pick up, like a hard drive; it is an intangible thing, like data. From this perspective, the database is the thing that contains all of your data, which takes physical form in disks. A database usually starts out with a finite amount of space, and can be expanded manually or automatically.

## Monitoring the Size of Your Database

You can check the size of your database like this:

1. In Enterprise Manager, click on the appropriate database.

2. Select **Space Allocated** in the taskpad.

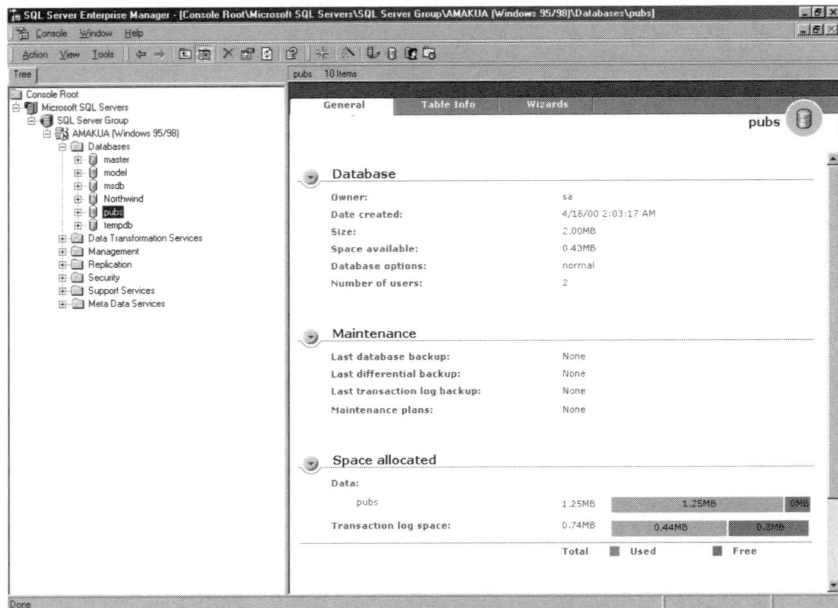

You can manually expand it like this:

1. In the Enterprise Manager, click on the appropriate database.

2. Select **General** in the taskpad.

3. Right-click on the database, and select **Properties**.

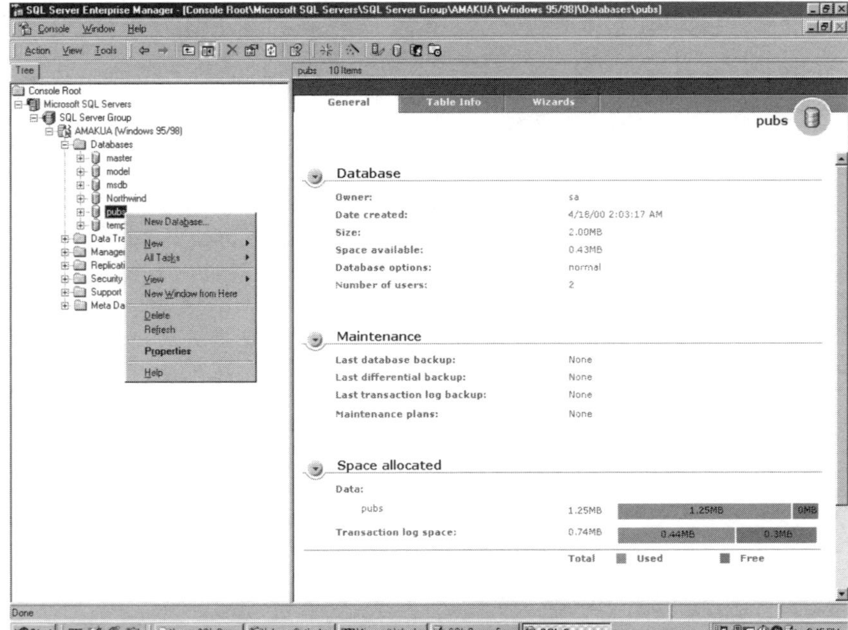

4.    Select the **Data Files** tab.

5.    Click inside the Space Allocated (MB) box of a database file and enter a larger number.

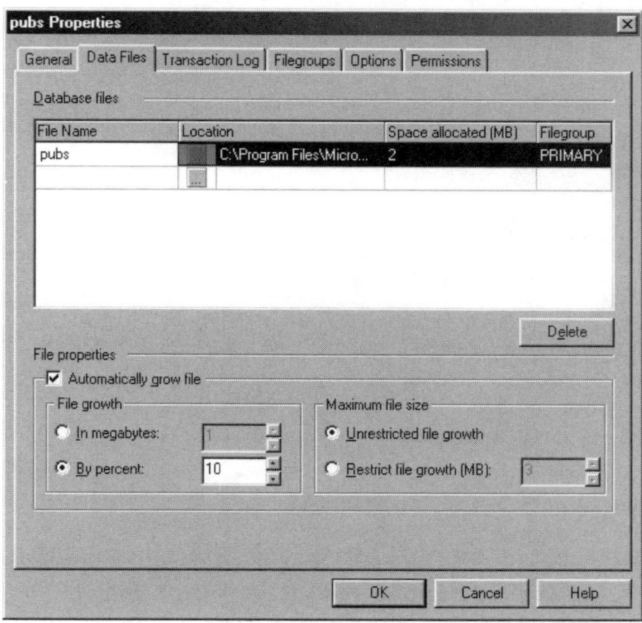

6.    Click **OK**.

You can tell it to expand automatically like this:

1.    Click on the **Data Files** tab.

2.    Check the **Automatically grow file** option.

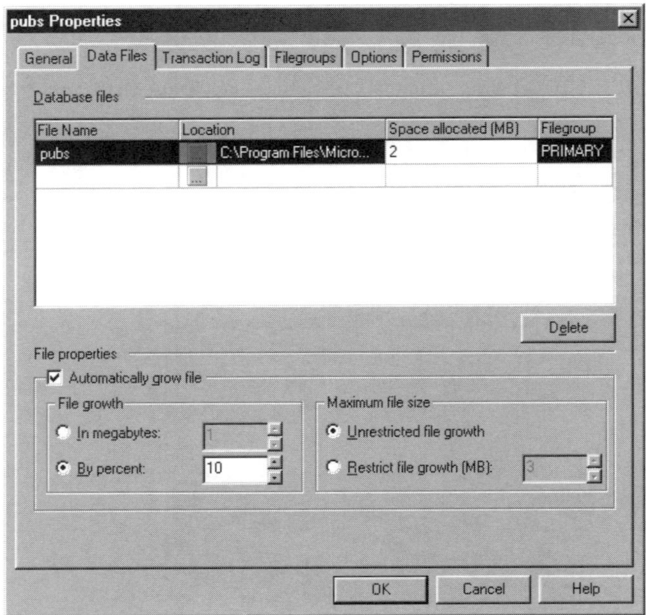

Note there are two options for automatic growth:

- **In megabytes** The file will be increased by exactly the number of megabytes specified.

- **By percent** The file will be increased by the percentage specified.

3. Click **OK**.

Now, here's where attention to detail is important: If the data fills up all the space in the database, and the database is not made bigger (manually or automatically), then you can no longer put data into your database. So, identify how full your database is by looking at the Space Allocated area in the database window.

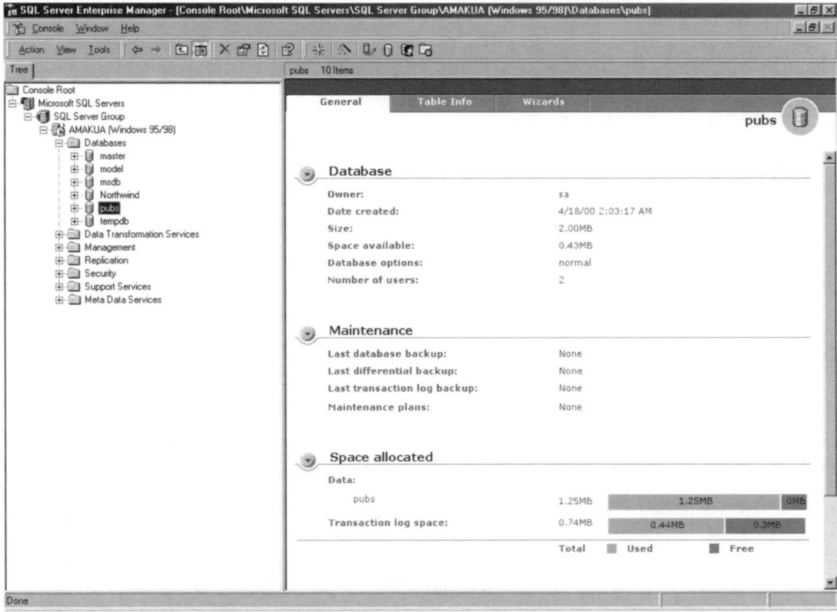

Every month or so, record how full your database is:

| Month | Space Used | Space Available (Allocated) |
| --- | --- | --- |
| January | 50 MB | 350 MB |
| February | 75 MB | 350 MB |
| March | 100 MB | 350 MB |
| April | 150 MB | 350 MB |

In the previous chart, we seem to have a nice, smooth growth of about 25 MB of data per month. This should lead you to predict that you fill a 350 MB database in 14 months (350/25=14). That is a reasonable guess. But you need to check your results. Perhaps you took on additional clients, there was a cold and flu (or tax) season, or some other event that drives your data needs. In April, we used an additional 50 MB, not 25. Does that mean that you are going to use 50 MB more each month? Or go back to 25? The answer: You can't know. That is why you have to pay attention. Watch your database space utilization closely. Use this data to predict when you might need to buy more disk space. Then act based on hard data.

# Chapter 11

# Updating Index Statistics

Updating your index statistics is the single most important thing that you need to do in order to maintain performance in your database. With Microsoft SQL Server 2000, this normally happens automatically. Under some circumstances, though (when you are loading lots of data, for example), the automated statistics update may not be running often enough to keep your system performing smoothly. In this chapter, we look at the procedures for manually updating your index statistics.

## The Cost-Based Optimizer

SQL Server has a cost-based optimizer. Let's take a moment and discuss what this means. When a query (request for data) is submitted (sent) to the server, there are a variety of methods the server may use to resolve the query (return the correct set of data). This ranges from a table scan (reading an entire table looking for the results) to using an existing index to creating an index automatically and dynamically (as you may guess, this is <u>not</u> efficient).

The *optimizer* is the software within the SQL Server which determines the best (read: fastest) approach to retrieving the data.

*Cost-based* means that the server evaluates all practical approaches to resolving the query, and uses that method.

How does the server determine the best method? Well, the answer to that question is itself a separate five-day class. The short answer is that the server breaks the query into a query tree and picks the best approach for each component of the tree based on its own internal statistics regarding the usefulness of each index. Like the table of contents in a book, statistics give the optimizer a place to start looking. If the statistics are missing, the optimizer must look at all the pages (as in the book). Worse, if the statistics are wrong, the optimizer must first follow the wrong path and subsequently look at all the pages in the book. You need to make sure that the SQL Server's optimizer has access to reasonably recent statistical information.

# Commands

Historically, these statistics needed to be updated manually. With the advent of Microsoft SQL Server 7.0, the server can now do this automatically. If, however, you are experiencing seemingly inexplicable performance problems, or if you are loading a lot of data or your initial data, you may need to instruct the server to update statistics for the table(s) involved. Here are the commands and system procedures that you can use to maintain your statistics pages:

| | |
|---|---|
| UPDATE STATISTICS | The base command which instructs the server to reset the information for a particular table or for a table's index. |
| SP_AUTOSTATS | Enables or disables the automatic statistics settings for a particular table or one or more of its indexes. |
| SP_UPDATESTATS | This command is your friend. It runs UPDATE STATISTICS against all of the tables in a database. |
| CREATE STATISTICS | Allows you to create the statistical information for columns that are not in indexes. |
| DROP STATISTICS | Removes statistics created by the CREATE STATISTICS command. |
| DBCC SHOW_STATISTICS | Retrieves and shows statistics for a specific table and index combination. |

# UPDATE STATISTICS

This command reinitializes the distribution of key values (statistics) for the specified table. It is run automatically when an index is created on a table that already contains data (so you do not need to run this command if you are dropping and rebuilding indexes).

### Syntax

```
UPDATE STATISTICS table
[
index
| (statistics_name[,...n])
]
[ WITH
[
[FULLSCAN]
| SAMPLE number {PERCENT | ROWS}]
]
[[,] [ALL | COLUMNS | INDEX]
[[,] NORECOMPUTE]
]
```

### Arguments

table

> The name of the table for which to update statistics. Index names are not unique within a database (though they are unique for a table), so you must specify the table name even if you are only updating the statistics for an index. We recommend, however, that you only update statistics for an entire table.

index

> This is the index for which statistics are being updated (unless of course this is for all indexes on a table).

statistics_name

> If you are going to create a set of statistics for non-indexed columns, this is where you can update those statistics independently.

n

> This is a placeholder indicating that multiple statistics_name groups can be specified.

FULLSCAN

Specifies that all rows in the table should be read to gather the statistics (rather than a random sampling). Using FULLSCAN is the same as using SAMPLE 100 PERCENT, but it cannot be used with the SAMPLE option.

SAMPLE number {PERCENT | ROWS}

This specifies the percentage of the table or the number of rows to sample when collecting statistics for larger tables. If the PERCENT, ROWS, or number option results in too few rows being sampled, SQL Server automatically corrects the sampling based on the number of existing rows in the table.

The default behavior is to perform a sample scan on the target table, with the SQL Server automatically calculating the optimal sample size.

ALL | COLUMNS | INDEX

This specifies whether the UPDATE STATISTICS statement affects column statistics, index statistics, or all existing statistics. If no option is specified (recommended), the UPDATE STATISTICS statement affects all statistics. Only one type (ALL, COLUMNS, or INDEX) can be specified for each UPDATE STATISTICS statement.

NORECOMPUTE

Specifies that statistics that become out of date are not automatically recomputed. Don't do this. Statistics become out of date depending on the number of INSERT, UPDATE, and DELETE operations performed on indexed columns. When specified, this option causes SQL Server to disable automatic statistics rebuilding. To restore automatic statistics recomputation, you will have to reissue the UPDATE STATISTICS command without the NORECOMPUTE option or execute SP_AUTOSTATS.

The UPDATE STATISTICS command should be run in the SQL Server Query Analyzer:

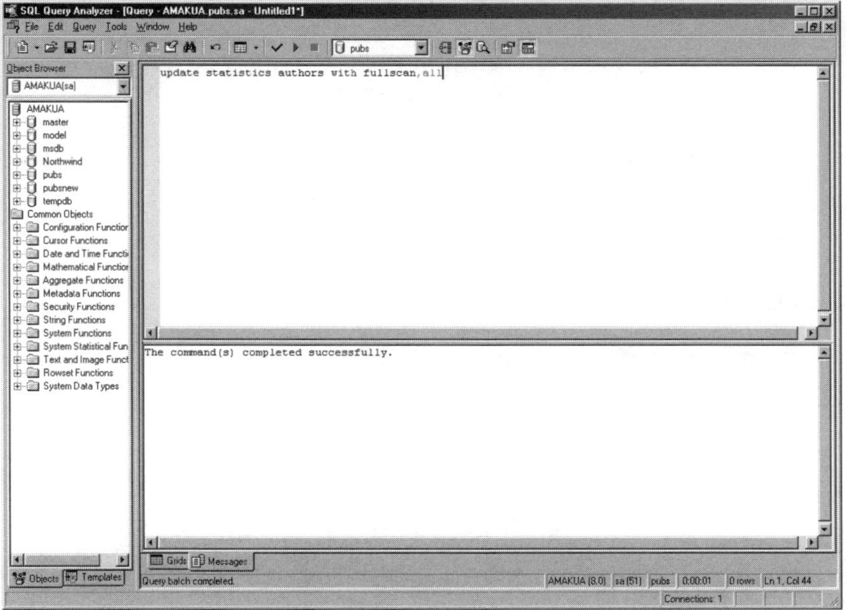

# SP_AUTOSTATS

This is how you change the way statistics are automatically managed. SP_AUTOSTATS will display or change the automatic UPDATE STATISTICS setting for a specific index or all indexes (recommended) for a given table in the current database.

### Syntax

```
sp_autostats [@tblname =] 'table_name'
[, [@flagc =] 'stats_flag']
[, [@indname =] 'index_name']
```

### Arguments

[@tblname =] 'table_name'
> This is the name of the table for which we will display or change the automatic UPDATE STATISTICS setting. If index_name is also supplied, SQL Server enables the automatic UPDATE STATISTICS setting for that index.

[@flagc =] 'stats_flag'
> This sets the automatic UPDATE STATISTICS setting for the specified table to enabled (ON) or disabled (OFF).

[@indname =] 'index_name'
> This is the name of the index for which to enable or disable the automatic UPDATE STATISTICS setting.

Note that a stored procedure can be called with or without the parameter names.

This statement:

```
EXEC sp_autostats authors, 'OFF', au_id
```

is equivalent to this statement:

```
EXEC sp_autostats @tblname = authors, @flagc ='OFF', @indname = au_id
```

The SP_AUTOSTATS procedure should be run in the SQL Server Query Analyzer:

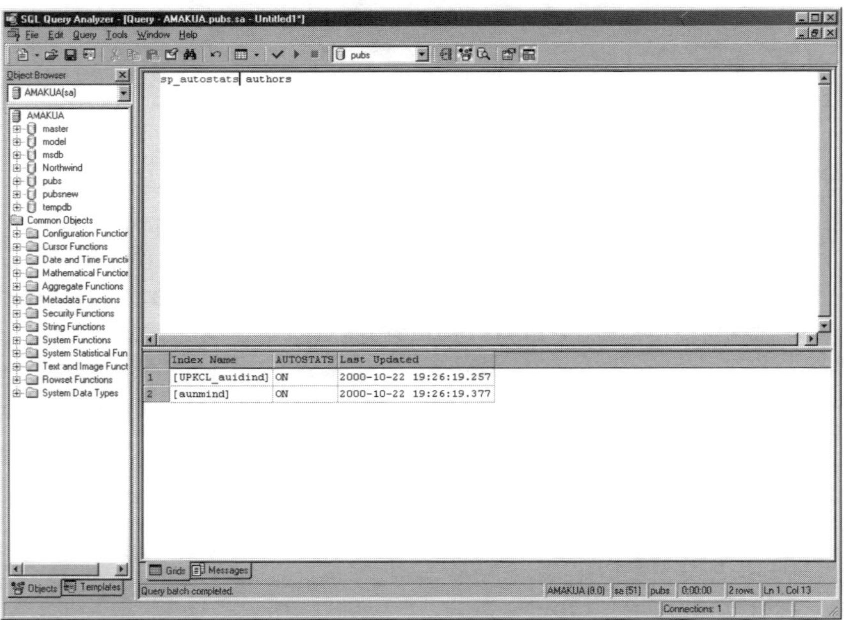

Note that there are two result windows, one listing the indexes, as shown above, and the other listing the messages:

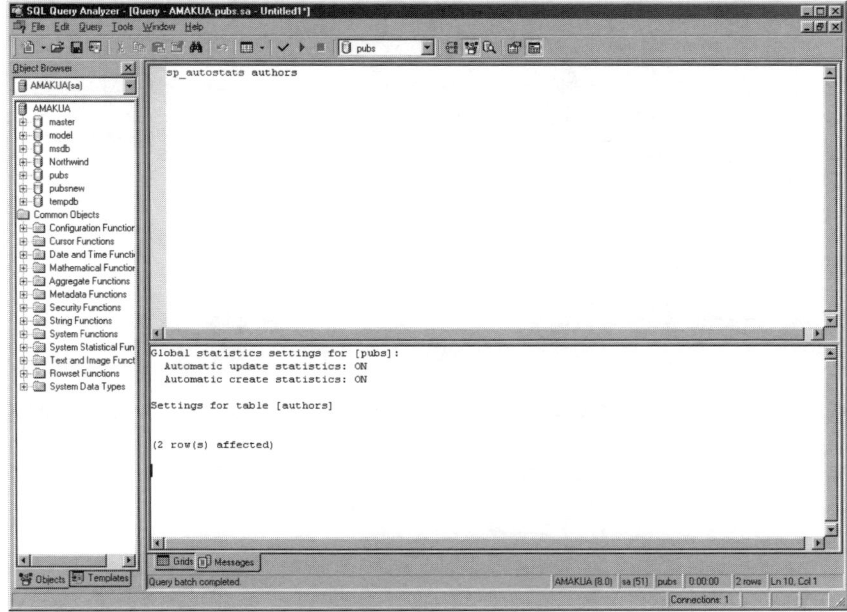

# SP_UPDATESTATS

This command is your friend if you are manually running UPDATE STATISTICS. It will run the UPDATE STATISTICS command on all user-defined tables in the current database. In the old days, we used to have to do these one at a time. This procedure builds a dynamic list and executes it.

### Syntax

```
sp_updatestats
```

The SP_UPDATESTATS command displays messages indicating its progress. When the update is completed, it reports that statistics have been updated for all tables.

The SP_UPDATESTATS command should be run in the Query Analyzer:

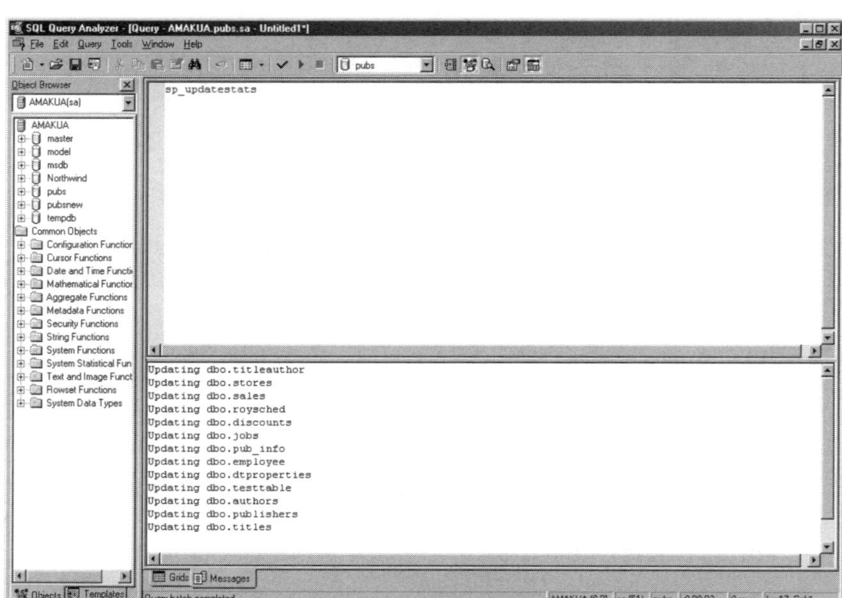

# DBCC SHOW_STATISTICS

For true geeks (like your authors), this command is fun because it shows you what the optimizer knows about your data. It displays the current distribution statistics for the specified target index on the specified table.

### Syntax

```
DBCC SHOW_STATISTICS (table, target)
```

### Arguments

table

> This is the name of the table for which to display statistics information.

target

> This is the name of the index for which to display statistics information.

The results returned indicate the selectivity of an index (this means the level of uniqueness, or lack of) which provides the basis for determining whether or not an index is useful to the optimizer. To see the last date the statistics were updated, you can use STATS_DATE. Here is an example of a query that uses STATS_DATE:

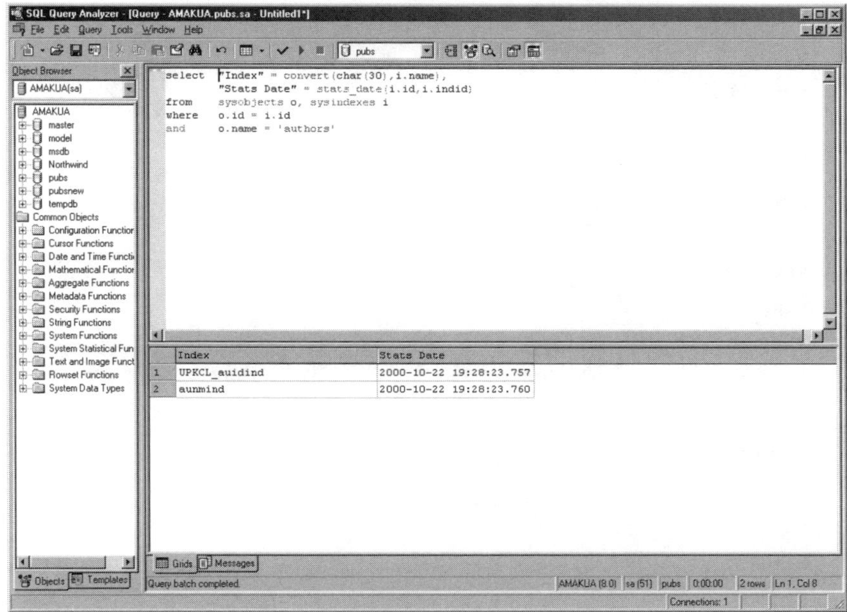

DBCC SHOW_STATISTICS should be run in the SQL Server Query Analyzer. It produces results similar to this sample output:

```
dbcc show_statistics (authors, aunmind)
--------------------------------
Statistics for INDEX 'aunmind'.
    Updated                 Rows  Rows Sampled Steps  Density  Average key length
    ------------------      ----  ------------ -----  ------   ------------------
    Dec 22 1999 9:53PM  23    23                      23       4.3478262E-2
                                                               24.52174
(1 row(s) affected)
    All density     Columns
    ------------    --------------------------
    4.5454547E-2    au_lname
    4.3478262E-2    au_lname, au_fname
    4.3478262E-2    au_lname, au_fname, au_id
(3 row(s) affected)
```

```
Steps
----------------
Bennet
Blotchet-Halls
Carson
DeFrance
del Castillo
Dull
Green
Greene
Gringlesby
Hunter
Karsen
Locksley
MacFeather
McBadden
O'Leary
Panteley
Ringer
Ringer
Smith
Straight
Stringer
White
Yokomoto
(23 row(s) affected)
DBCC execution completed. If DBCC printed error messages, contact your system
administrator.
```

The following set of columns and their descriptions reflect output from the DBCC SHOW_STATISTICS command.

| Column Name | Description |
| --- | --- |
| Updated | Date and time the statistics were last updated |
| Rows | Number of rows in the table |
| Rows Sampled | Number of rows sampled for statistics information |
| Steps | Number of distribution steps |
| Density | Selectivity of the index |

| Column Name | Description |
| --- | --- |
| Average key length | Average length of a row |
| All density | Selectivity of the specified column prefix in the index |
| Columns | Name of the index column prefix for which All density is displayed |
| Steps | Number of histogram values in the current distribution statistics for the specified target on the specified table |

# Index Maintenance

Indexes are storage structures that are used to improve performance for your queries. You can think of an index as the table of contents of a book. It doesn't tell you where each word is, but it assists you in narrowing down where you look.

As you add rows of data, remove rows of data, or update (and correspondingly move) data, the indexes no longer point at the data properly, forcing the computer to search the data without using them. This would be like having to look through an entire book to find which section you want to read. The solution to this problem used to be to drop and rebuild the indexes. With the current release of SQL Server, instead, we will simply run the DBCC REINDEX command.

## Rebuilding Your Indexes

Of all the maintenance tasks that are performed worldwide on Microsoft SQL Server, index maintenance is the most neglected. This is because the amount of work to maintain them used to be excessive, the rewards for maintaining them properly are seemingly intangible, and the penalties for not maintaining them are not especially severe unless you have a high-transaction volume system. The consequence of not rebuilding your indexes, one way or another (DBCC DBREINDEX is recommended), is simply data fragmentation (which wastes space and slows down index access).

If your database is under 100 MB, you may simply not notice any effects of failure to rebuild your indexes, but maintaining the indexes periodically is still a good idea. How often do you want to do this? This depends on the size and volatility of your system. If you have a system under 1 gigabyte in size, and your volatility is below a transaction per second, monthly is probably fine. If your volume is higher, consider rebuilding more often.

## DBCC DBREINDEX

This command rebuilds one or more indexes for a table in the specified database. We recommend you rebuild all indexes for each table each time. This makes it more difficult to forget one.

### Syntax

```
DBCC DBREINDEX
( [ 'database.owner.table_name' [, index_name [, fillfactor ] ] ]
) [WITH NO_INFOMSGS]
```

### Arguments

'database.owner.table_name'
> Name of the table for which you want to rebuild the index. If you are within the database, you can specify the name of the table only.

index_name
> This is the name of the index to rebuild. Again, we suggest you simply skip this parameter and do all indexes for the table.

fillfactor
> The percentage of space on each index page to be used for storing data when the index is created. Fillfactor replaces the original fillfactor, which was specified when the index was created, as the new default for the index and for any other non-clustered indexes that are rebuilt because a clustered index is rebuilt. When fillfactor is 0, DBCC DBREINDEX uses the original fillfactor.

WITH NO_INFOMSGS
> This option suppresses all informational messages (that is, those with severity levels from 0 through 10).

The DBCC DBREINDEX command rebuilds an index for a table or all indexes defined for a table. Since they are rebuilt dynamically, any indexes that are built to enforce either PRIMARY KEY or UNIQUE constraints can be rebuilt without having to drop and re-create those constraints. This saves you from having to find or build the data definition language (DDL) statements that are usually used to drop and then re-create the indexes.

**Note:** If you specify either index_name or fillfactor, you must specify all of the preceding parameters.

The DBCC DBREINDEX command is not supported on system tables.

Output from DBCC DBREINDEX returns a result set that looks something like this :

```
DBCC execution completed. If DBCC printed error messages, contact your
system administrator.
```

DBCC DBREINDEX is executed using the Query Analyzer program.

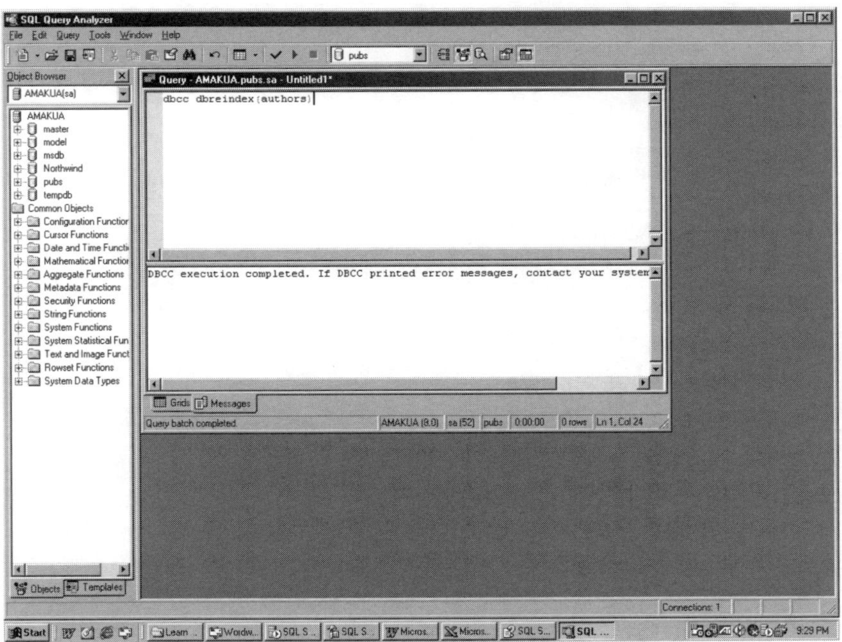

# Chapter 13

# Alerts, Operators, and Jobs

There's an old saying that goes "a watched pot never boils." It would be nice to say that "a watched server never fails," but that is usually not the case. Often times, the watched server never fails until you turn away for a second to look at something else. This leaves the poor administrator with a dilemma: Stay and watch the server 24 hours a day, seven days a week, 365 days a year, or get someone or something else to do it and maintain some semblance of a life.

There are often many tasks that must be performed regularly in order for a database to run smoothly. There can often be enough tasks and conditions that an administrator must look for that little time can be left for anything else. So, to ease the burden on the administrator, SQL Server has procedures and tools to automate most of the common administrative tasks.

## SQL Server Agent

One of the tools that handles these administration tasks is the SQL Server Agent. This program acts as an administration assistant. The Agent scans the NT application log and looks for the errors the administrator specifies. If any of the errors are found, the SQL Server Agent can e-mail or page an appropriate operator. If a job has been specified in response to a particular error, the job will be executed. In order for alerts, operators, and jobs to function, the SQL Server Agent must be running and have been started with an account that has the proper permissions and settings.

To start the SQL Server Agent:

1.  Click the **Start** button.

2.  Choose **Programs|Microsoft SQL Server|Service Manager**. (This might also be in the icon tray.)

3.  Choose **SQL Server Agent** from the Services box. If the server is up, Stop is an available option; you need go no further. If Start is an available option, you need to start the service.

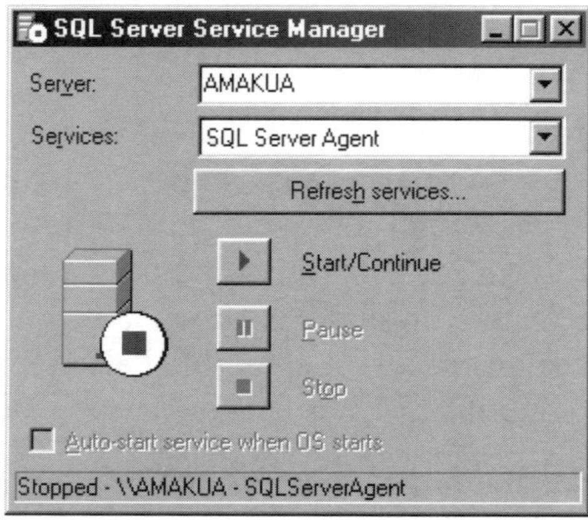


4.  Click the **Start/Continue** button. When the agent is up, the Stop button is highlighted.

In order for mail and paging to function with the SQL Server Agent, it must be configured.

To configure the SQL Server Agent to work with Windows messaging:

1.   In Enterprise Manager, open the **Management** folder.

2.   Right-click **SQL Server Agent**.

3.   Select **Windows Messaging Settings** from the Mail profile list box.

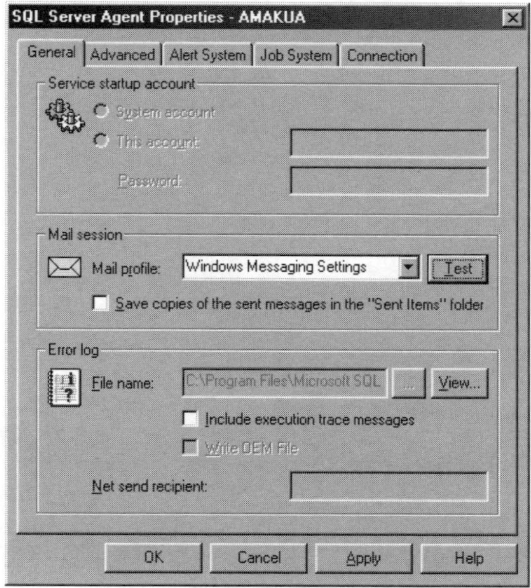

4.   Click the **Test** button to test the messaging settings.

5.   Click **OK** when finished.

## Creating Alerts

In order for the SQL Server Agent to perform its job, it must be told several things. The Agent must be told what to look for, what tasks to perform, and who to notify. These are the alerts, jobs, and operators. Alerts are alarms; they are what the Agent should be looking for. If any specified events happen, it will notify the appropriate people.

To create an alert:

1.   In Enterprise Manager, open the **Management** folder.

2. Open the **SQL Server Agent** item.

3. Right-click **Alerts**.

4. Click on **New Alert**.

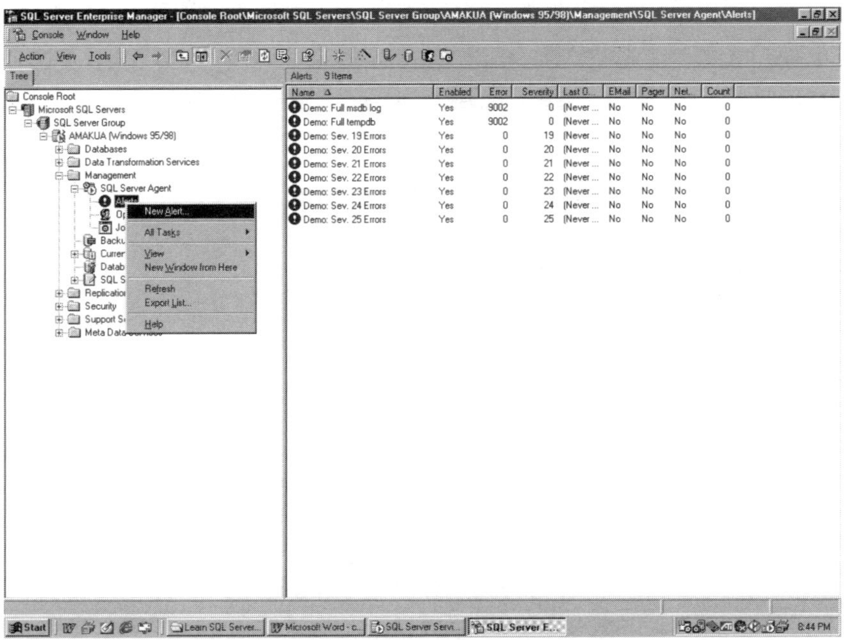

5. Enter the name of the new alert in the dialog box that appears.

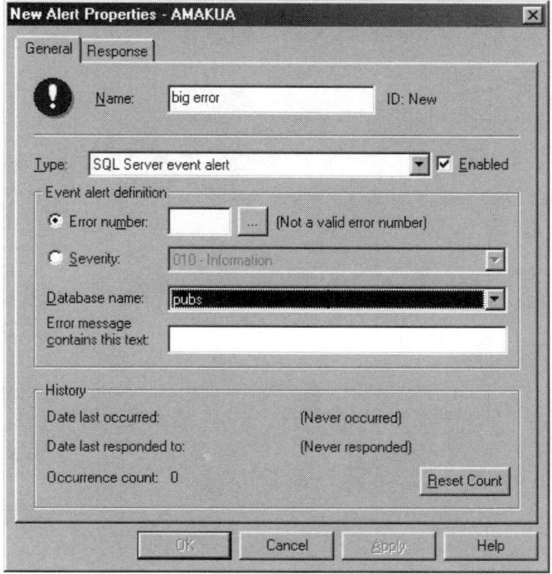

6.  Choose the type of alert from the Type drop-down box.

7.  Choose **Error number** or **Severity**. Error number allows alerts to be defined for a specific error number. Severity allows SQL Server to define alerts based on the type of error or its severity. For this example, the selection is Error number.

8.  To locate a particular error, click on the button with the ellipsis next to Error number. This will provide a search screen to locate a specific error. Type a search phrase in the Message text contains box and click the **Find** button.

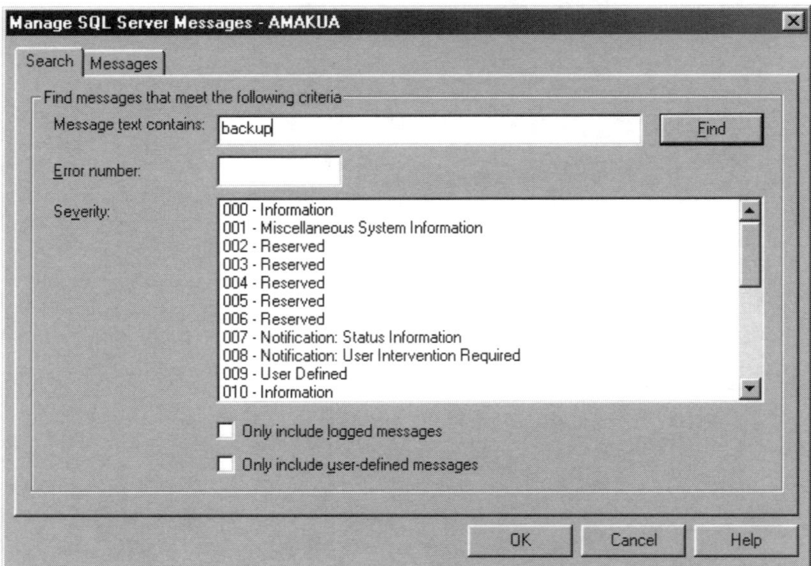

A list of related messages will be provided.

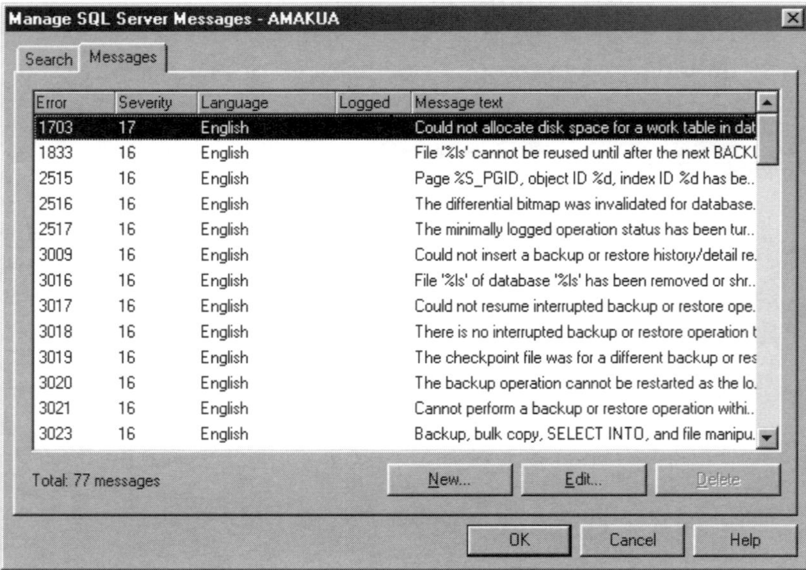

9. Note the error number, and click on **OK**.

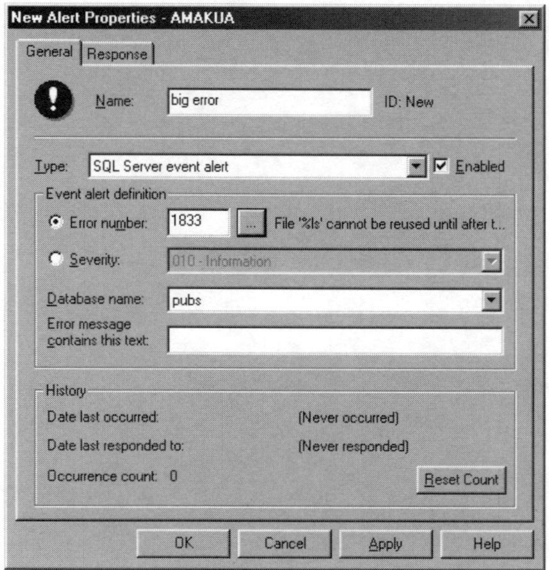

10. After entering the error number and filling in other information, click **OK**.

## Creating Operators

Now that the alerts have been defined, the next step is to decide who needs to know when the alert happens. These people are the operators. An operator is a systems administrator who will be notified if an error is found.

To create an operator:

1. In Enterprise Manager, open the **Management** folder.

2. Open the **SQL Server Agent**.

3. Right-click **Operators**.

4. Click **New Operator**.

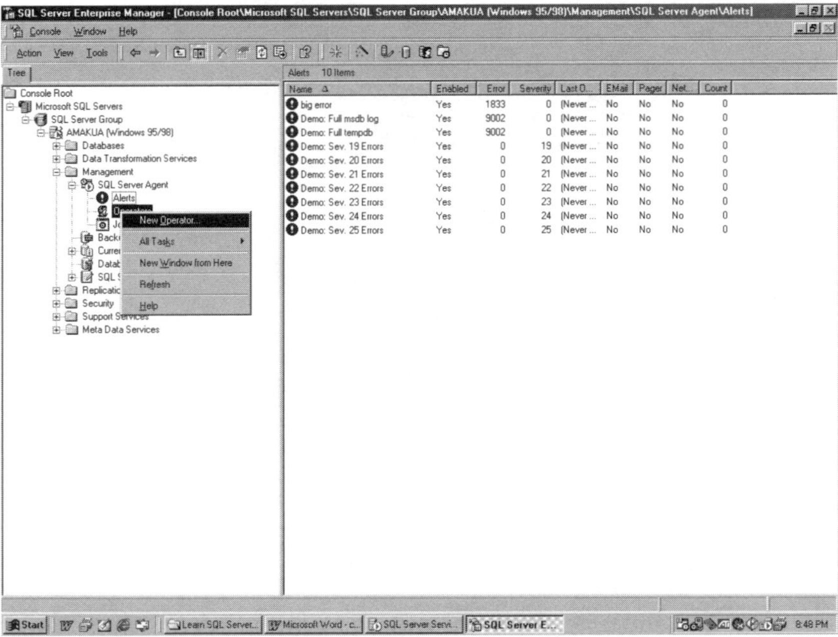

5.    Type the name of the operator in the Name box.

6.    Enter the e-mail address of the operator in the E-mail name box.

7.    Enter the pager e-mail name in the Pager e-mail name box.

8.    Enter the net send address in the Net send address box.

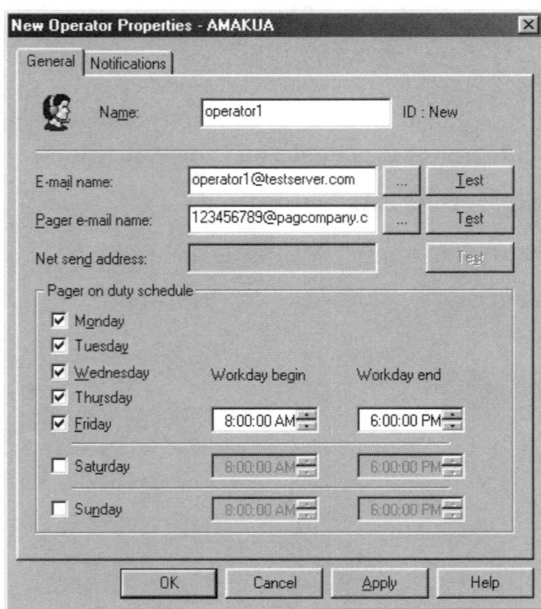

To define the notifications this operator should receive:

1. Click the **Notifications** tab.

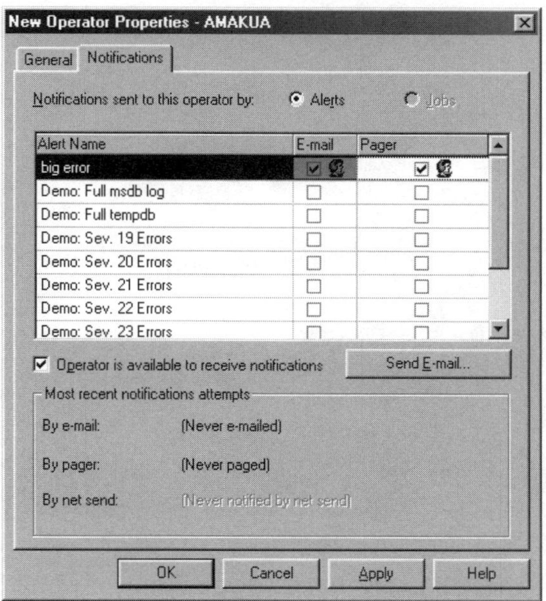

2. Check the necessary notifications for this operator.

3. Click **OK**.

# Creating Jobs

A job is a task that the SQL Server should automatically perform. There are three kinds of jobs that the SQL Server Agent can perform.

- A Transact-SQL command (SQL statements or programs)

- An operating system command (command prompt command)

- An ActiveX script ( a program written in VBScript or JavaScript)

To set up a job:

1. In Enterprise Manager, open the **Management** folder.

2. Open the **SQL Server Agent**.

3. Right-click **Jobs**.

4. Select **New Job**.

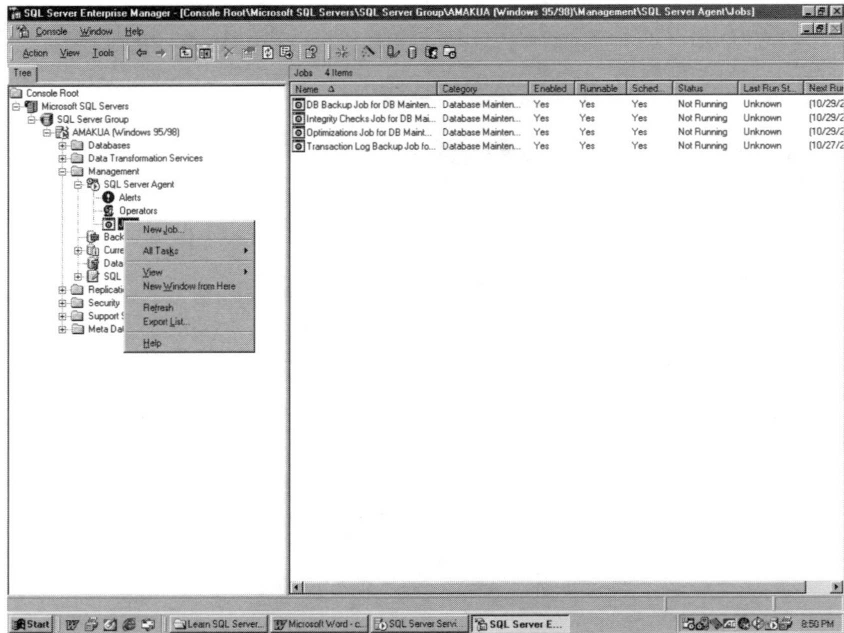

5.  Type a name for the job in the Name box of the New Job Properties dialog.

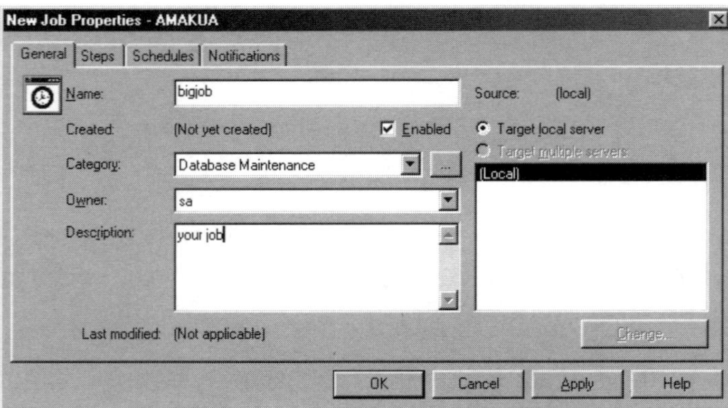

6.  Type a description for the job in the Description box.

7.  Select a category for the job from the Category box. Jobs can be Transact-SQL commands, but they may also be operating system commands or ActiveX programs.

8.  Click the **Steps** tab.

9.  Click **New**.

10.  Enter a name for the step.

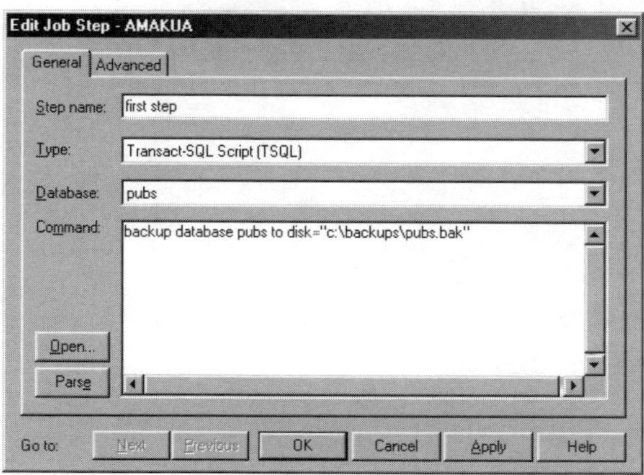

11.  Select the type of step (for the example, use Transact-SQL).

12.  Select the database involved.

13.  Enter the Transact-SQL command or script to be executed.

14.  Click **OK**.

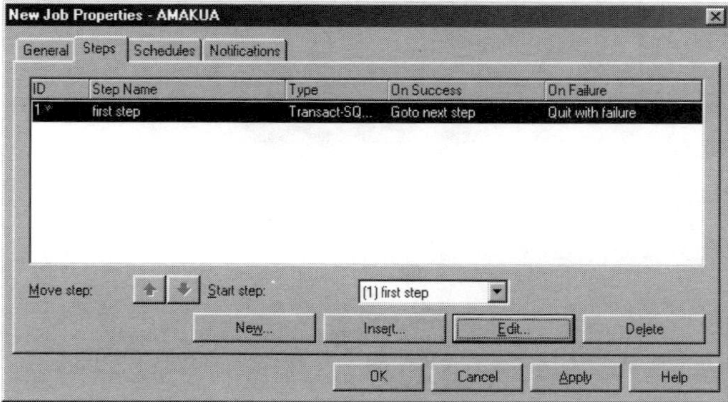

To determine a run schedule for the job:

1.  Select the **Schedules** tab in the Properties dialog.

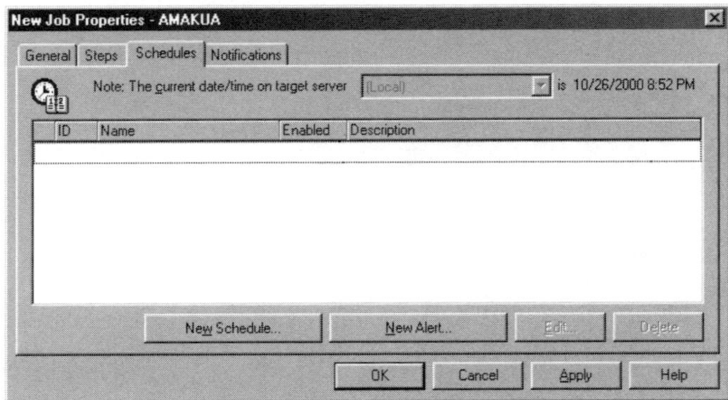

2. Select the appropriate job.

3. Click **New Schedule**.

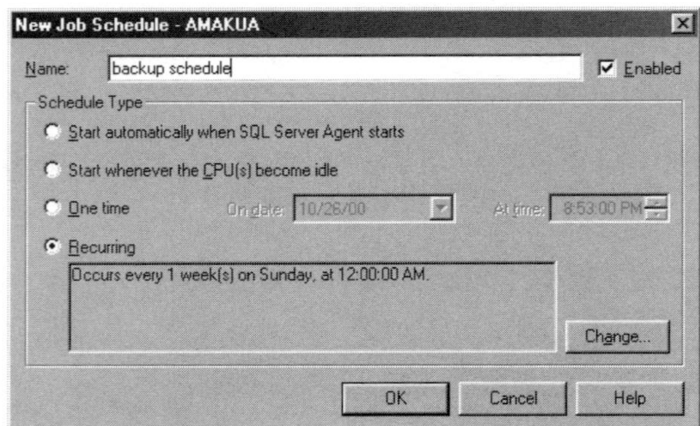

4. Decide when this task will run and select one of the following options:

*Start automatically when SQL Server Agent starts*
This option is self-explanatory.

*Start whenever the CPU(s) become idle*
This option means the task will run when the CPU is not busy with other tasks.

*One time*
When this is selected, a valid date and time must be provided.

*Recurring*
This is for a repeating scheduled task.

For the example, Recurring is selected.

To alter the schedule, click the **Change** button.

5.    Select whether it is a daily, monthly, or weekly task (the example is Daily). Select any days the job should be executed. Select the time for the job to be performed in the Daily frequency section.

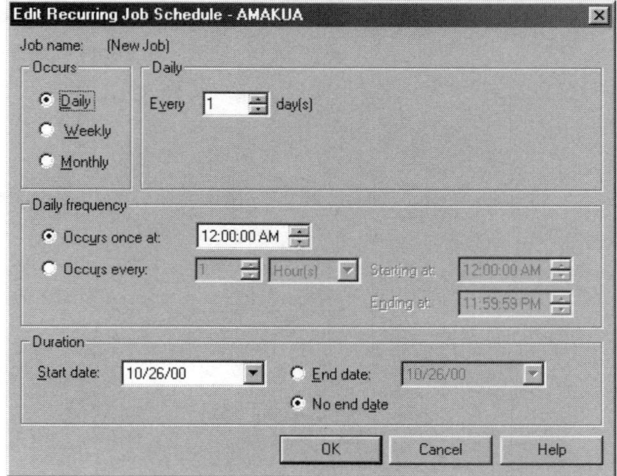

6.    Click **OK**.

7.    If any operators need to be notified of the job, click on the **Notifications** tab. Check off the appropriate types of notification from the different types—E-mail, Pager, or Net Send. Select the appropriate operator from the drop lists. Select when the operator should be notified of the job's conditions.

The choices are:

- When the job succeeds

- When the job fails

- Whenever the job completes

With these automation tools, the SQL Server Agent will be able to know what errors or conditions are critical to the server. The Agent will be able to notify the appropriate administrators when these errors occur and the Agent will be able to perform specific maintenance tasks on its own. This will allow the administrator to spend more time dealing with other issues rather than the day-to-day operations of the server.

# Some Rules to Work By

Following are some frequently asked questions and the answers, as well as some general tips given by DBAs from around the country. Special thanks to Darren Green, Sajal Kumar, Ryan Malayter, Tammy Moisan, John Scances, Richard Scherrer, Patrick Scribner, Lara Siren, Robert White, and Andrew Wiegand.

Know how to get in touch with Microsoft Support. Have the appropriate telephone numbers and be prepared to pay to get your system back if it is mission critical. Do not rely on a purchased package for all of your backups; perform some normal backups as well. Think of this as insurance. It is not lucky to have coverage; it is lucky never having to file a claim. If there is a problem, run a complete system backup at that point so you can at least get back to where you are. Do this before "trying things." The current situation may not be as bad as it looks, but could be made worse than it looks.

## Blocking Problems

### Problem

What is blocking and how do I determine if there is blocking on my SQL Server?

### Resolution

Blocking occurs when two users are attempting to access the same resource. If one user has a lock on the record in a table, and then another user attempts to access that record, the second user will be blocked by the first user.

Blocking can be identified by executing the SP_WHO stored procedure in Query Analyzer. Another version of SP_WHO is SP_WHO2, which returns some extra information in a format that is more readable than SP_WHO.

Once you have executed SP_WHO2, examine the BlkBy column. If you see any numbers in that column, then there is blocking on your server. Each number in the column represents a user that is blocking another user.

If you need the blocking resolved immediately, you can execute the kill command to kill the user's process (i.e., kill <number>, where <number> is the number in the BlkBy column). Also, you can open SQL Profiler and attempt to determine the SQL being executed by the blocking user. You want to trace the SQL:Stmt:Completed event (located in the TSQL group) and filter on spid, where spid equals the number in the BlkBy column.

# Blocking Process/Timeout

### Problem

We have provided an Access front end to a SQL back end. We have installed the most current ODBC drivers on all computers. We use a database of parts for all jobs. Each employee is responsible for specific jobs in the database. There are one or two employees who are concerned with all jobs. When an employee opens up a query for a specific job and then another employee opens a query for all jobs and one tries to update, everyone is locked out. The following error occurs to all users:

```
ODBC - update on a linked table "Table name" failed. [Microsoft][ODBC
SQL Server Driver] Timeout expired(#0).
```

I have done lots of reading on locks, blocks, and deadlocks and I am getting the impression that SQL Server 2000 determines the locking setup and that I should not intervene.

### Resolution

What you are probably experiencing is not a SQL issue but an Access issue. There are two places to set a timeout in Access, one is global and the other is per query. More than likely your per query timeout needs to be extended.

# Indexing

### Problem

I received this error message when trying to reindex all indexes in a database:

```
DESCRIPTION: 17052 Table Corrupt:
Object ID 0, index ID 0, page ID (1:1172119).
The PageId in the page header = (0:0).
```

The error message repeats with different page IDs. I am unable to identify the offending table or index in the sysobjects or sysindex tables with "Object ID of 0" or "Index ID 0."

### Resolution

This is most likely a transient error caused by activity in the database. Try to run DBCC in single-user mode to be sure. There is no object with an ID of 0; that's why I believe this to be a bogus error. Index ID 0, however, is your data (Index ID 1 if there is a clustered index present).

# Indexing/6.5 to 7.0 Upgrade

### Problem

I've just upgraded my database from SQL Server 6.5 to SQL Server 7.0 and I notice there are many new indexes that did not exist in my 6.5 database. All of these new indexes start with "_WA". Where did they come from?

### Resolution

These are not really indexes but statistics on data distribution for columns in your tables. SQL Server uses these statistics to determine the best execution plan for queries. By default, SQL Server will automatically create statistics on your columns. You can determine if SQL Server is automatically creating statistics with the following SQL:

```
sp_dboption <database name>
```

Do you see an option called "auto create statistics"? If so, SQL Server is automatically creating statistics. In general, this is a good thing and you should leave this option turned on.

# Overallocated Memory

### Problem

I have overallocated memory for SQL Server and now it will not start. What can I do?

### Resolution

To recover from this:

1.  Stop SQL Server and SQL Executive. Also make sure that SQL Enterprise Manager isn't running.

2.  Go to the <sql>\binn directory and type **sqlservr -c –f**. This will start SQL in single-user mode with a minimum config.

3.  Ignore the text messages in this window—but wait for them to finish appearing (shouldn't take more than 10-20 seconds). SQL Server is now started.

4.  Go to another window and start ISQL/W and connect locally with the SA userid.

5.  In ISQL/W issue the following commands :

    ```
    sp_configure memory, <new memory value>
    go
    reconfigure
    go
    ```

6.  Now go back to the window SQL is running in; type **shutdown** and press **Enter**.

7.  SQL Server should shut down. If it doesn't, press **Ctrl+C** to shut it down.

8.  Now you should be able to start SQL normally and connect.

# Installing SQL Server

## Problem

I'm having trouble installing SQL Server. What could be going wrong?

## Resolution

Try the following checklist of things that could go wrong. I have never known anyone not to install SQL after following these instructions. (If you're the first, then let me know.)

1.  Make sure you have administrator level permissions on the machine in question, as SQL needs to create registry entries, services, etc.

2.  Make sure the machine is of the required spec to run the version of SQL you are installing (i.e., if it is SQL EE then make sure you have NT EE; for SQL 2000 you need a 100% PENTIUM compatible chip or an Alpha).

If you have tried to install SQL before, then manually clean up all the files/registry entries as follows:

- Remove the <sql> directory and everything under it

- Remove the <sql> dir from the path (use Control Panel|System for this)

- Remove the SQL registry entries using regedt32|regedit. These are:

### (All versions)

- HKEY_LOCAL_MACHINE\System\CurrentControlSet\Services\MSSQLServer

- HKEY_LOCAL_MACHINE\Software\Microsoft\MSSQLServer

### (6.0 and above)

- HKEY_LOCAL_MACHINE\System\CurrentControlSet\Services\MSDTC

- HKEY_LOCAL_MACHINE\System\CurrentControlSet\Services\SQLExecutive

### (7.0 and above)

- HKEY_LOCAL_MACHINE\System\CurrentControlSet\Services\SQLServerAgent

- HKEY_LOCAL_MACHINE\Software\Microsoft\Microsoft SQL Server 7

- HKEY_LOCAL_MACHINE\Software\Microsoft\MSSQLServ65

If you have lost permission to any of the registry keys, then log on as administrator and take ownership of them starting at the highest relevant level. Use regedt32 and check the box to take ownership of all subkeys as well.

If SQL is complaining about not enough space being there, this could be due to a known bug when there is between <n> times 4,295,917 KB and <n> times 4,367,417 KB. To get around this, either create temporary files to use space up, or start the SQL setup program as follows. Spacing is important.

```
<sqldir>\i386\setup /t SpaceChecking = Off
```

SQL Server is dependent on network functionality—even for the setup routines. Specifically it needs to use named-pipe/mailslot functionality. These usually require a network card to be present. If you don't have a network card, then go to Control Panel|Networks, choose Add Adapter and then add the Microsoft loopback adapter—which is just a dummy driver, no hardware involved. This needs to have working network protocol(s) bound to it. Let whichever protocols you have use default parameters, <u>except</u> for TCP/IP. If you are using this, do <u>not</u> specify the DHCP assigned address; use 192.168.1.1 as the IP address and 255.255.255.0 as the subnet mask. This is a standard RFC1918 non-routed IP address so it shouldn't clash with any dial-up address you may be given by an ISP. If you are using the IPX/SPX protocol, accept the default frame type of 802.3.

If the server service does not start after installing the loopback adapter and you get the message "The server service was terminated" with the following error: "Not enough server storage is available to process this command in the event log," then you need to reinstall your NT service pack to synchronize your NT networking files.

# SQL Server Version

## Problem

How do I determine what version of SQL Server I'm using?

## Resolution

Execute the following extended stored procedure in Query Analyzer and examine the ProductVersion field:

```
exec master.dbo.xp_msver
```

# Transaction Log is Full

## Problem

How do I recover from a full log error?

## Resolution

1. Issue log backup with TRUNCATE_ONLY for database.
2. Create a table in the problem database, insert a row, and issue a few updates. I do 100 updates in a while loop; this will move the active VLF to an earlier physical location.
3. Issue DBCC SHRINKDATABASE with NOTRUNCATE to mark a shrinkpoint:

   ```
   DBCC SHRINKDATABASE( @dbName , NOTRUNCATE )
   ```

4. Issue log backup with TRUNCATE_ONLY for database to force the shrink:

   ```
   BACKUP LOG @dbName WITH TRUNCATE_ONLY
   ```

5.  Now issue FULL DATABASE BACKUP.

After all that, you should have a backup of your database with a pretty clean log file. The log should show up as being almost completely unused.

The following stored proc will execute all this logic, and can be run to recover from a full transaction log. It can be set up to run automatically from a performance monitor alert.

```
CREATE PROC dbo.LogFull @dbName VARCHAR(128) , @backupLoc VARCHAR(128)
AS

/*****************************************************************
* Stored Procedure: LogFull
*
*
* Purpose: Recovers from log full errors
*
* Input Parameters: @dbName VARCHAR(128) - pass in the name of the
* database that has a full log
* @backupDir VARCAHR(128) full path to store backup file
*
* Output Parameters: NONE
*
* Return Status: Always 0
*
* Usage: EXEC admin.dbo.LogFull 'database_name' ,
'd:\sqlbackups\dbdump.BAK'
*
* Local Variables: <list all local variables>
* @NOW DATETIME Current date/time
* @tblName VARCHAR(128) name for a temporary table created by this
procedure.
*
* Called By: to be invoked by the DBA when a log fills up
*
* Calls: NONE
*
* Data Modifications: NONE
*
* Result Set: NONE
```

```
*
* Permissions: SYSADMIN
*
*************************************************************************/
DECLARE @NOW DATETIME
DECLARE @tblName VARCHAR(128)

IF @dbname IN ( 'master' , 'tempdb' )
BEGIN
 RAISERROR ('CANNOT BACKUP LOG on master or tempdb' , -1 , -1 )
 RETURN 0
END
--
-- Issue log backup with TRUNCATE_ONLY for database
--
 BACKUP LOG @dbName WITH TRUNCATE_ONLY
--
-- Create a table in the problem database,
-- Insert a row,
-- Issue a few updates.
-- This will move the active VLF to an earlier physical location.
--
-- Create a table name using spid and datetime:
SELECT @tblName = 'logShrink_' + REPLACE ( REPLACE ( @dbName +
 + ' ' + CONVERT( VARCHAR(16) , @@SPID )
 + ' ' + CONVERT( VARCHAR(35) , @NOW , 113 ) , ':' , '_' ) , ' ' , '_'
)

EXEC (' use ' + @dbName
 + ' SET NOCOUNT ON CREATE TABLE ' + @tblName + ' ( col1 int )
 INSERT ' + @tblName + '(col1) VALUES(1)
 DECLARE @I INT
 SET @I = 0
 WHILE ( @I < 101 )
 BEGIN
 UPDATE ' + @tblName + ' SET col1 = @I
 SET @I = @I + 1
 END
 DROP TABLE ' + @tblName )
--
```

```
- Issue DBCC SHRINKDATABASE to mark a shrinkpoint
-
 DBCC SHRINKDATABASE( @dbName , NOTRUNCATE )
-
- Issue log backup with TRUNCATE_ONLY for database to move allocated
pages to front of files
-
 BACKUP LOG @dbName WITH TRUNCATE_ONLY
-
- NOW ISSUE FULL DATABASE BACKUP:
-

 BACKUP DATABASE @dbName TO DISK = @backupLoc

GO
```

# Practice Makes Perfect

Practice, practice, practice....

Be sure to practice all manners of restores whenever possible, from the entire database to just the log to rolling back a single transaction. This way you will know what to do when the pressure is on and not panic when the business units are breathing down your neck asking why the db is down. Arbitrarily pick a database backup that you have on tape and restore it to disk and run through your disaster recovery steps. There is no way you can be too prepared for when things go wrong.

# Problems with Comments

If block commenting (/* ... */) has been used to comment many lines of code in a batch file that will be executed using osql from a bat file, the blocking does not apply to the word "GO." This results in error because "GO," even within a commented block, signifies the end of the batch and complains about the commenting not being complete. At the same time it ends up executing the lines of codes that you thought you had blocked.

For instance, in the following case, SELECT USER_NAME will be executed:

```
select getdate()
go
/*
select user_name
go
*/
select getdate()
go
```

# Protect Your Data

In my opinion, a DBA's #1 job is to protect the data on his servers. All other DBA job tasks (performance tuning, managing data replication, helping developers, etc.) are absolutely secondary. So, I suggest that the new SQL Server DBA first create a complete backup and recovery plan and test it thoroughly.

I use a script to do native SQL backups to disk of all databases. Then use whatever backup software you like to copy these SQL server backup disk devices to tape. This method gives you three big benefits:

- An immediate restore capability—it's right there on disk, and there is no need to call your off-site storage for the tapes.

- Circumvention of any bugs that third-party SQL Server agents may introduce. There have been such bugs in the past. Using a native SQL backup gives you one place to call (Microsoft PSS) in the event of a SQL restoration failure.

- Decreased SQL backup window. Dumping to disk is almost always faster than dumping to tape. Backing up SQL backup device files to tape can happen at any time—even during business hours.

You can use batch file scripts to store several days worth of data. For example, I have seven folders on one of my backup disks, labeled BACKUP1 through BACKUP7. Before I back up to disk on any given day, I run a .BAT file which performs the following actions:

- Deletes the directory BACKUP7.

- Renames BACKUP6 to BACKUP7, then renames BACKUP5 to BACKUP6, and so on for each directory, ending by renaming BACKUP1 to BACKUP2.

- Creates a new BACKUP1 folder to hold the day's backup.

If using your SCSI hot swap drives for backups seems cost-prohibitive, I point out that you can get an 80 GB IDE drive for about $300. SQL Server data is highly compressible, so using NTFS compression on an 80 GB disk will enable you to back up 160 GB or more to a SQL backup file. Any organization should be able to afford adding a large IDE disk to every SQL server.

You can still send your tapes off-site for fire and flood disaster protection.

# For Further Information

If you would like further information on SQL Server, or a place to go online to ask experts for help, here are some good places to start.

http://www.soaringeagleltd.com
http://people.mw.mediaone.net/overthrow/index.html
http://www.microsoft.com/sql/
http://www.microsoft.com/mcp/certstep/mcdbaben.htm
http://www.pinpub.com/sqlpro/home.htm
http://www.sqlpass.org/
http://www.deja.com/dnquery.xp?search=word&svcclass=
    dncurrent& showsort=date&ST=QS&query=
    ~g%20comp.databases.ms-sqlserver
http://support.microsoft.com/support/sql/papers.asp
http://www.geocities.com/~dsnydersql/links/links.htm
http://www.sqlmag.com/index.html
http://www.sqlserver.com/
http://www.swynk.com/sqlhome/scriptlibrary.asp

# The Wizards

*Wizard* is a term used by Microsoft to describe tools that try to automatically figure out some of the tasks that might otherwise require a great deal of work, research, and/or thought. This appendix covers the SQL Server wizards that have not already been discussed in this book. We will recommend settings and some changes that you may have to make for your particular database system.

You will find the database wizards in Enterprise Manager. Just click on the database name and the General screen will pop up. Click on the Wizards tab.

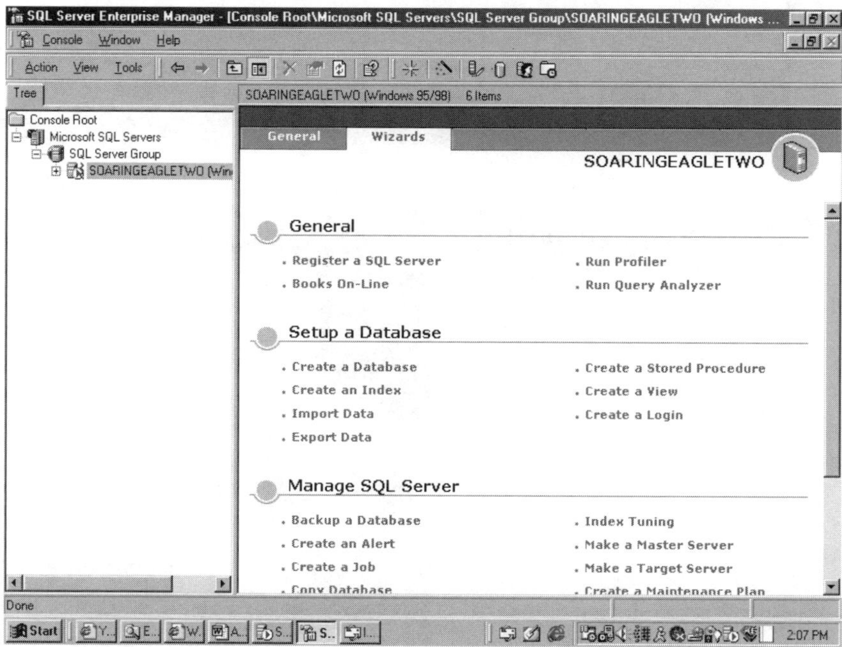

# The Create Database Wizard

You can use the Create Database Wizard, rather than manually create database statements, to create your database initially. To use this, double-click on the **Create a Database** selection (making sure that you have selected a server in the drop-down tree on the left).

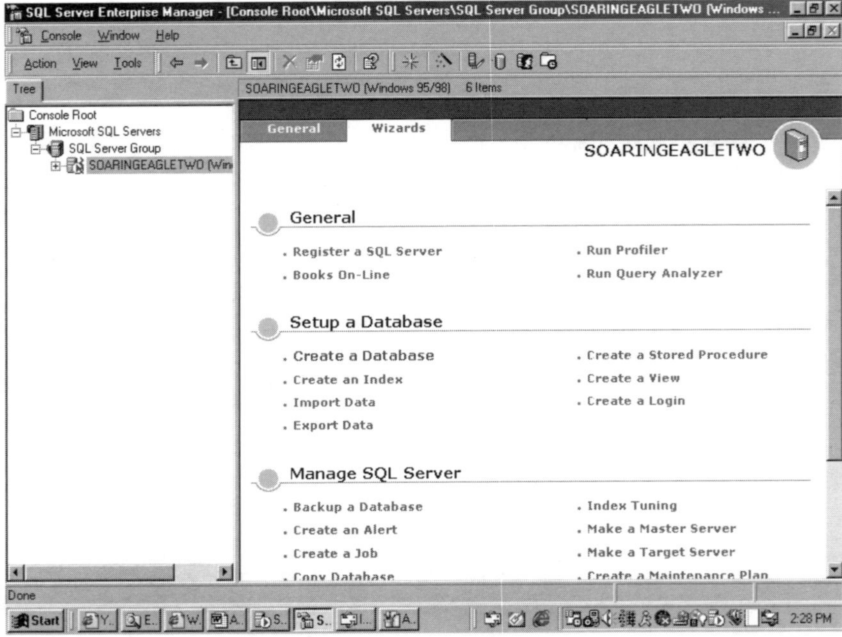

The welcome window will appear.

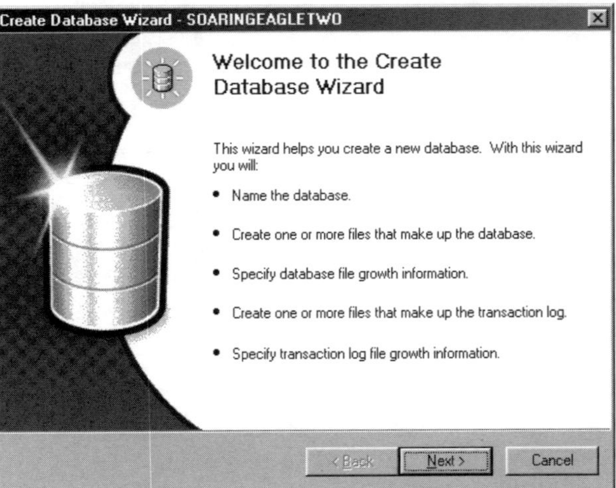

Click **Next** and the following window appears.

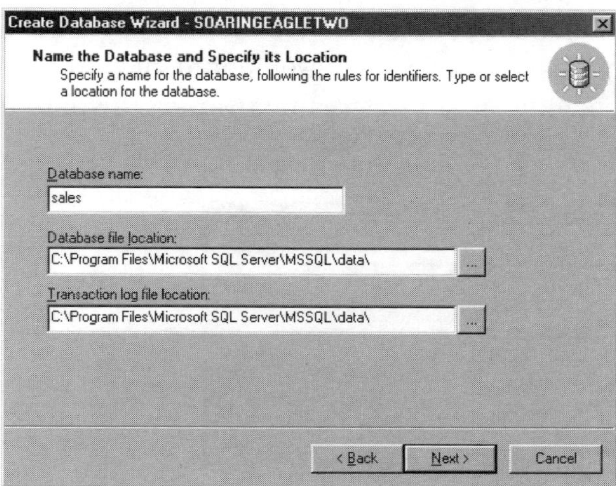

You will have to decide upon a name for the database. We recommend less than 30 characters, and we further recommend you exclude spaces and punctuation marks. The location is the place where you want the server to preallocate space for the database. If possible, this should be a physical disk that is set aside for this purpose.

Next, name the database files on this screen:

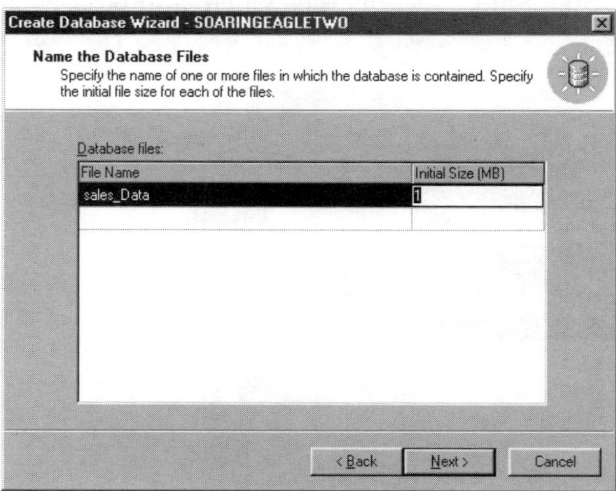

File names should correspond with normal file naming conventions for your operating system. File size is much more easily managed if you set it to automatically grow as needed. Remember, your unit of backup is the database, so if you keep it small and only grow it as necessary, you can back up the least amount of database, while still being able to use all of the space on your disk. There is no reason not to allow the database to start small. You might consider restricting the file growth to the size of your disk.

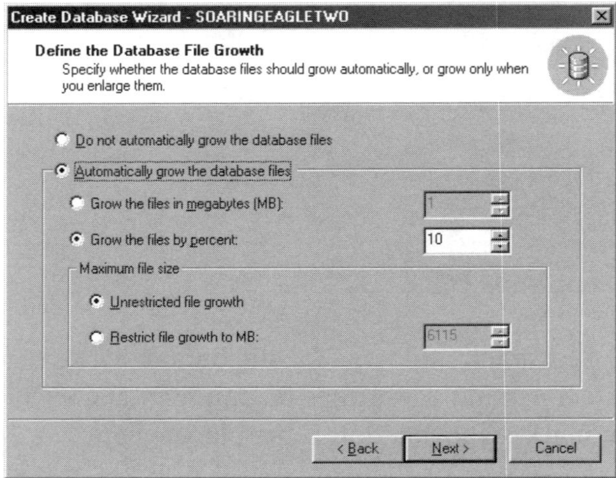

The transaction log file also meets naming conventions for your operating systems. You should name the database file and log file something similar but different, so that you know which is which, and which files are for which databases.

Click **Next**.

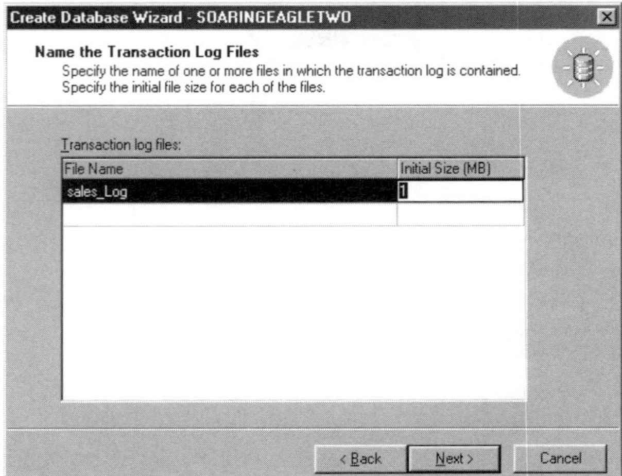

As with database file growth, transaction log file growth should be set to automatically grow as needed.

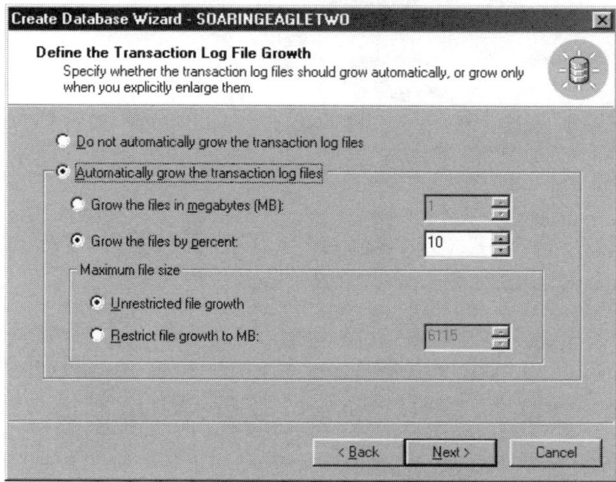

Click **Next**. To complete the creation of your database, click **Finish**.

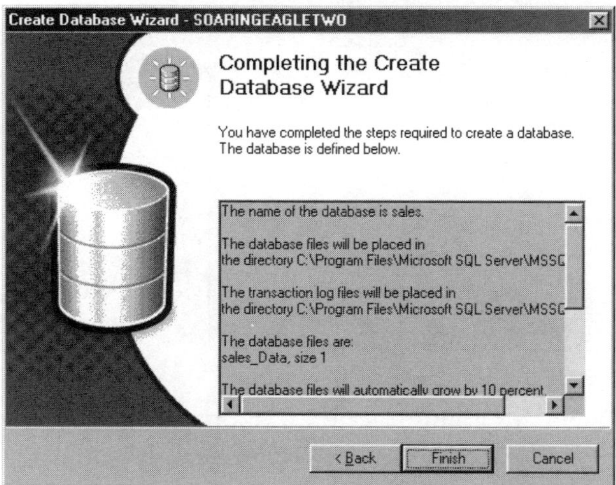

A message will appear to confirm that the database was successfully created.

The wizard will then give you the option to create a maintenance plan for your database.

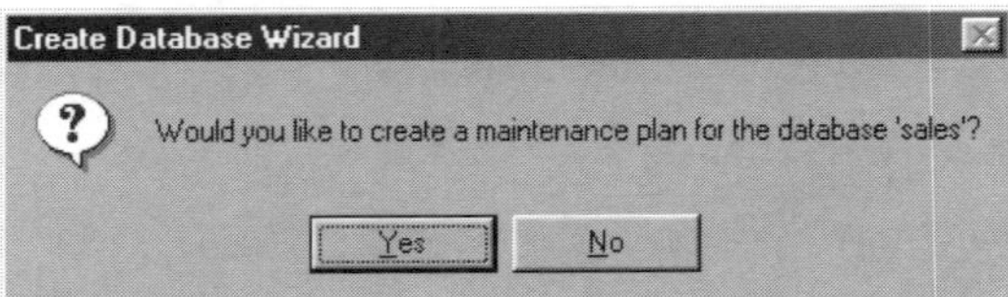



# The Database Maintenance Plan Wizard

This topic was already discussed at length in Chapter 2, but is repeated here for convenience. If you clicked Yes in the previous window, you will see the welcome screen to the Database Maintenance Plan Wizard.

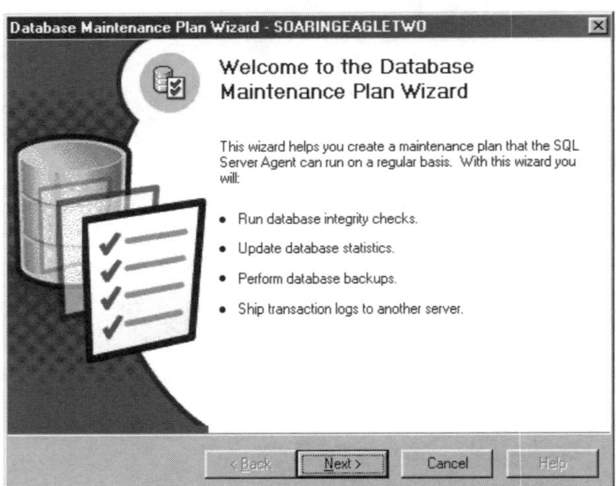



Click **Next**. Here we are going to build a maintenance plan for only one database, the Sales database which we have already created. Click on **These databases** and scroll down until you find your database. Select your database and click **Next**.

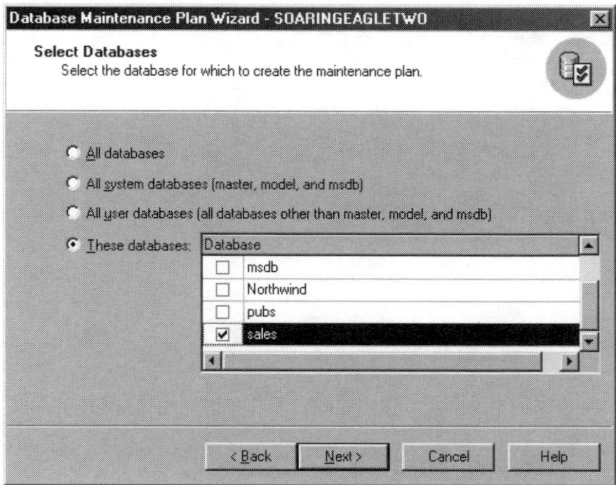

Make sure you check the first and third check boxes (statistics update automatically if you reorganize the pages). The numbers selected here are a good start, unless your database vendor has recommended alternate settings.

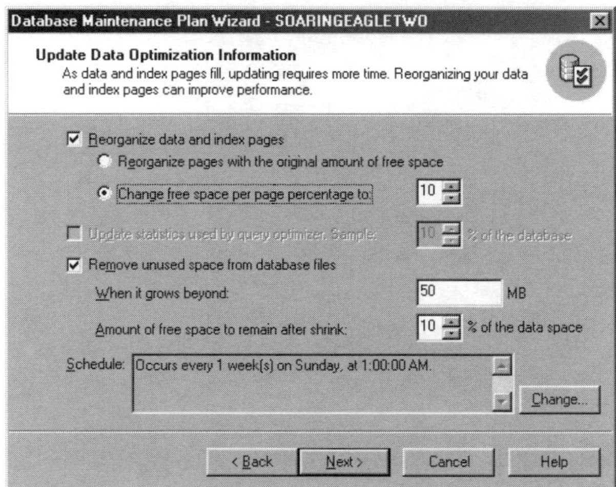

You can alter your schedule by clicking the **Change** button. You can create many schedules, and name them accordingly.

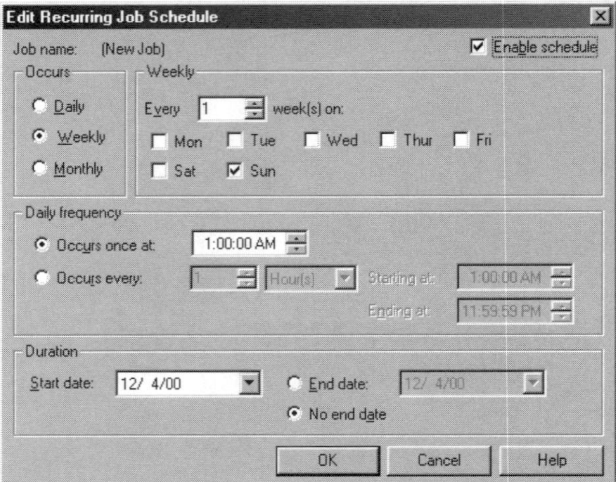

Click **OK** and **Next** to schedule database and internal data integrity tests.

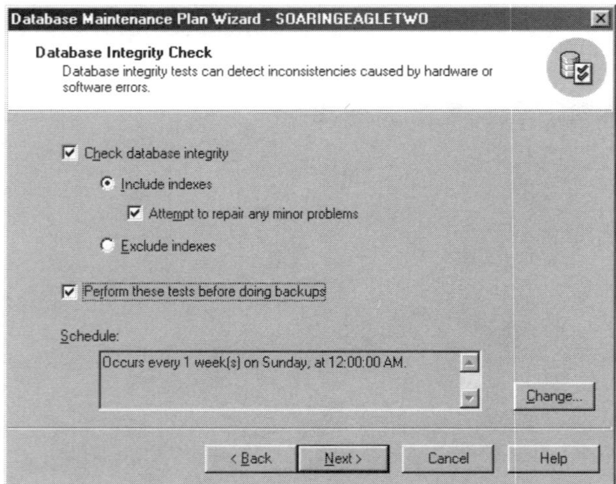

Be sure to click **Perform these tests before doing backups**.

Press **Next** to finish or the **Change** button to customize a schedule.

Remember this schedule window? You can schedule maintenance to be performed all at once or at different times. All of this should be scheduled when the system is not in heavy use. Press **OK** when you are finished.

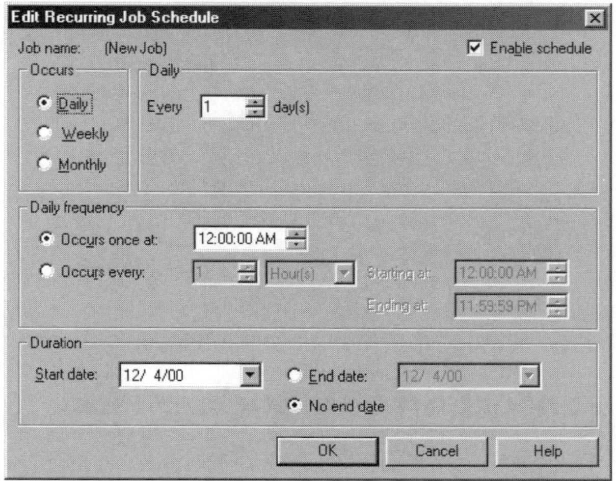

## Specify the Database Backup Plan

The next step in the wizard is to specify where, when, and how the backups will take place. This would be a good time to refer to your backup plan. Be sure that you are backing up to the correct device. Be sure that you are backing up often enough for your environment. Remember to check to be sure that the backups occurred. Then get the backup off-site.

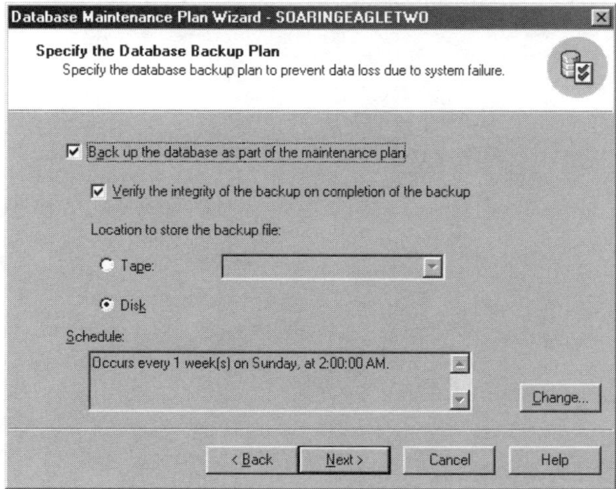

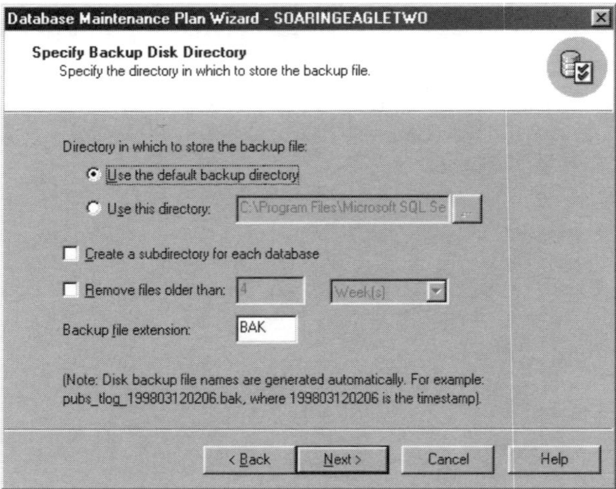

## Specify the Transaction Log Backup Plan

Remember that if your transaction log fills, SQL Server will pause. Therefore, the decision to back up this log is crucial. You will want to monitor the transaction log to recognize normal growth patterns, understand high-volume cycles, and determine the best time to perform backups for your database. Please refer to Chapter 8.

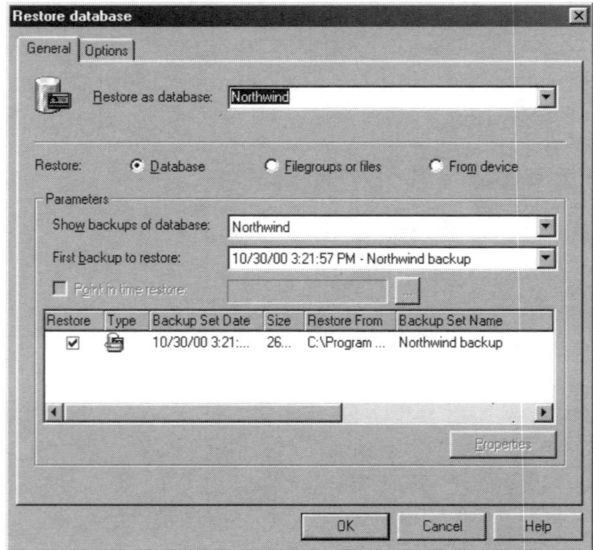

As you can see, this process is similar to specifying database backups. However, you may want to be careful with your selection for the Remove files older than option. Think about how volatile your data needs are and the space you have on your hard drive or disk(s).

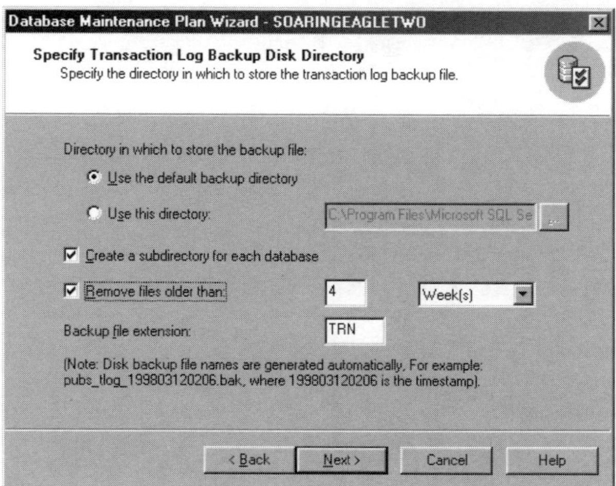

Select your reporting option in accordance with your business environment. Do not skip this step. An actual record of the maintenance plan occurring may be helpful for a multitude of tasks and problem solving issues over time.

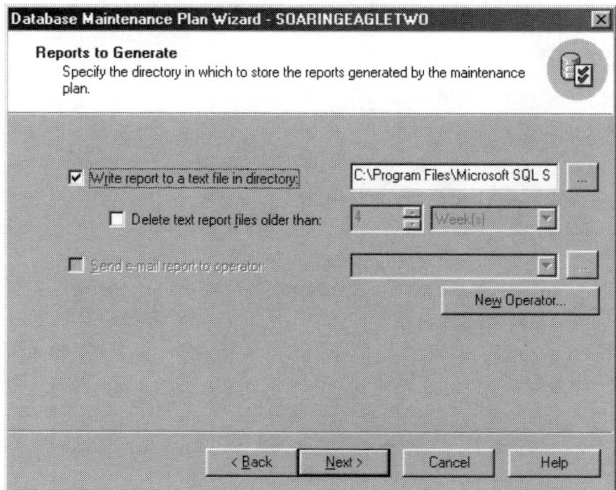

You will notice on this screen that you may e-mail the operator and/or yourself a report generated by your automatic maintenance plan. This is an excellent way of keeping in touch with the status of your database systems. Enter the name and the e-mail address of the recipient of the report; then click **Apply** and **OK**.

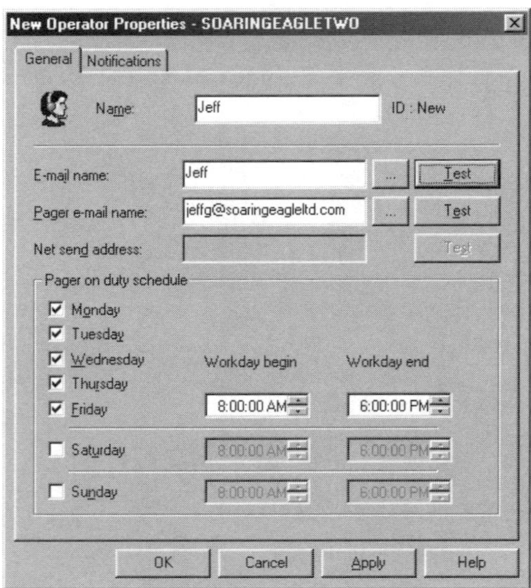

As you can see, the e-mail name appears in the Send e-mail report to operator window.

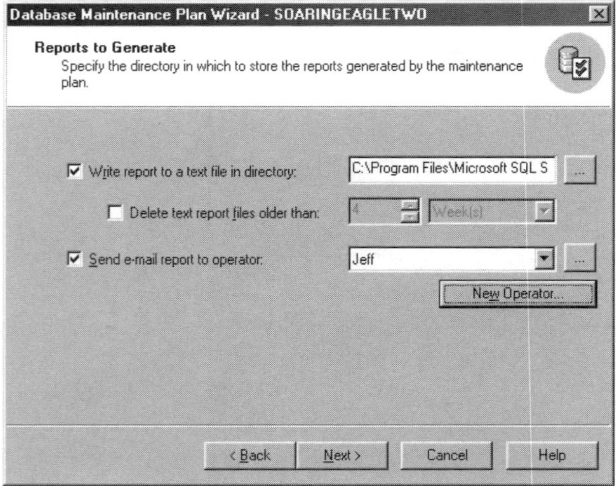

The next window allows you to keep a copy of the maintenance records on either a remote or local server. If you have the option to keep this information on a remote server, then do so. Otherwise, keep it on your local server and limit the amount of rows you want this record to take up in your database.

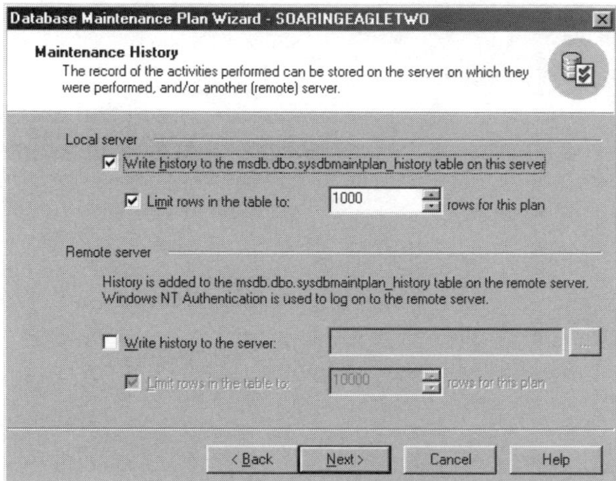

Click on **Next** for the final step in this wizard, naming your database plan to coincide with the database. Then click **Finish**.

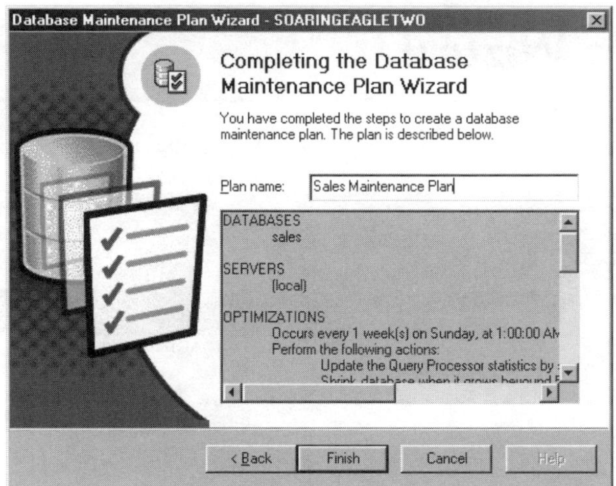

To see your newly created database maintenance plan, search down the directory, and click on **Database Maintenance Plans**.

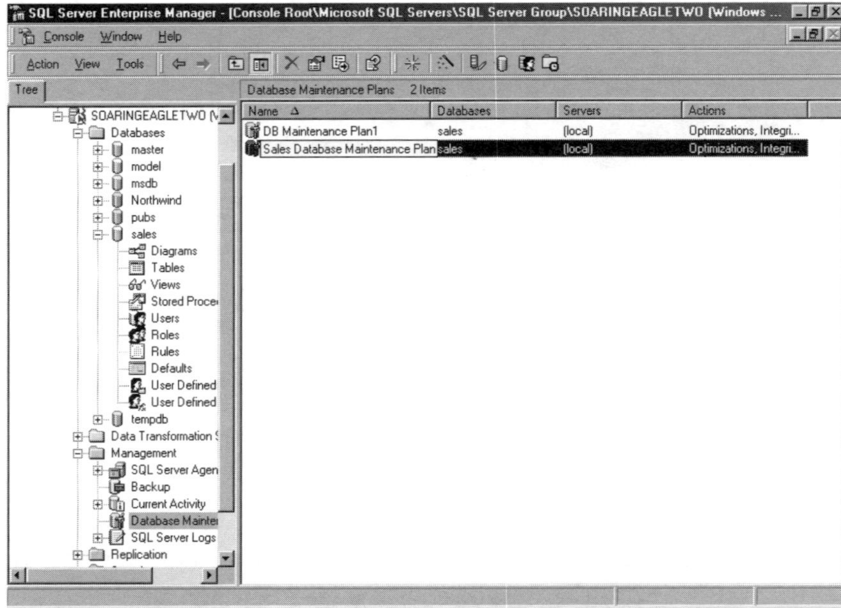

# The Create Login Wizard

The Create Login Wizard helps to give users access to the SQL Server.

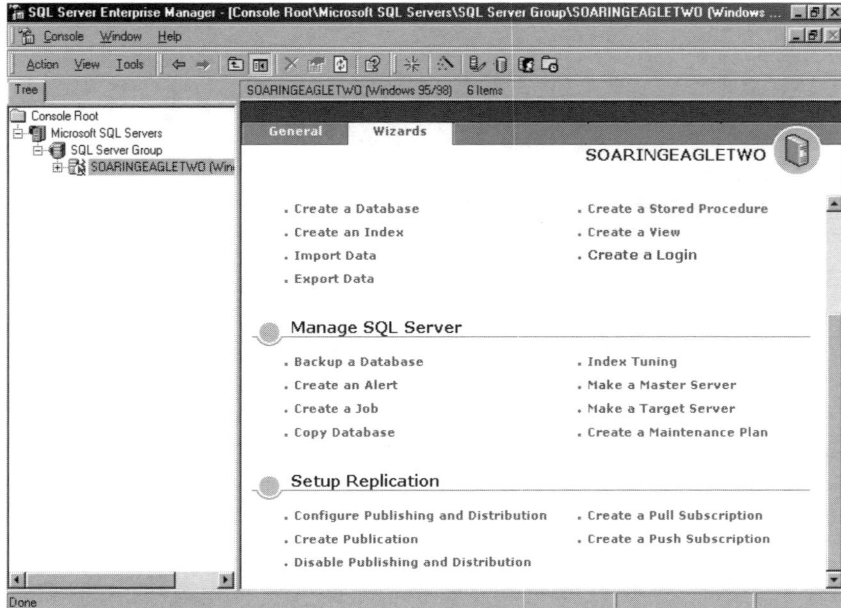

The initial wizard screen should look familiar by now:

Use the authentication recommended by your software vendor. Here, we are using SQL Server authentication, rather than NT authentication.

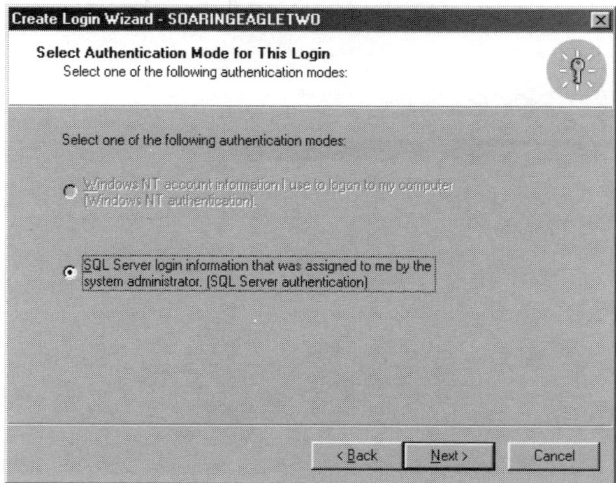

For security reasons, we recommend passwords be at least six characters and include special characters and/or numbers.

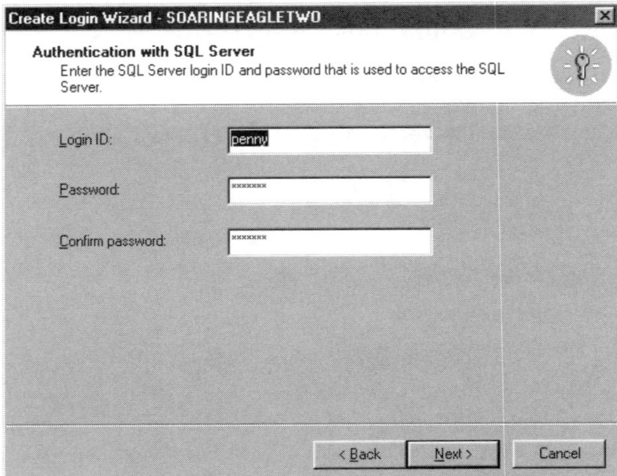

Most of your users will not have any of the following options checked, unless special roles were created by your software vendor.

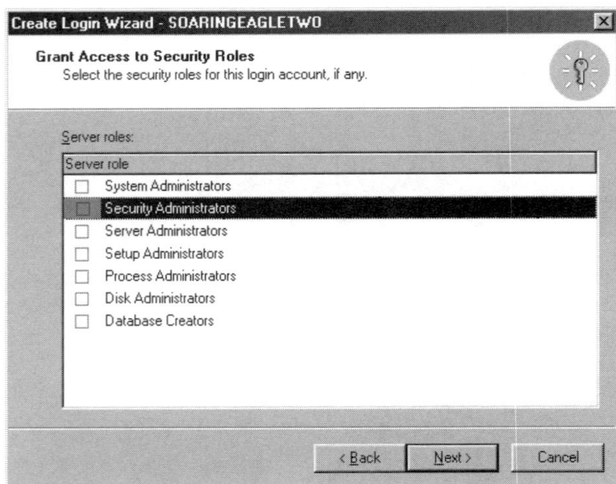

Grant the user access to one or more databases.

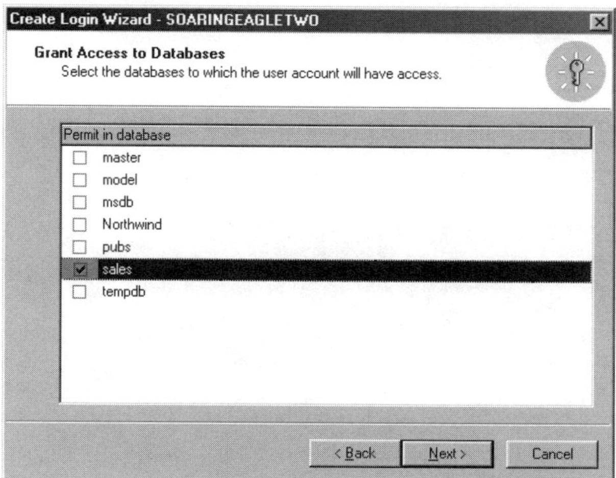

Access to the server does not guarantee access to any of the user databases. Give users access to the appropriate database.

Click **Finish** to confirm your selections and complete the wizard.

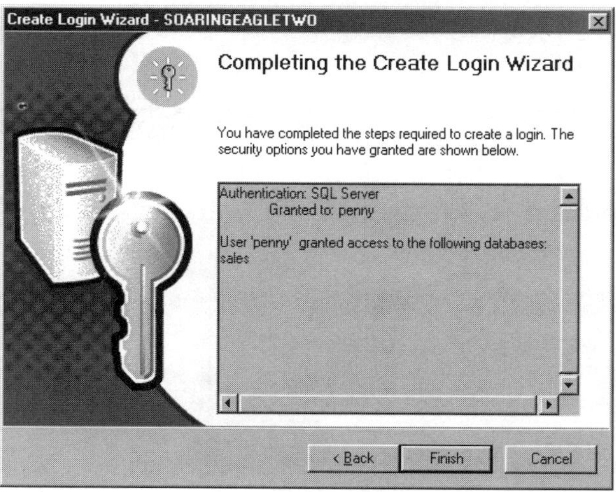

# The Backup Wizard

The Backup Wizard exists to help you automate the backing up of your databases to a specific device on a specific schedule.

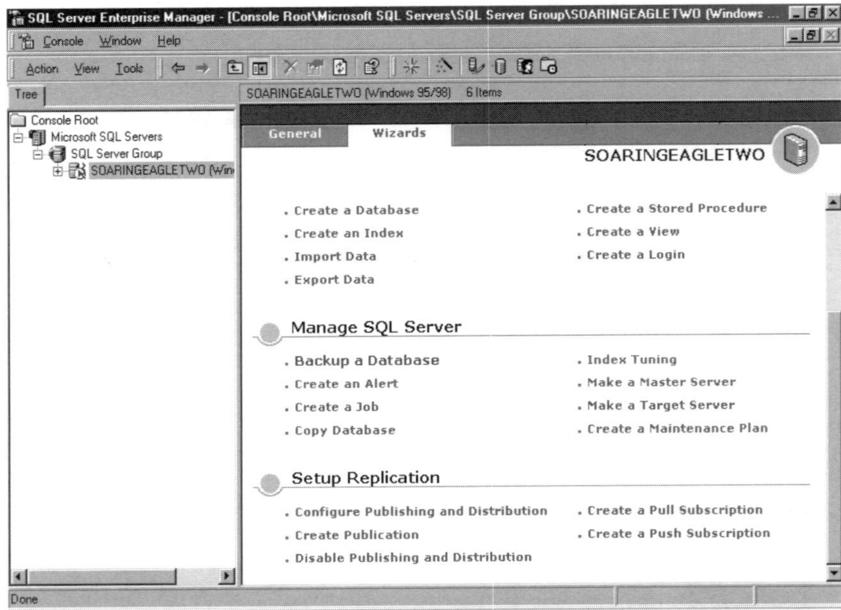

If you click **Backup a Database**, you will get the familiar wizard starting screen:

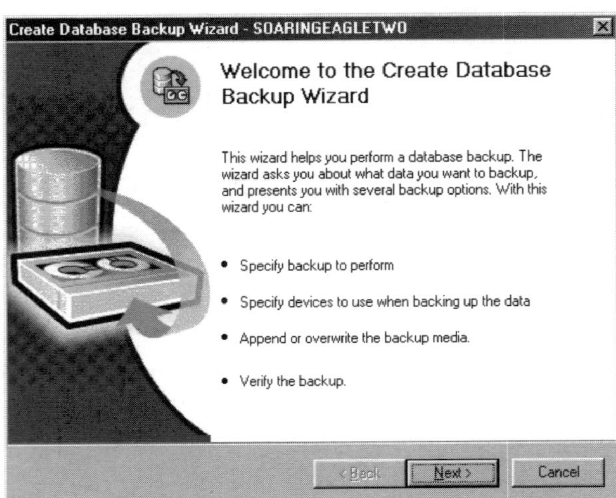

Click **Next** to get to the following screen, which allows you to pick the database for which you'd like to set up a backup plan.

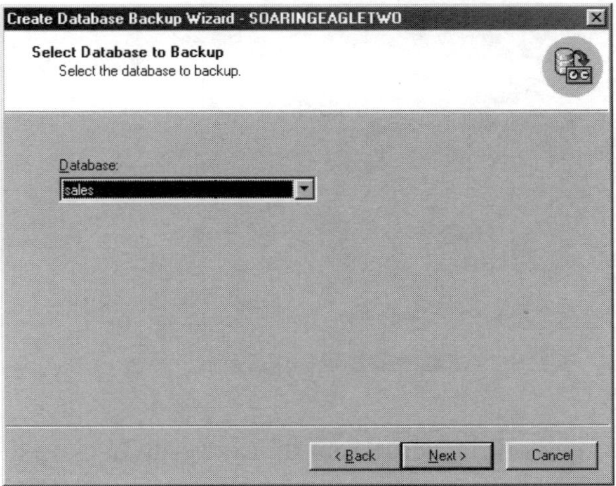

Since we have been using the Sales database that we have just created, we will continue to use this as an example. The description here is optional. If you have only one database, the description is not necessary. Click **Next**.

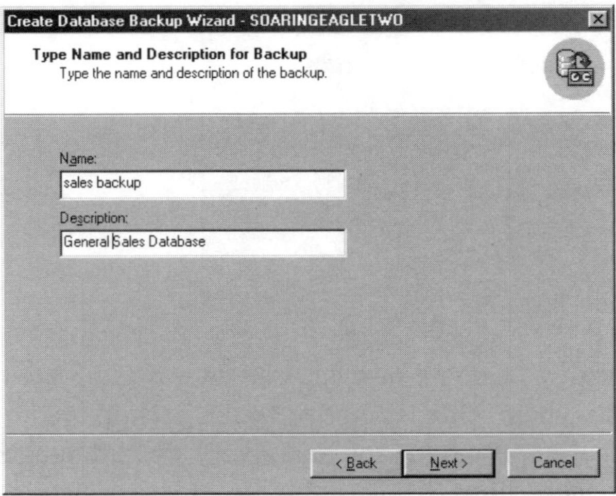

If you are going to automate your backups we suggest that you use the complete backup scenario. Ignore the differential backup and the transaction log options given to you on this screen.

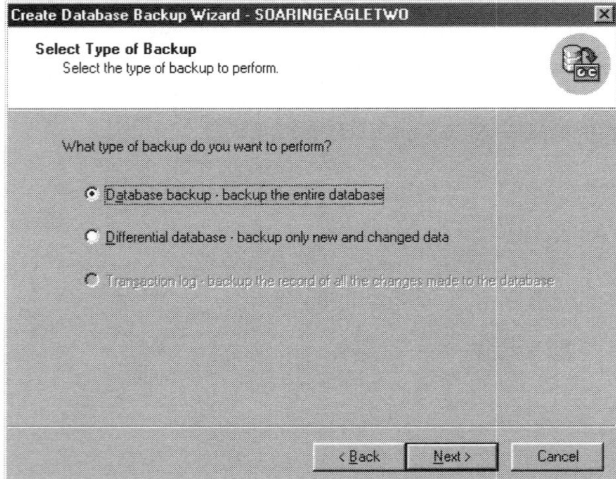

You will have to click on the scroll box that lists the backup devices in order to create a new backup device.

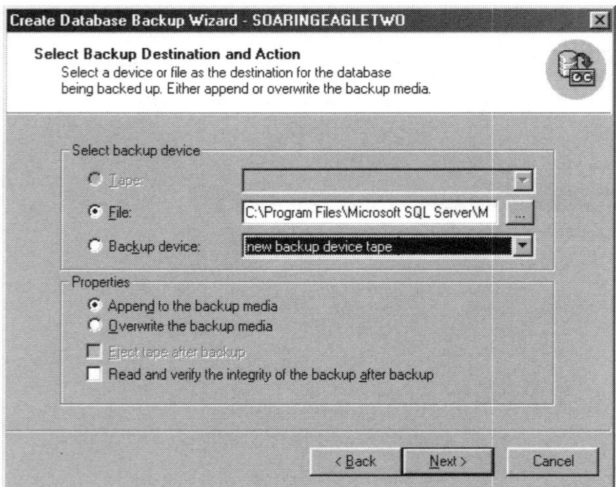

Whether you decide to append or overwrite your backup media, there are two paths to follow here. One is Append to the backup media. If, for example, you have a very large tape and a very small database, you may want to simply collect all of the database backups on a single tape, which might sit in the tape drive until it is needed (note that this is <u>not</u> a substitute for getting your backups off-site). The other is to replace the contents of a backup media each time. We prefer to use fresh media each time and remove the media from the site. The next couple of screens will first follow the Append to the backup media path.

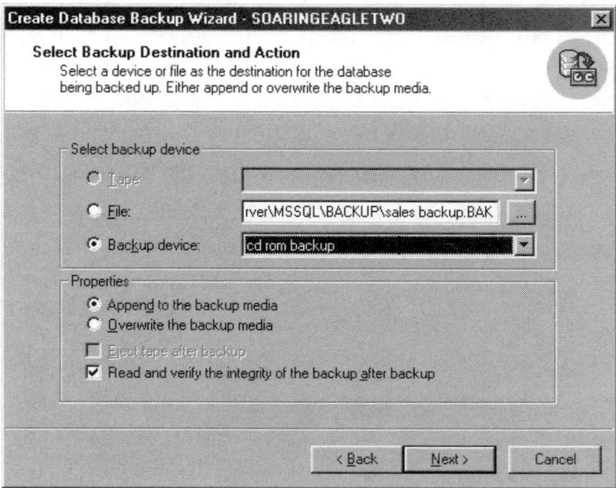

Choose your backup device, and also choose **Read and verify the integrity of the backup after backup**. This will ensure that you do have a viable backup and that your data will be clean when you need to run a restore from backup. Then click **OK**.

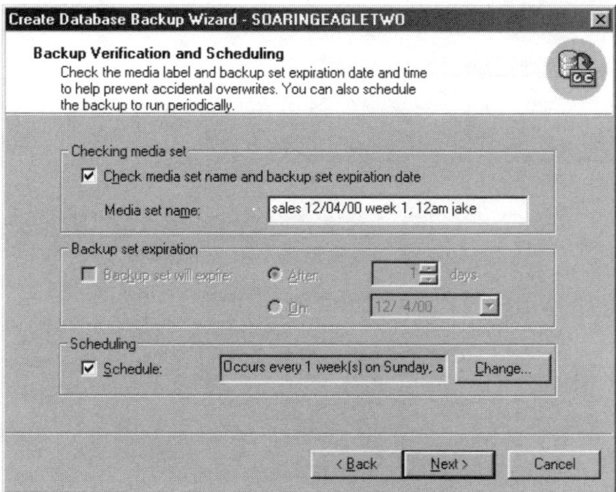

When you choose Append, the Backup set will expire option is not active. Choose a descriptive media name and schedule your backup. You can change the schedule by selecting the **Change** button.

Enter a descriptive media set name. As you are going through this naming process, follow the naming conventions that you have set up to be sure that anyone following through this process later will know exactly what to do. This will help resolve any human error issues in tracking problems and processes later.

Many of the other windows have been deleted from this process in SQL Server 2000. In SQL Server 7.0 you had to run through some windows that allowed you to initialize the media, etc. However, this has all been automated for you in SQL Server 2000.

So you have now completed an automatic append to media backup process.

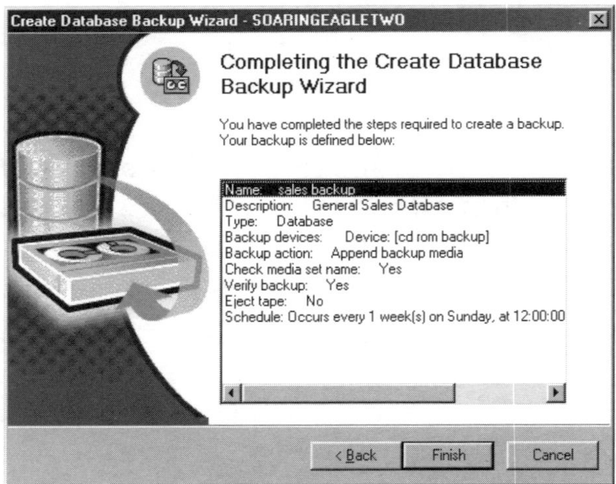

If you choose to overwrite the backup media in the Select Backup Destination and Action window, the wizard will skip directly to the Initialize Media window.

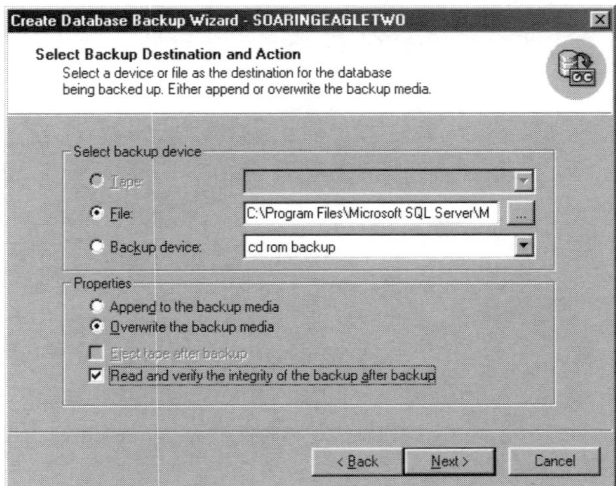

This screen asks you to choose a name to set for the tape description. Remember in Chapter 8 we discussed appropriate naming conventions and the importance of establishing them. If you have not set a naming convention when you have come to this point, stop for a couple of minutes and describe one in a document that is available to others and then stick with that convention unless a change has been documented. Be sure that it is descriptive enough to identify the tape quickly and precisely under stressful conditions.

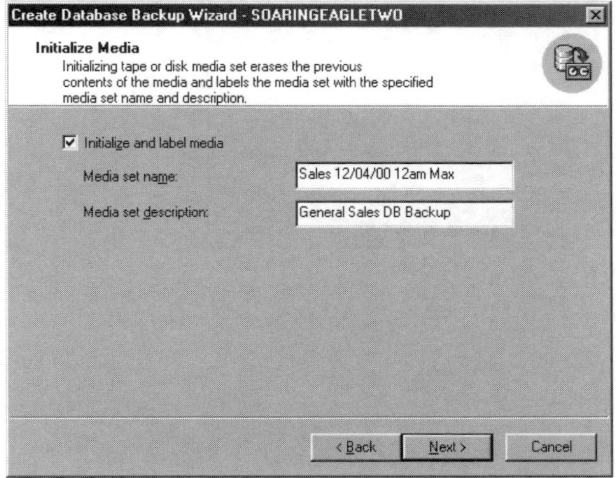

As you can see, the Backup set will expire selection now becomes active since it is relevant to this type of media backup. Consider all of the aspects of your system processes as you choose these expiration and scheduling suggestions. For example, if you back up daily, you may want to keep that backup for at least one week. If you back up weekly, you may want to keep that backup for a full month.

Review this screen to be sure that everything seems to be correct and click on the **Finish** button.

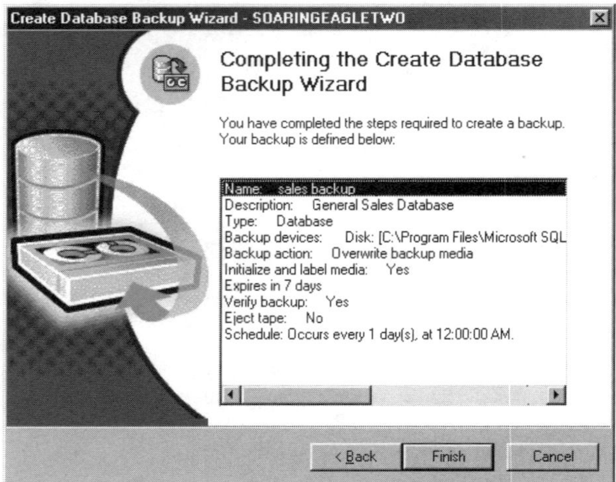



Your automated backup processes are complete.

Now remember to take the backup media out of the drive, label it, and then take it off-site.

# The Create Alert Wizard

Alerts, jobs, and operators are objects that are created to define automated problem solving techniques. We are going to create an example of how to set up an alert to notify you that someone has tried to enter your system without authorized access.

Click **Create an Alert**.

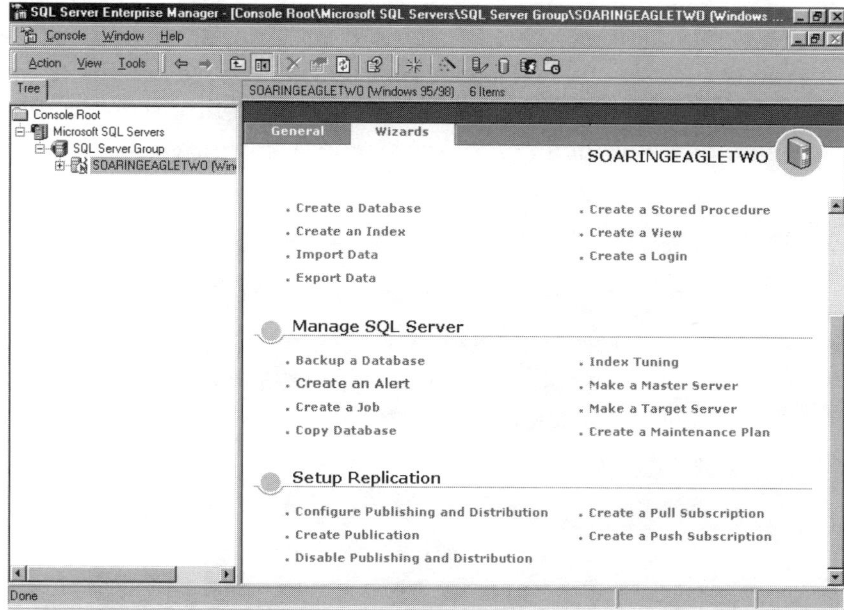

The Create Alert Wizard will appear. Click **Next**.

If you select the down arrow in the For any error of severity box, you'll see that many selections are pre-described for you. Click **Next**.

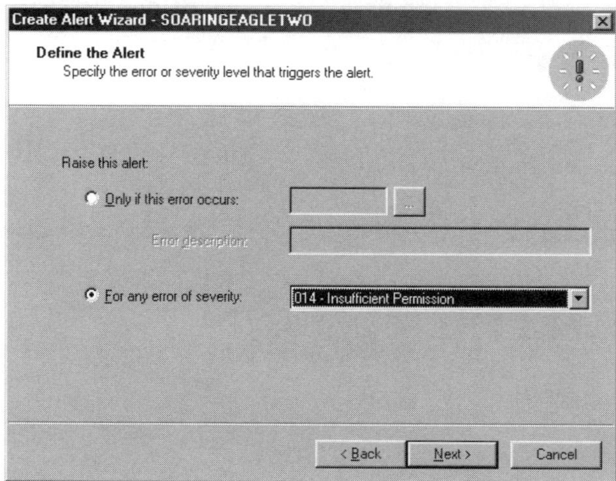

You can choose any database by selecting the drop-down arrow. For this type of alert we have decided that we want to be notified if anyone is trying to get into any of the databases without authorization. We have not put any data in the Error message contains this text box since we want to keep this open to any message. Click **Next**.

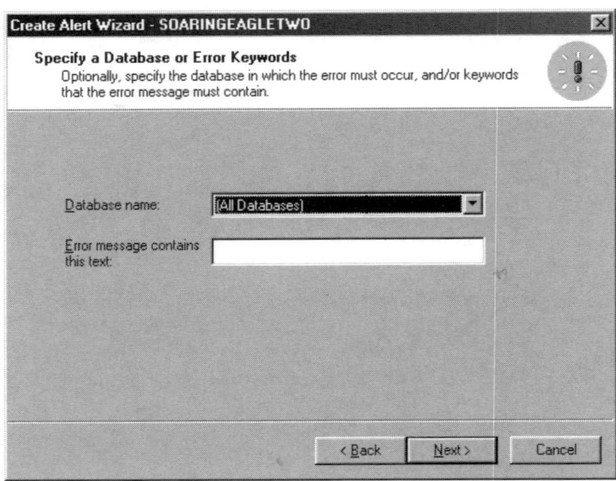

In order to use the Define Alert Response screen you must create a new job. You will see a scroll box labeled Job to execute; **(No Job)** should show up in the box. Scroll up and choose **New Job**.

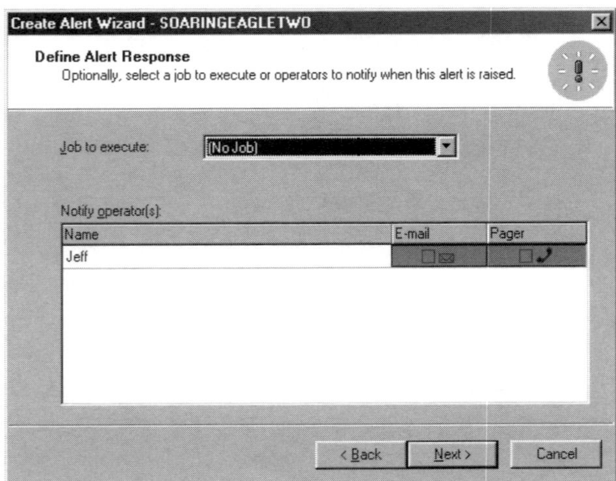

Here you are able to edit the properties of the job you are creating.

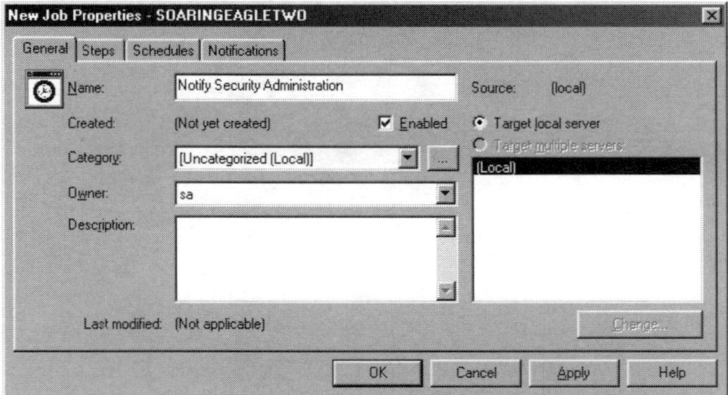

You must have a step but our step is a non-event so set these parameters by selecting the **New** button.

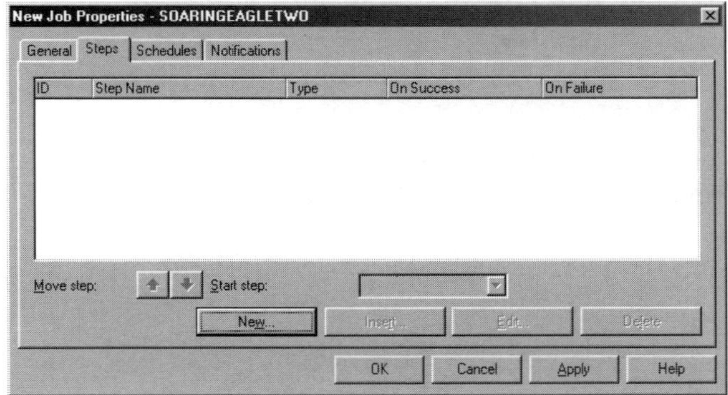

Type **non event** in the Step name box. To select the correct type, scroll down to the Operating System Command (CmdExec) selection. Enter the letters **cd** in the Command box for "change directory," which is something that will not have any effect on the system. In this case, we are only interested in the end of the job, which is the notification of the administrator. Press **OK**.

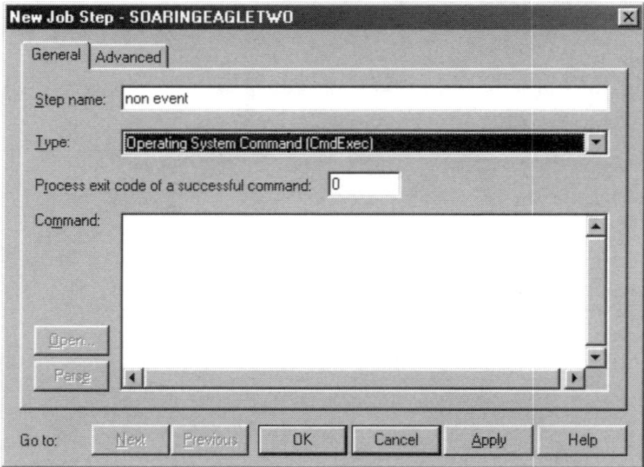

The new step name and type automatically appear in the Steps tab of the New Job Properties window.

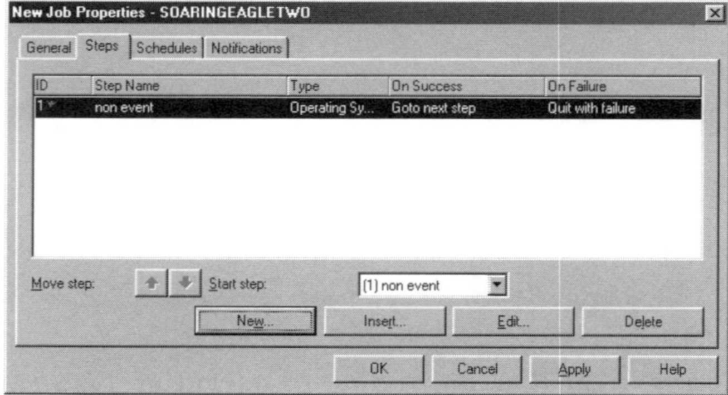

For this particular alert, select the **Notifications** tab. Then be sure that the correct person is to be notified and select a process of phone or e-mail. The only automatic process you want to occur is to notify you of an authorized user. Then click **Apply**.

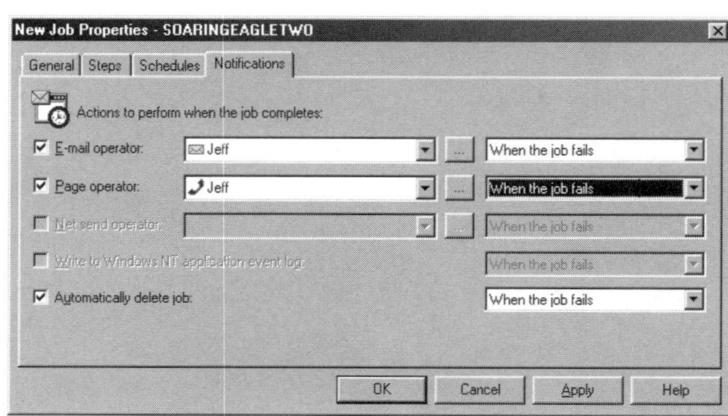

This screen should pop up if you have been successful.

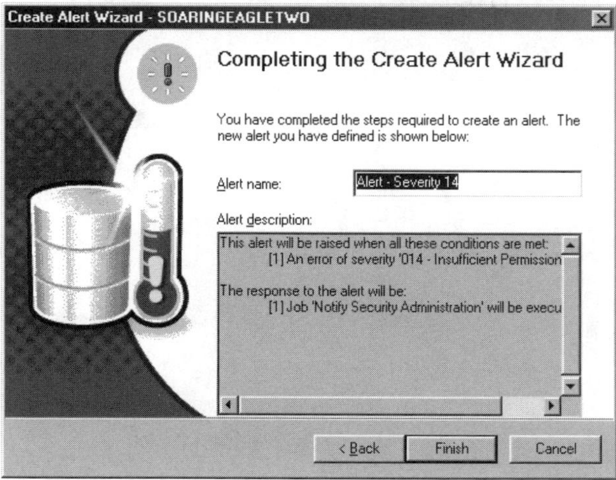

Click **Finish** to confirm your selections.

The wizard is complete.

You can see the alert that you have just created by going to the SQL Server Agent. Here you can see all of your alerts, operators, and jobs.

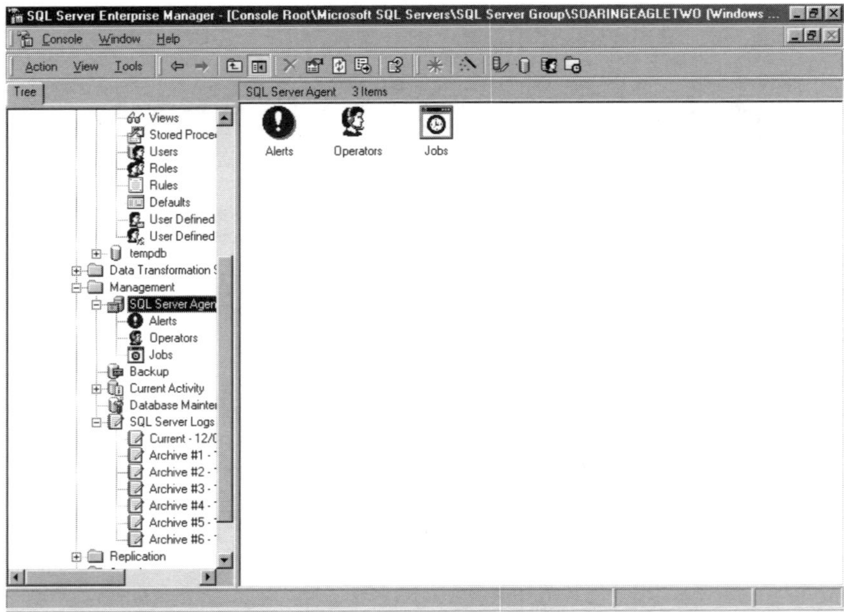

Click on the **Alerts** folder to see the alert that you have just created.

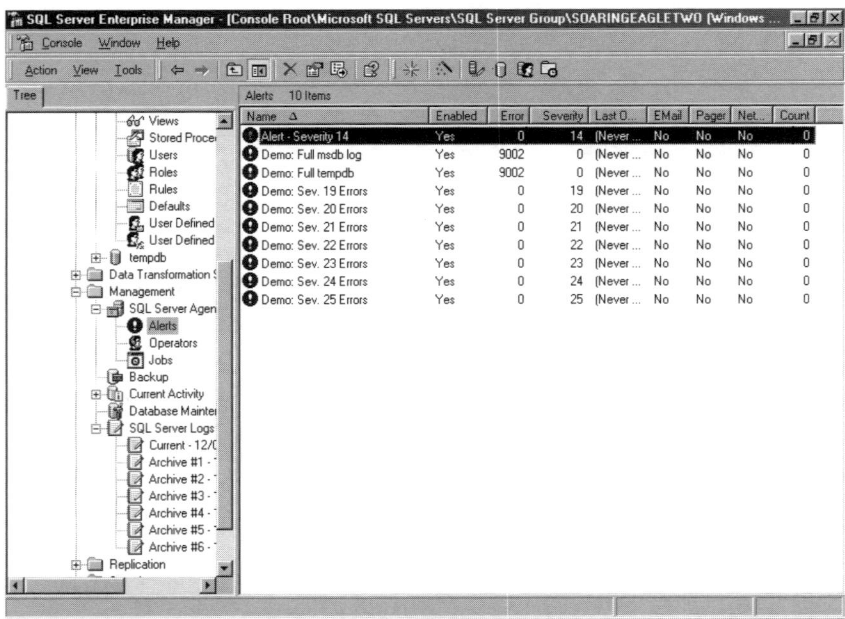

# Replication

Sometimes it may be necessary to hold information in more than one place. This can be like keeping copies of your work at home and at the office. However, if you make a change to your work at home, how does the office know what you have done? The same can be true of databases. Sometimes an application may be developed that will require data from other databases. These databases may not even be on the same server but the data will need to exist in more than one database. The data will need to be replicated from one database to the other.

## Types of Replication

*Replication* is the mechanism provided in SQL Server that allows for data and stored procedures to be distributed to other databases. These databases receiving the copied data can be on the same server as the source, or they can exist on other servers. This distribution mechanism also ensures that should the copied data be altered, the change will be reflected throughout the distributed data. In other words, the data will be synchronized so that one copy of the data will match all other copies. Microsoft uses a publish and subscribe model for replication. This model has three key components: the Publisher, the Distributor, and the Subscriber.

The Publisher is the server that provides the data being distributed to other databases. The Distributor is the server with the task of taking the published data and passing it along to all the other servers that require it. The Subscriber is the server that will request information from a Publisher.

Using this model, SQL Server 2000 supports three types of replication:

- Snapshot replication
- Transactional replication
- Merge replication

## Snapshot Replication

Snapshot replication involves taking a "snapshot" of the published data at a particular time. This snapshot is a copy of the schema of the published objects and the data stored in them. A snapshot agent actually takes the snapshot. The snapshot agent will copy the schema and all the data in it. This snapshot is sent to the distribution agent which will send the data to the Subscribers. The Subscribers will not merely receive changes to the data; they receive a whole new set of data to replace the old data. The old data will be dropped and replaced with the schema and data from the snapshot.

This can be similar to newspaper delivery. A newspaper is prepared at a publisher and distributed by a newspaper carrier to the subscribers. When the subscribers receive the paper, it replaces the newspaper from the previous day.

## Transactional Replication

While snapshot replication is a relatively simple form of replication, it can take a lot of time and resources on the server if the tables are very large. This is because snapshot replication forces data to be completely rewritten. An alternative to rewriting entire tables is transactional replication. Transactional replication only distributes the changes to data. If only some rows are modified in a database, then only the modifications are distributed to the Subscribers.

## Merge Replication

The third and more complicated form of replication is merge replication. The previous two forms of replication are simple in the sense that the source of the data modifications is the Publisher. However, if other people are using the data in the Subscriber databases, it might be required that a Subscriber be allowed to change the replicated data from a Subscriber server rather than a Publisher. These changes should not only be present in the server where the change was made but also distributed to other subscribing servers.

## Snapshot Replication Example

As an example, we will walk through the steps to set up a snapshot replication environment.

Setting up a Distributor:

1.    From the Tools menu, select **Wizards**.

2.    Expand the **Replication** option.

3.    Select **Configure Publishing and Distribution Wizard**.

4.    Click **OK**.

The following figure is an introduction window.

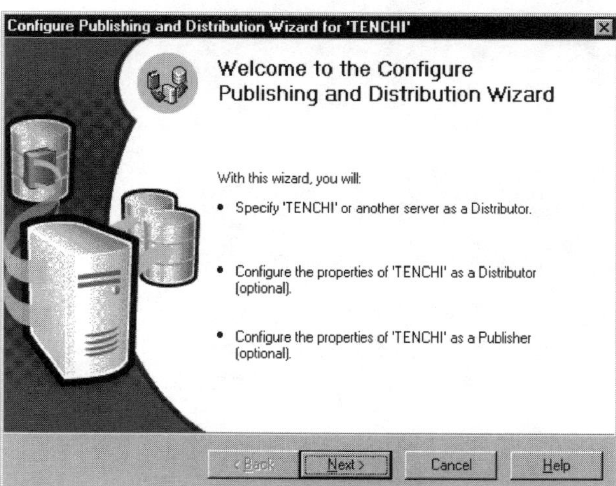


5.    Click the **Next** button. The next window asks if the current server is the one being configured as a Distributor. Select **Next**, to use the local server as a Distributor. (Remote servers can also be used by selecting the Use the following server option and clicking **Add Server**.)

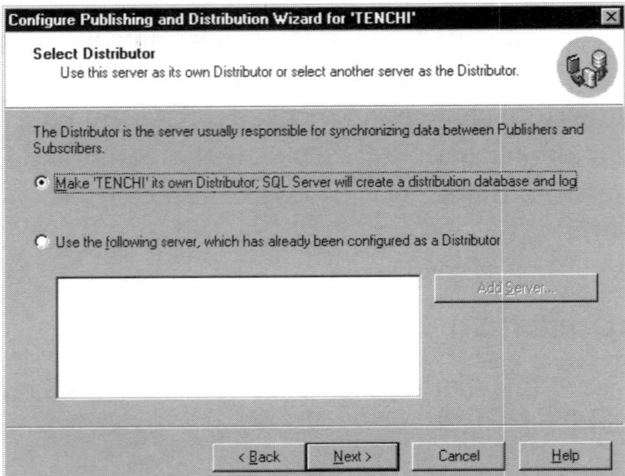

6. Click **Next**. This screen lets you decide whether to use the default distribution settings for SQL Server or customize the distribution settings. The default is to customize.

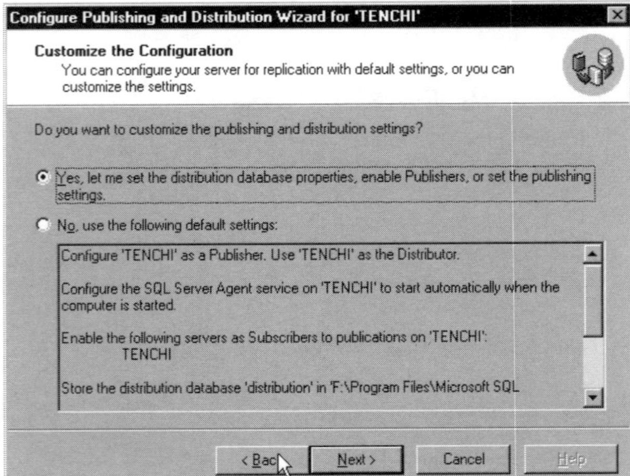

7. If Yes is chosen, the next step is to decide what to name the distribution database and where the distribution database files will be located.

   For now, select **No, use the following default settings**.

8. Click **Next** to access the final page in the wizard. Click **Finish** to complete setup of the Distributor. SQL Server will then execute a script to set up the distribution database and all necessary Subscriber and Publisher settings.

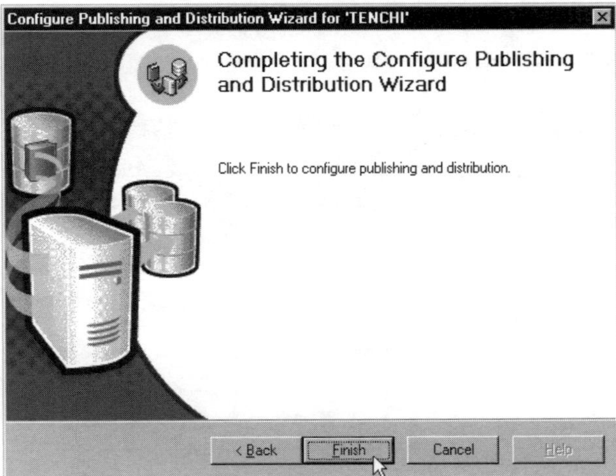

9.  A dialog box will appear when the configuration is complete. Click
    **OK** to finish the process

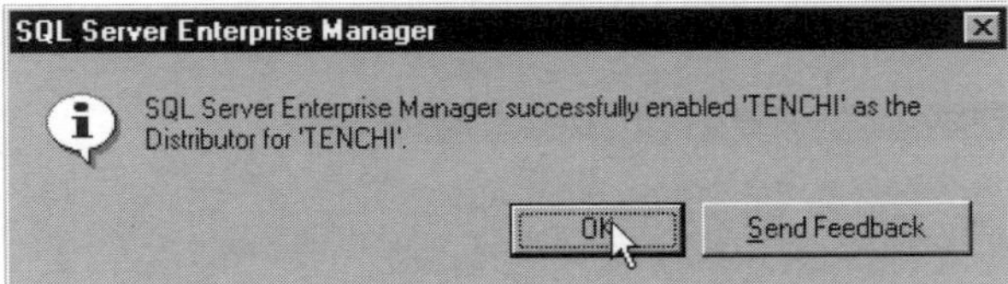

Setting up a Publisher:

1.  Select **Wizards** from the Tools
    menu and choose **Create Publica-
    tion Wizard**, which is located
    underneath Replication.

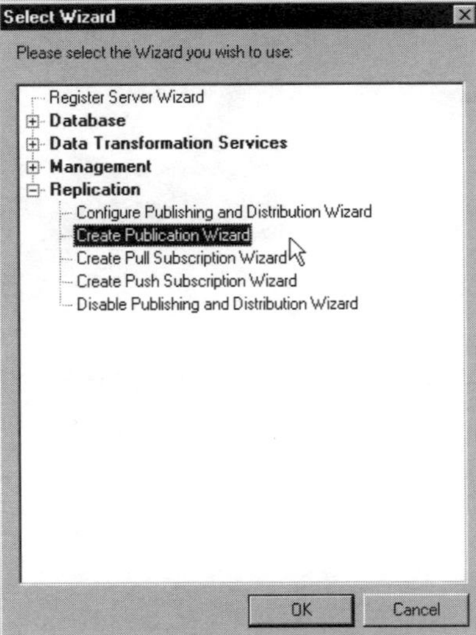

2. Select a database that can be used for publication. Then click the **Create Publication** button.

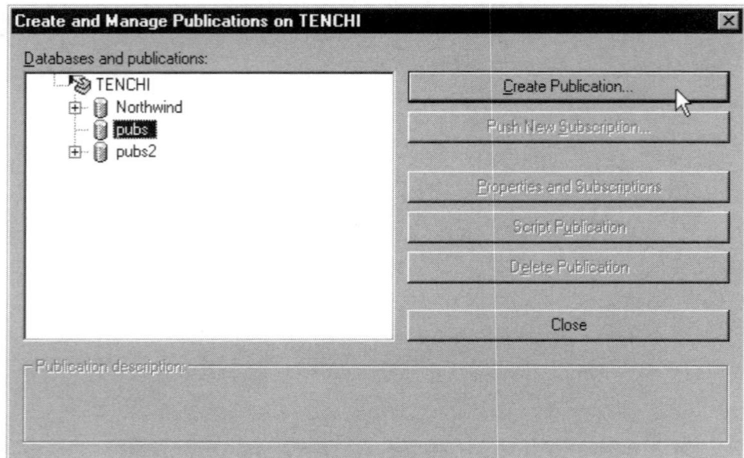

This starts the Create Publication Wizard.

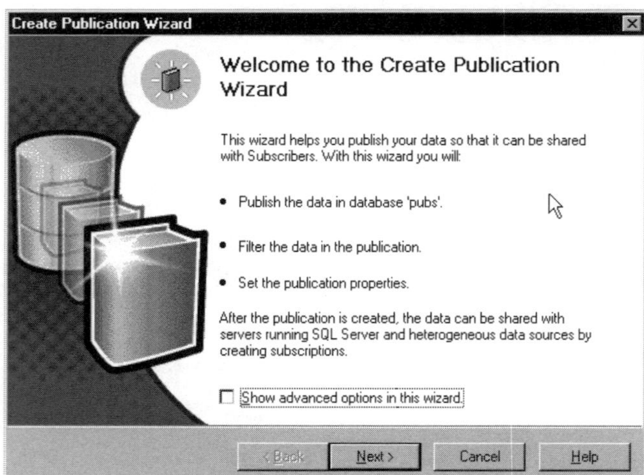

3. Click **Next** to move to the first step. Here you choose the database from which to publish data.

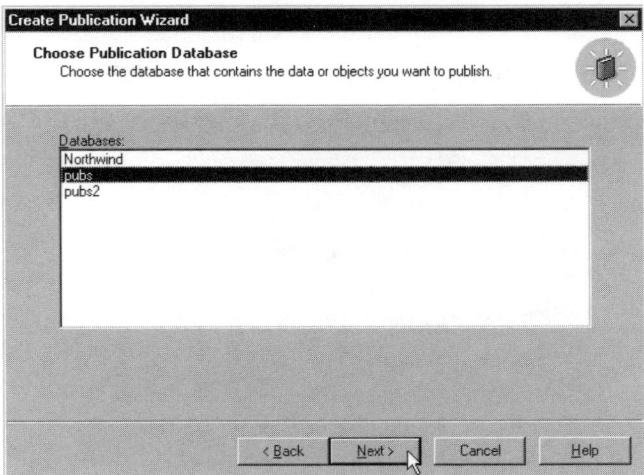

4. Click **Next**. The next step is to configure the type of publication. The choices are Snapshot, Transactional, and Merge. For this example, choose **Snapshot**.

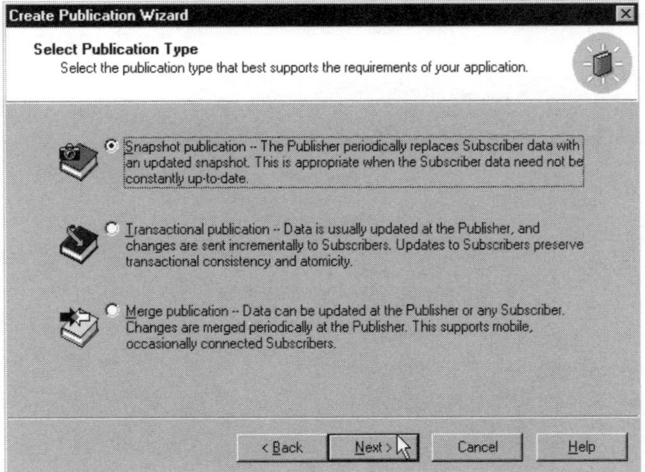

5. Click **Next**. The next step is to configure how replication will communicate to other databases. If all the other database servers are SQL Servers 2000 servers, then choose the default option. If any of the Subscriber databases are not SQL Server 2000, then choose the appropriate option.

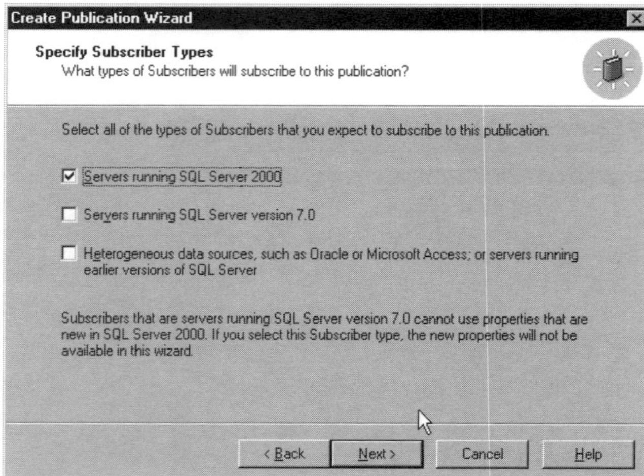

6.  Click **Next** to move on. Now you are ready to define the publication. Check any tables that you wish to publish for the publication. By default, SQL Server will provide an article name for each object being published. Clicking the button with the ellipses for the object may change the article name.

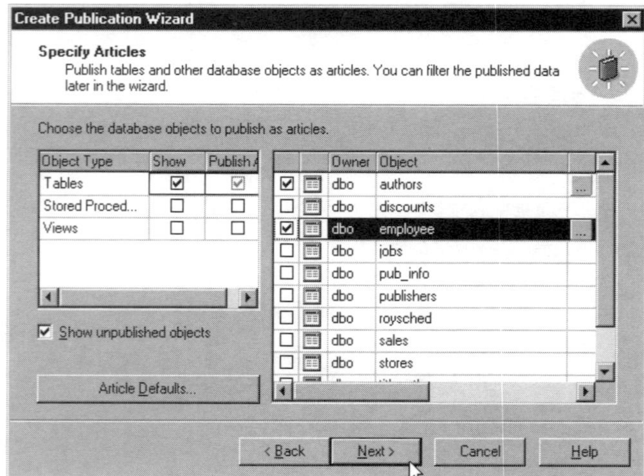

7.  Click **Next**. Enter a name and a description for the publication.

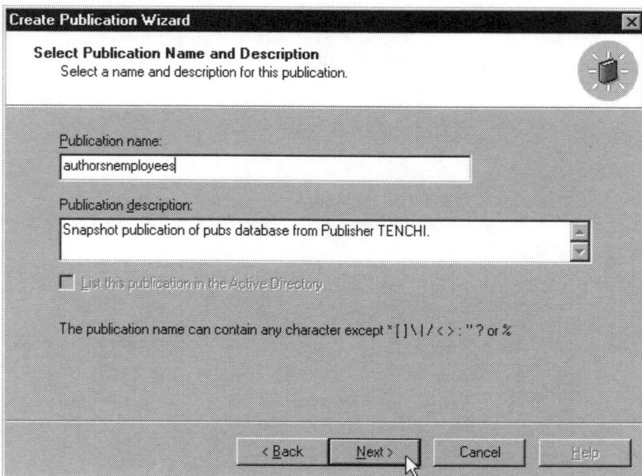



8. Click **Next**. This window will ask if you would like to define any data filters, enable anonymous Subscribers, or customize any other properties. The default is No.

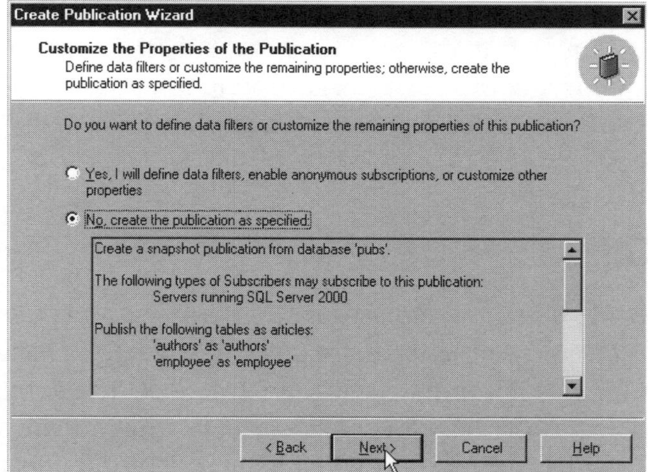



9. Click **Next** to access the final page in the wizard.

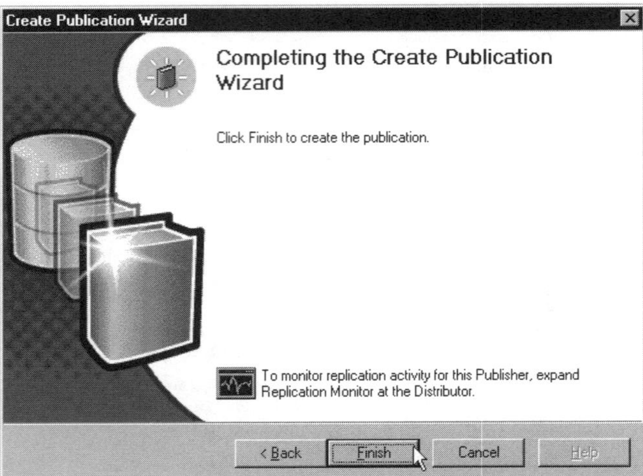


10. Click **Finish** to complete the process.

After the publication is created, Enterprise Manager will return to the Create and Manage Publications window from the beginning of the publication process. However, we should now have a publication available. The only thing left to do is create a new subscription to use it. This can be done by clicking the Push New Subscription button or, if you have closed this window, by selecting Tools|Wizards and selecting Push Subscription Wizard.

## Push vs. Pull

For transactional and merge replication, Subscribers can be defined as *push* or *pull*. Normally Subscribers are push Subscribers. This means that the data transfer was not initiated by the Subscriber. The data is pushed to the Subscriber. Subscribers for snapshot replication are always push Subscribers. A pull subscription is when a Subscriber initiates the data transfer. The Subscriber requests that replicated data be transmitted to the database. The Subscriber is pulling the data from the Distributor.

Setting up a subscription:

1. Select **Tools|Wizards|Push Subscription Wizard**.

2.  Click **Next**. Select which server or servers will be used as the Subscriber.

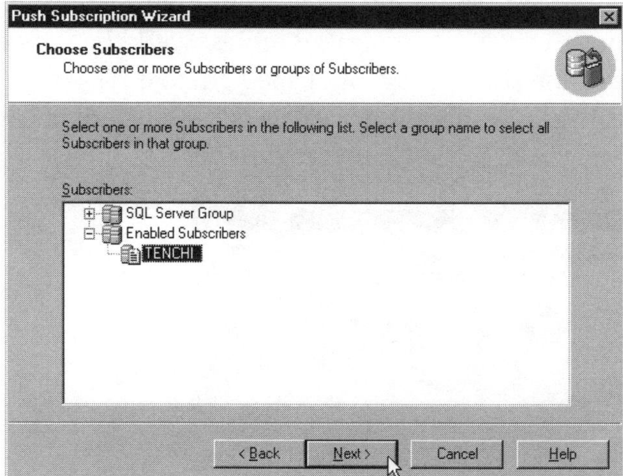

3.  Click **Next**. It is required that the database receiving the subscription exist on the server. If the database has a different name, enter the new name in the box or choose from a list of databases by clicking the **Browse or Create** button. This button will also allow you to create a new database to store the replicated data if one does not already exist.

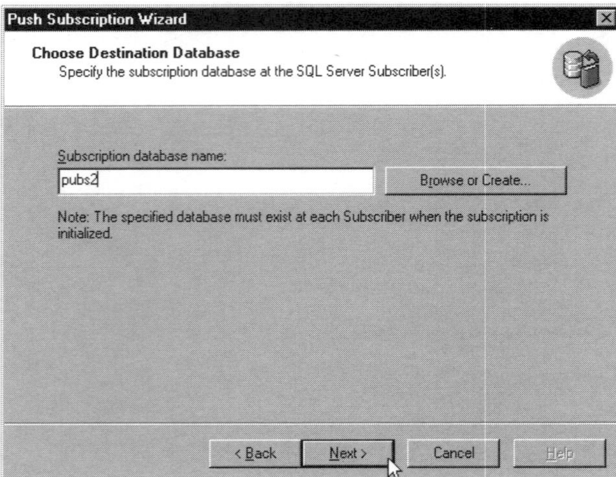

4. The next step is to determine when the Distributor will transmit the data to the Subscriber databases. This can be done continuously or on a schedule. For snapshot replication, continuous transmission is not a good option because the replicated tables would be dropped and re-created any time there was a published change. Therefore, creating a schedule is best. The default schedule is to replicate hourly. (This can be altered by clicking the **Change** button.)

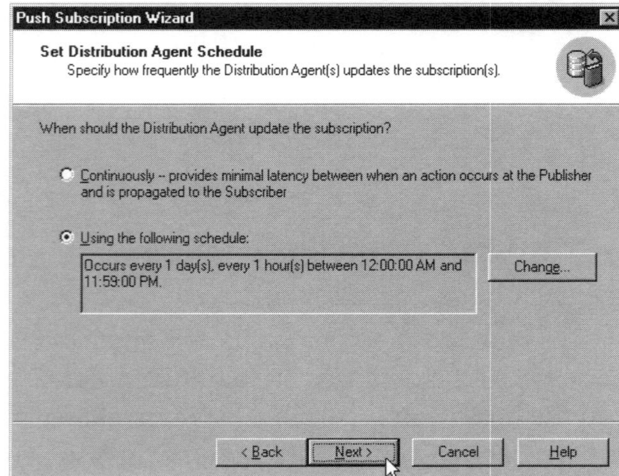

5. Click **Next**. SQL Server needs to know if the Subscriber database needs to have the replicated data and tables built as part of the replication process. If the data already exists, select No. If the data does not exist, select the default Yes; this will force SQL Server to use a

snapshot agent to take an image of the present published data so it can be replicated to the other databases. It is also recommended to check the **Start the Snapshot Agent** option to start this process as soon as possible.

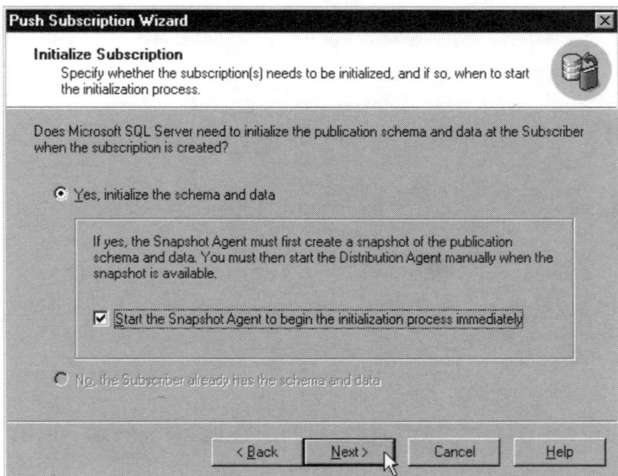


6. Click **Next**. The next step is more of a system check. In order for the replication to work, a SQL Server Agent must be running on the machines involved in replication. Putting a check in front of all the servers in the list will ensure that when the subscription is created, the necessary agents will be started as well. If you leave out any required agents, replication will not work until the agents are started.

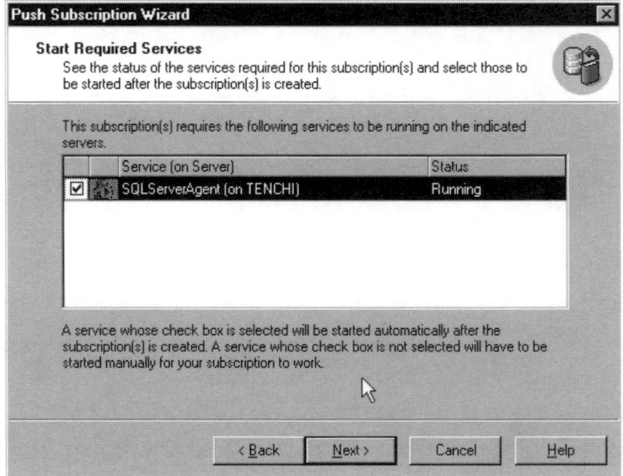

7.  Click **Next**. Then click **Finish** to complete the process.

Replication should now be configured. However, it is possible that the data will not be immediately available until the initial snapshot has taken place. This is true of all forms of replication.

# Installing Microsoft SQL Server 2000

This chapter guides you step by step through the installation process of Microsoft SQL Server 2000.

## Hardware Requirements

Listed below are the requirements for installing and running Microsoft SQL Server 2000.

### Intel or Compatible System

Pentium or compatible processor, 166-megahertz (MHz) or higher

### Operating System

- SQL Server 2000 Enterprise and Standard Editions

  - Microsoft Windows NT® Server version 4.0 Service Pack 5 (SP5) or later

  - Microsoft Windows NT Server 4.0 Enterprise Edition with SP5 or later

  - Microsoft Windows® 2000 Server

  - Microsoft Windows 2000 Advanced Server

  - Microsoft Windows 2000 Datacenter Server

- SQL Server 2000 Evaluation and Developer Editions

- Any listed operating system for SQL Server 2000 Enterprise and Standard Editions
- Microsoft Windows 2000 Professional
- Microsoft Windows NT Workstation 4.0 with SP5 or later

- SQL Server 2000 Personal and Desktop Editions
  - Any listed operating system for SQL Server 2000 Enterprise and Standard Editions
  - Any listed operating system for SQL Server 2000 Evaluation and Developer Editions
  - Windows 98
  - Windows Millennium Edition (Windows Me)

**Memory (RAM)**

- Enterprise Edition: 64 megabytes (MB); 128 MB recommended
- Standard Edition: 64 MB
- Evaluation Edition: 64 MB; 128 MB recommended
- Developer Edition: 64 MB
- Personal Edition: 64 MB for Windows 2000; 32 MB for other operating system

**Hard Disk Space**

- 95 to 270 MB for server; 250 MB for typical installation
- 50 MB for minimum installation of Analysis Services; 130 MB for typical installation
- 80 MB for Microsoft English Query

# Installing the Software

Insert the Microsoft SQL Server 2000 compact disc in your CD-ROM drive. From the Start menu choose **Run**. The auto setup should automatically be in the window

The installation window will appear. Choose **Install SQL Server 2000 Prerequisites**.

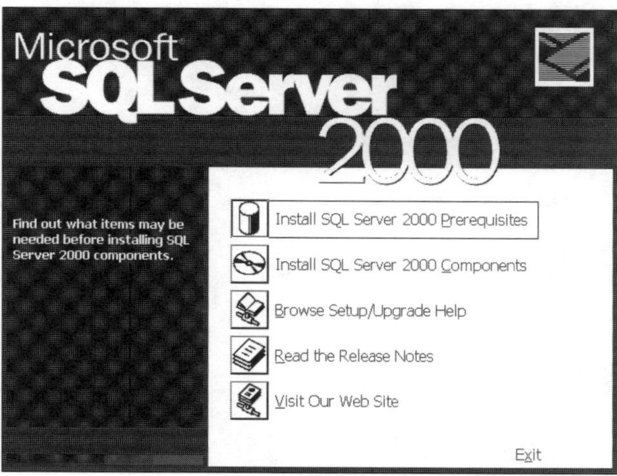

Select **Install Winsock2 Update for Windows 95**. Remember to only install this if you are running Microsoft Windows 95.

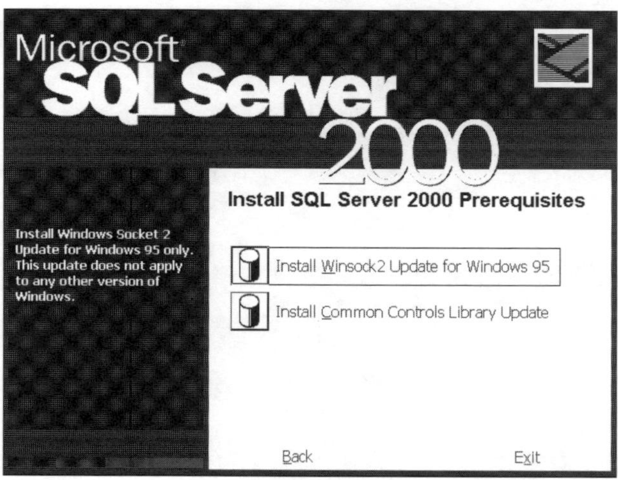

If you are running Windows 95, you will also need to install the Common Controls Library Update. This allows SQL Server 2000 to run on Windows 95.

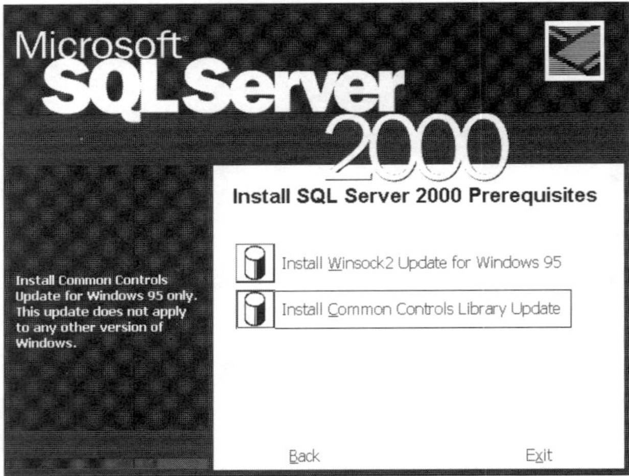



If you need to install the Common Controls Library Update, click **Yes**.

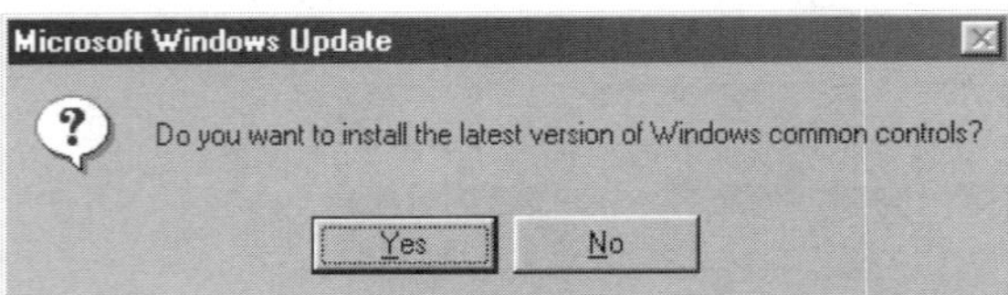



Click **Yes** to accept the license agreement.

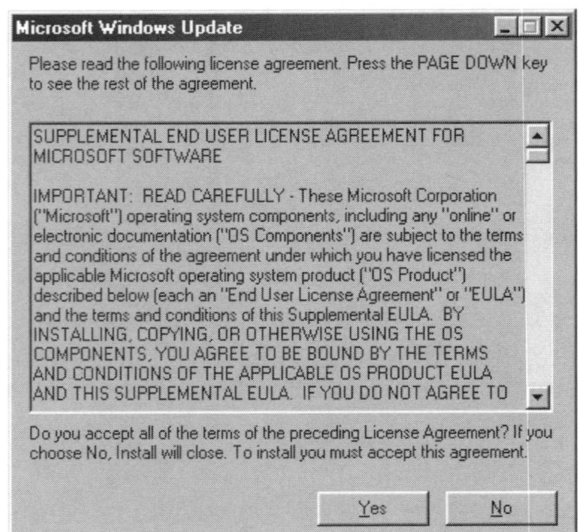

The following window will appear when installation is complete. Click **OK**.

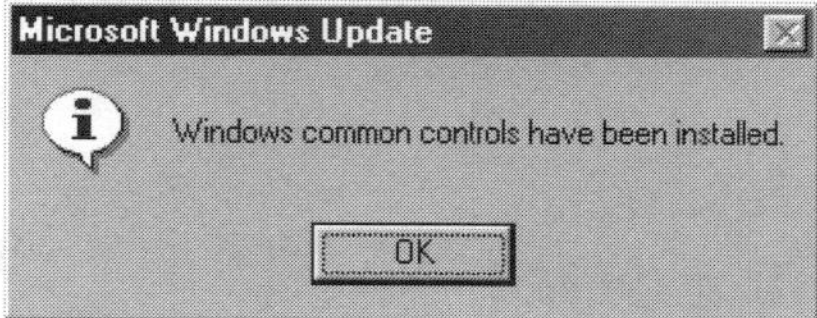

In the next window you can click Yes to restart your computer, but for this example, choose **No** to return to the opening screen and finish the installation.

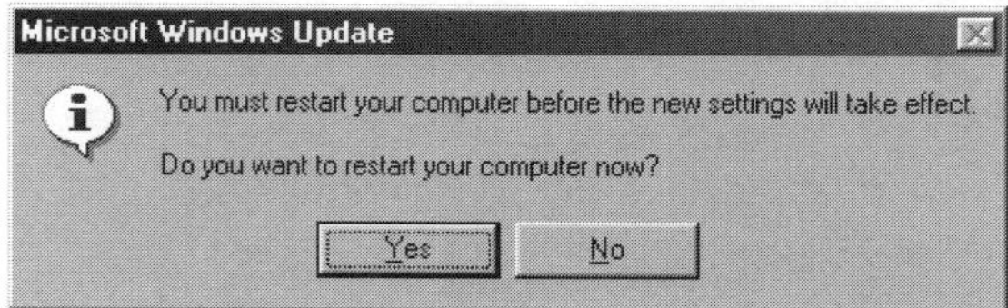

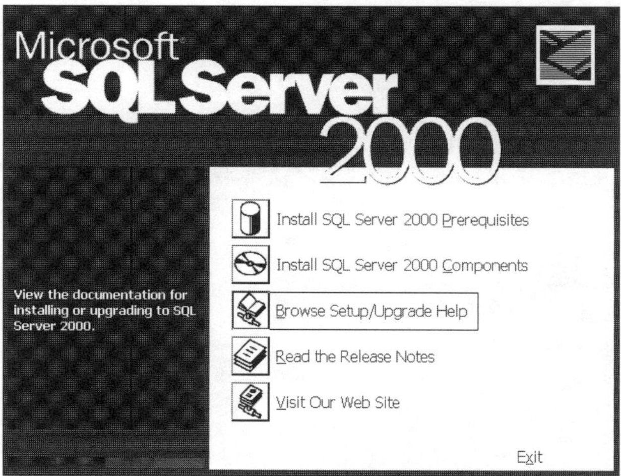


Click on **Browse Setup/Upgrade Help**. This is a nice little help file that you can use to help you with the install process. You may want to review a few topics before continuing the install of Microsoft SQL Server 2000. If there is information there that you think you need, then print out the topic so that you have it to refer to as you complete the install process.

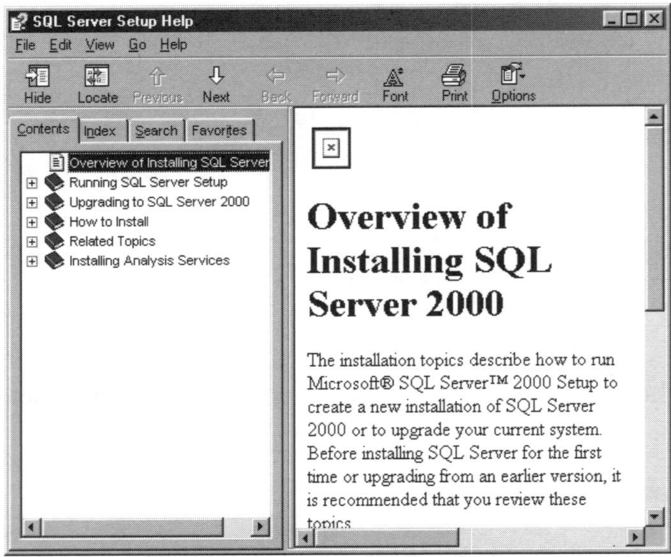

Close this screen and go back to the original installation screen. Select **Install SQL Server 2000 Components**.

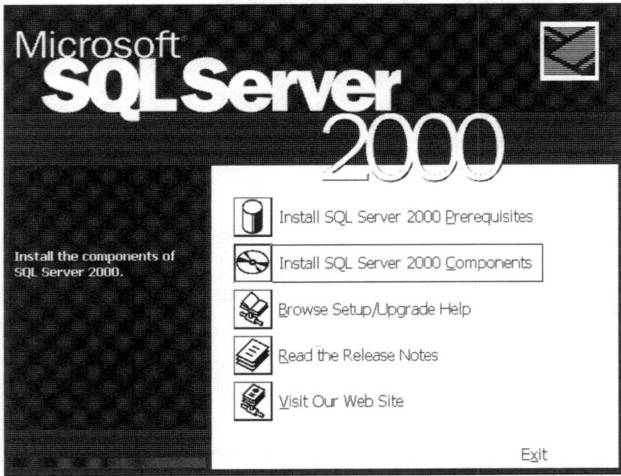



Select **Standard Edition**.

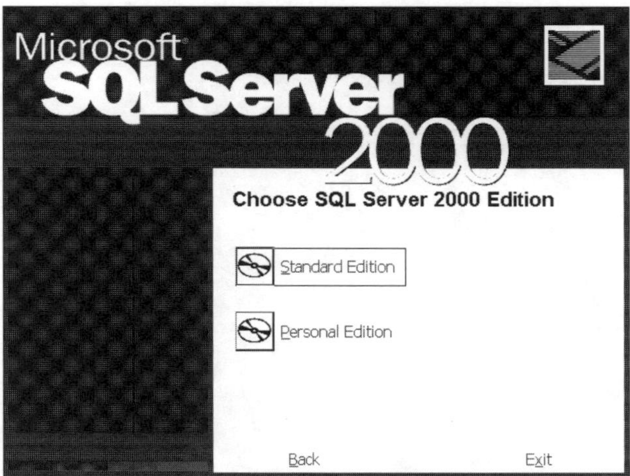

After choosing Standard Edition, you will need to select which component to install. For now, select **Database Server - Standard Edition**.

The installation wizard will automatically begin to load, and the progress window will appear.

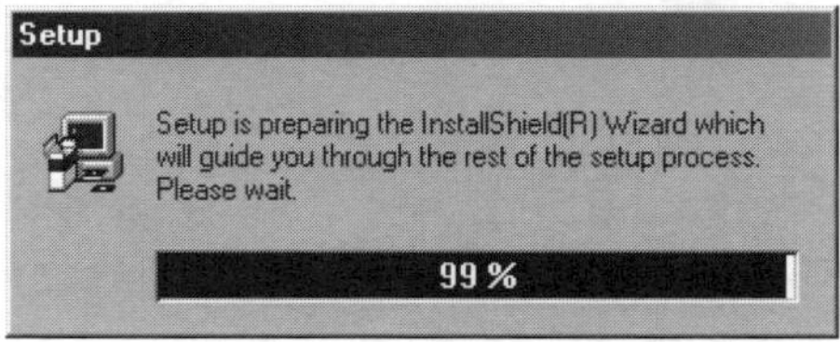

When the Welcome window appears, choose **Next.**

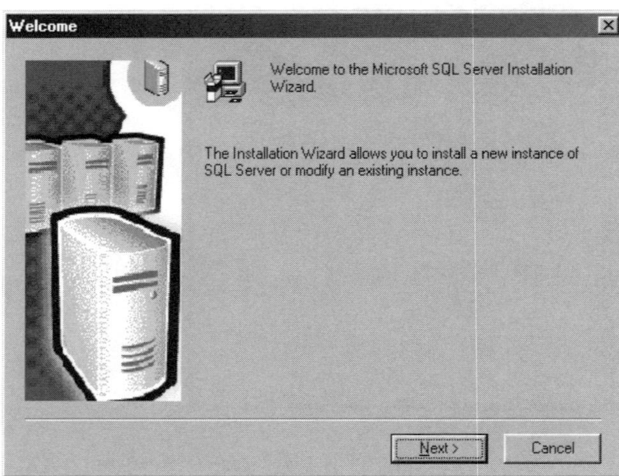

The Computer Name window allows you to input the computer on which you would like to install the software. If you are installing this program on your local area network, choose the Remote Computer option. You can then type the computer name.

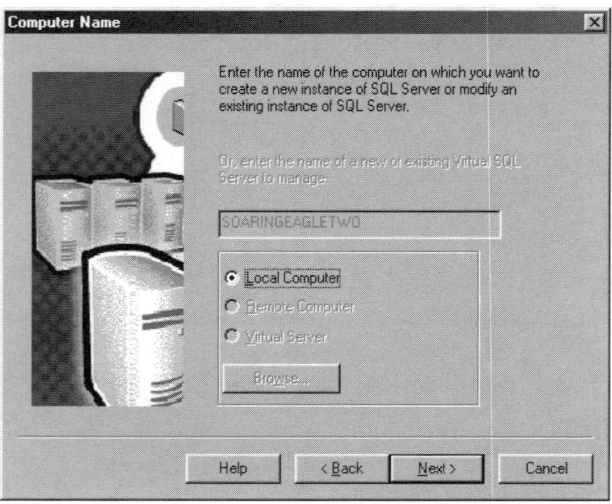

In the Installation Selection dialog box, choose **Create a new instance of SQL Server**. Note that there is an option to upgrade, remove, or add components to an existing instance of SQL Server. (We will discuss upgrading from Microsoft SQL Server 7.0 to 2000 in Appendix F, "Upgrading to Microsoft SQL Server 2000.") Click **Next**.

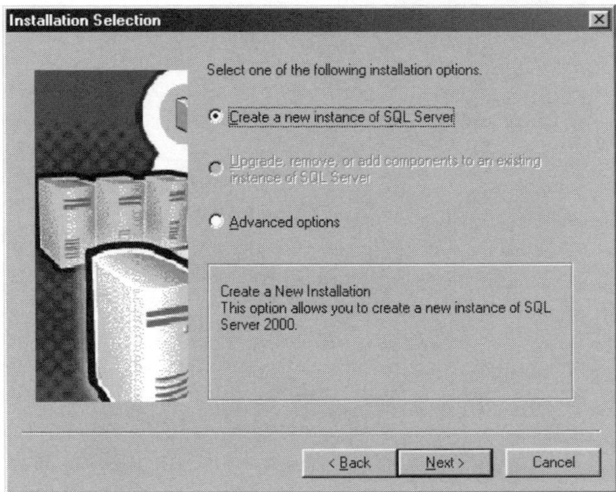

Enter your user information. You must enter your name, but entering your company name is optional. Click **Next**.

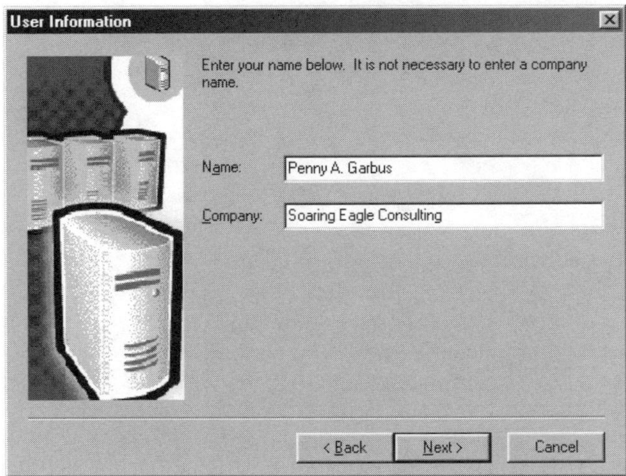

Click **Yes** to accept the license agreement.

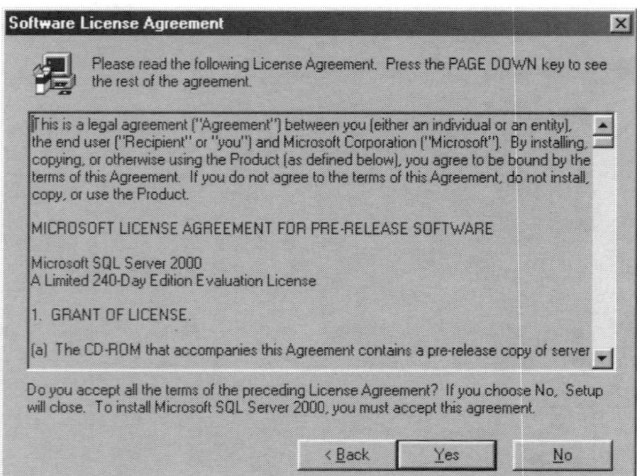

In the Installation Definition window you can choose what type of installation you would like. Select **Server and Client Tools**, then click **Next**.

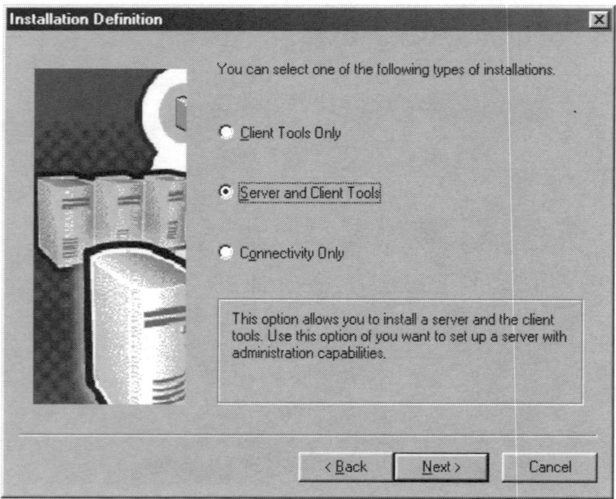

Choose a name for this installation instance. If the Default check box is checked, a default name will be present. To choose your own name, unclick the Default check box and fill in the Instance name field. Then click **Next**. It is possible to have more than one instance of SQL Server running on one machine. Please note that it is a good idea to keep a record of this name in a book (preferably in the manual you use to record all of your database management procedures). You may also want to record where all of the program files for Microsoft SQL Server are kept.

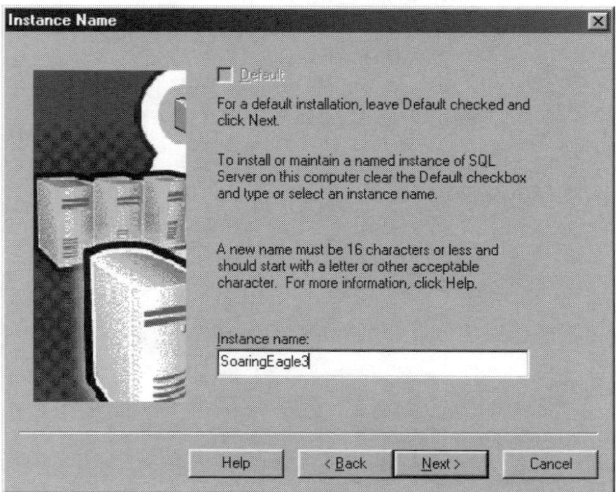

In the Setup Type dialog box, choose **Typical**. The destination folders are selected automatically. If you would like to choose another destination, click **Browse** and select or create a new file folder in which to install this program.

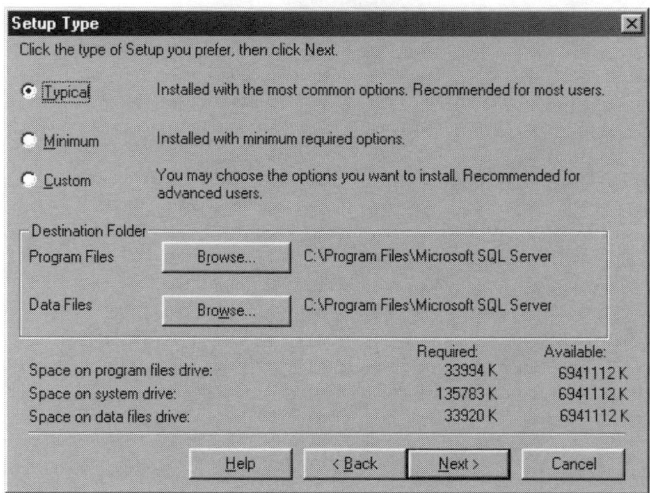

Notice the required hardware setup. Just take a moment to validate the resources of your computer to be sure that you can have a successful install. Click **Next** to continue installing Microsoft SQL Server 2000.

In the Authentication Mode dialog box, accept the default setting, enter your password, and click **Next**. You may skip the password requirement but this is not a good idea in most business environments.

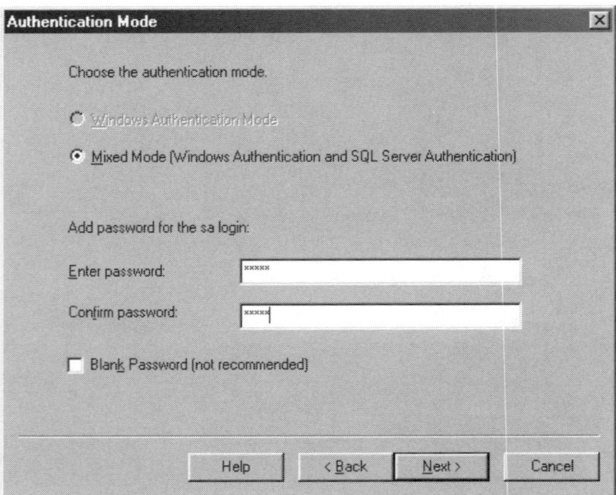

The Start Copying Files dialog box lets you know that the setup process is complete. Click **Next** and allow the install to begin.

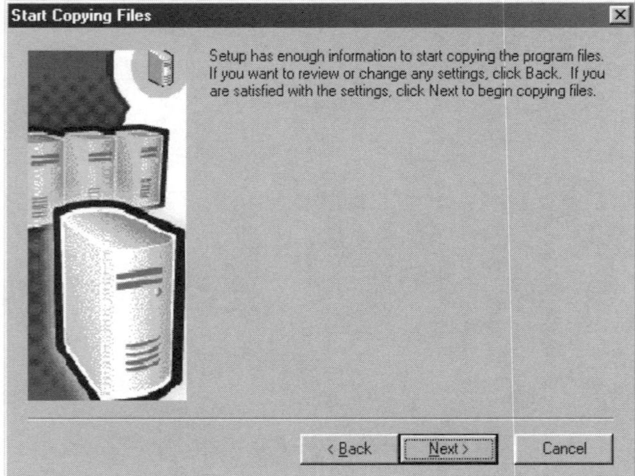

Many screens will pop up automatically to let you know how the installation process is advancing. This screen is a graphical interface showing you the percentage of the software that is currently installed. The installation takes at least three minutes, depending on your CD-ROM reader speed and the processing power of your computer.

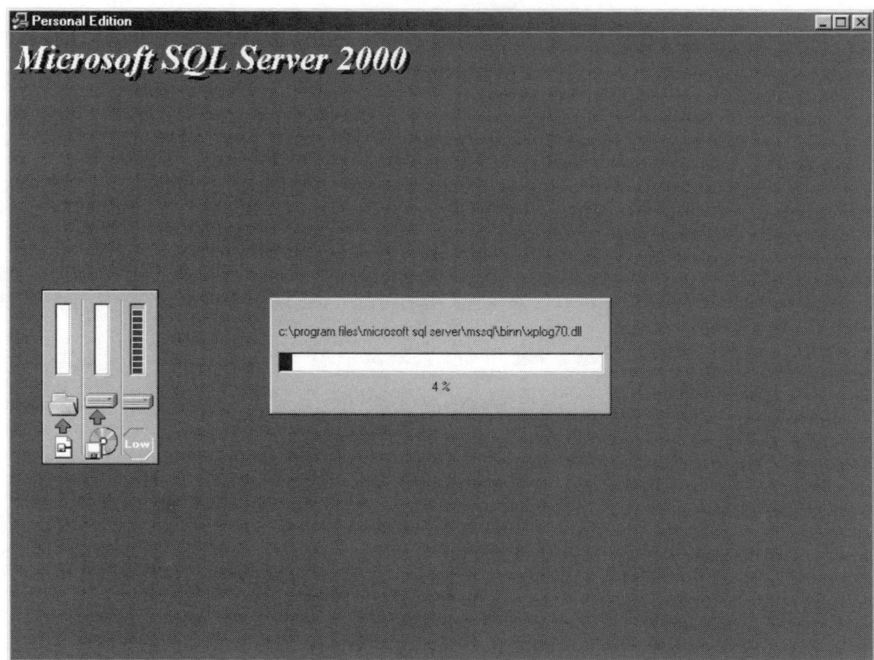


The Setup Complete screen notifies you that the Microsoft SQL Server 2000 installation has been completed and asks you whether you want to restart your computer now or later. To be sure that the installation is totally complete and successful, select **Yes, I want to restart my computer now** and click **Finish**. But first make sure that you do not have any other programs running.

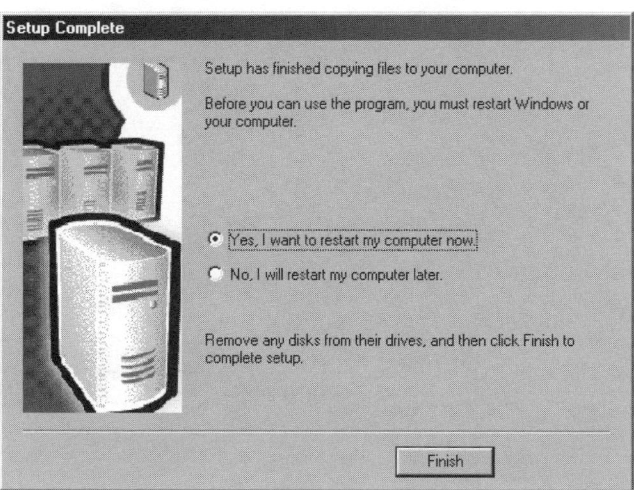

## Testing the Installation of SQL Server 2000

Follow these steps to test the installation:

1. Start Microsoft SQL Server 2000 by entering from a command prompt. For the default instance, use the following. (The term *instance* refers to the name you gave to your server when you installed Microsoft SQL Server 2000. Remember we named ours SoaringEagle 3.)

   ```
   Net start mssqlserver
   ```

   For a named instance, include the instance name, for example:

   ```
   Net start MSSQLSERVER SoaringEagle3
   ```

2. Connect to SQL Server by entering:

   ```
   Osql /Usa /P
   ```

   For a named instance, include both the server and the instance name, for example:

   ```
   Osql / Usa /P /S Machine/SoaringEagle3
   ```

   When osql connects, this osql prompt appears:

   ```
   1>
   ```

3. If osql cannot connect and an ODBC error is returned, enter a simple query, such as:

   ```
   SELECT @@SERVERNAME
   GO
   The osql utility returns the server aname:

   SELECT @@SERVERNAME
   GO
   The osql utility returns the server aname:

   1> SELECT @@SERVERNAME
   2> GO
   ```

   ```
   SoaringEagle3
   ```

```
(1 row affected:
1>
```

4.  Verify that you have checked a SQL Server 2000 server by entering:

```
SELECT @@VERSION
GO
```

The osql utility returns the version information.

5.  Quit the osql utility by entering:

```
Exit
```

Remember that this information and more can be found on your Microsoft SQL Server 2000 compact disc. You may refer to this file at any time. Just put the disc into your CD-ROM drive and the install screen will appear. Click on **Browse Setup/Upgrade Help**. Use this help as you would any other Windows help system.

# Upgrading to Microsoft SQL Server 2000

While it is not absolutely necessary, it is recommended that older databases be upgraded to SQL Server 2000. This will allow your older databases to incorporate the latest tools and processes available in SQL Server 2000. However, if there is any doubt that the database will function after the upgrade, it is possible to run both systems simultaneously. They can co-exist on different servers or, if the hardware configuration is powerful enough, on the same server.

Before any upgrade process, it is always a good idea to make sure that it is possible to restore the server if something should go wrong. In other words, make sure you have a recent backup and that the database has been checked to be free of any errors. The last thing anybody wants is for an upgrade of a production system to fail and the database to be completely lost.

Depending on your needs, Microsoft provides two distinct paths for upgrading a database. The first method, an installation upgrade, involves upgrading the entire server. For this, SQL Server 2000 will overwrite the old SQL Server 7.0 binaries and upgrade all of the databases so they are ready for use with SQL Server 2000. The second option is to do a database upgrade. Database upgrades are accomplished using the

Database Copy Wizard. The database is copied into SQL Server 2000 and upgraded in the copy process.

# Installation Upgrade

Installation upgrades allow for a one-stop upgrade solution for an entire server and its databases. However, should anything go wrong in the upgrade process, the database server may need to be completely re-installed from backup copies. The upgrade process and its failure recovery process can be time consuming. The upgrade process should be performed when no one is using the server, as it will be shut down and restarted several times and any changes by users could destroy the integrity of the database.

Follow these steps to perform an installation upgrade:

Start the installation process using the install CD-ROM (as described in Appendix E).

Follow the installation process described in Appendix E until the Installation Selection screen is reached

Select **Upgrade, remove, or add components to an existing instance of SQL Server**. Click **Next**.

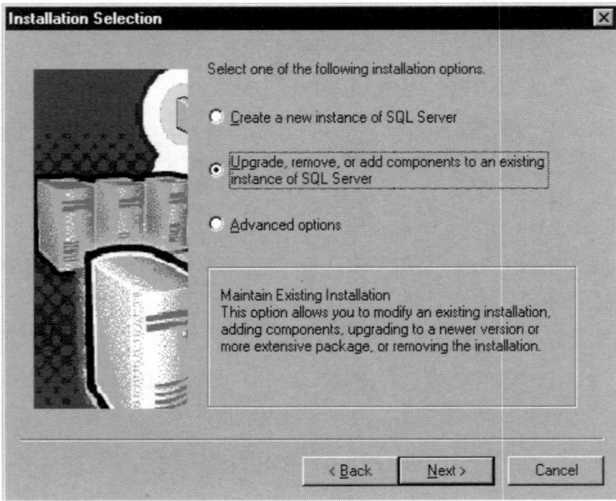

Select the instance of SQL Server to be upgraded (if there is more than one instance). If this is the default instance of SQL Server on the machine, click **Next**.

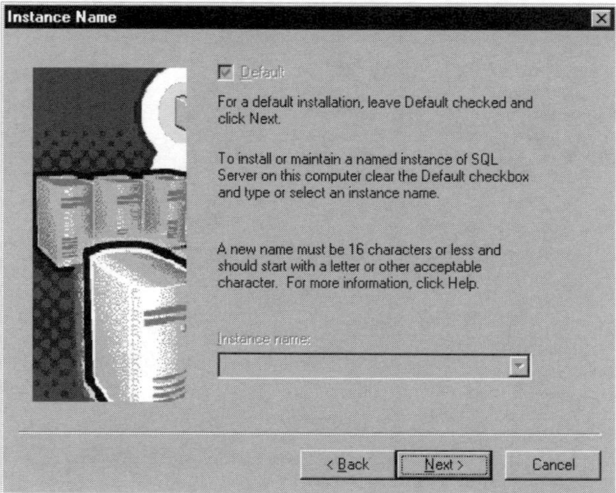

Select **Upgrade your existing installation**. Click **Next**.

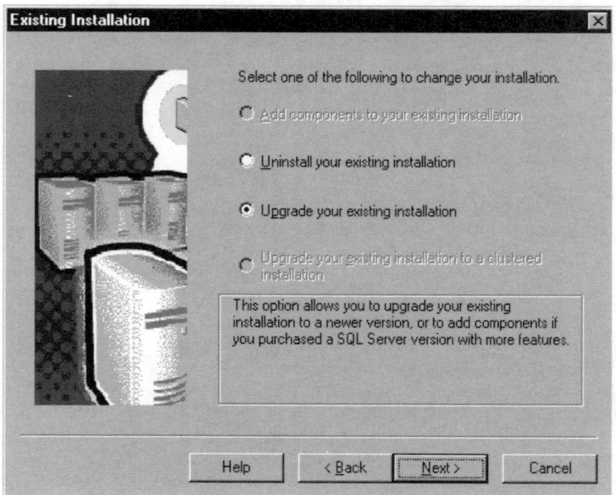

This next option will upgrade the SQL Server tools, such as Query Analyzer and Enterprise Manager. Select **Yes, upgrade my SQL Server Tools and data**. Click **Next**.

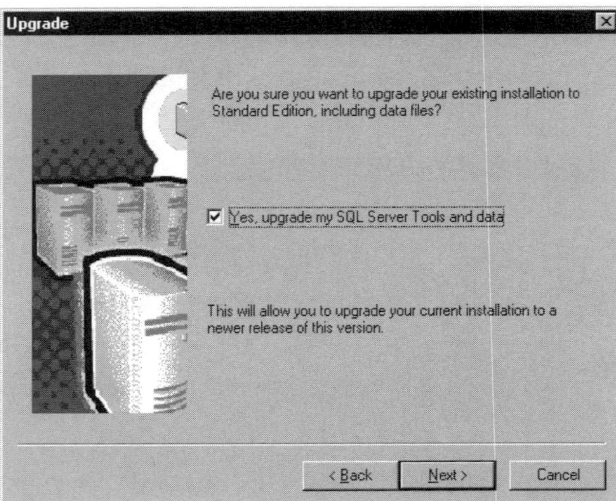

The upgrade program needs to know the sa password. Enter the sa password in the provided box, or if NT authentication is being used, select the **Windows NT authentication** option. Click **Next**.

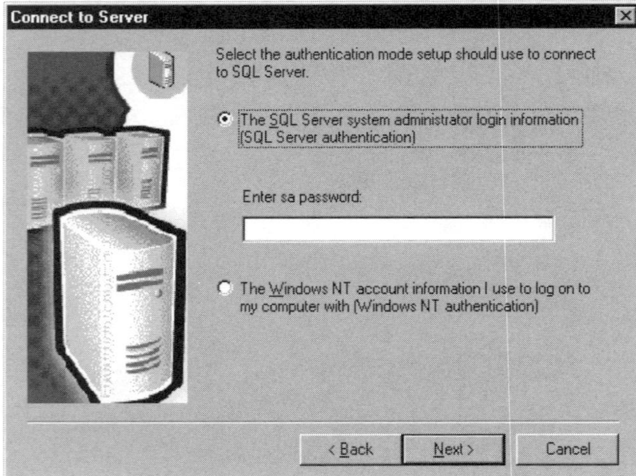

The next screen is a warning. This is the last chance to change any settings before the upgrade process begins. If the choices are final, click **Next**.

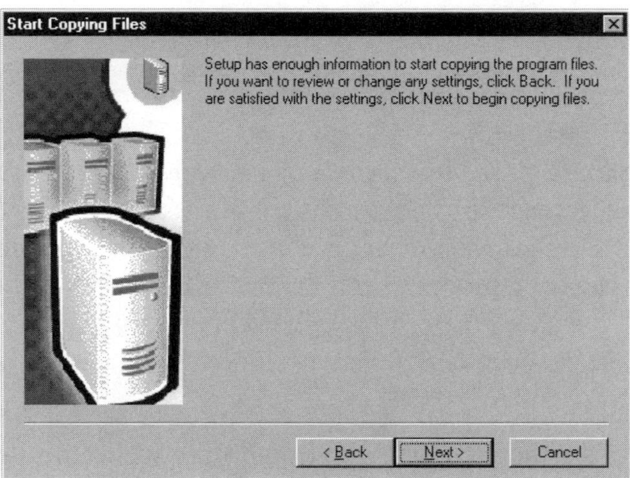

At this point SQL Server will begin the actual upgrade process. It is important not to interfere with the process after it starts. The actual time to complete the upgrade will vary based on the hardware in the server and the size of the databases.

When the upgrade is completed, the following screen will be displayed.

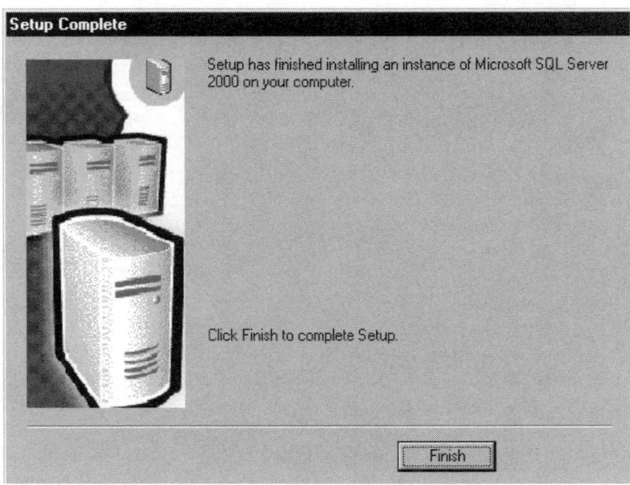

Click **Finish** to end the process.

# Database Upgrade

If the database cannot afford to be shut down during the upgrade process or if the database is to be moved from one server to another, SQL Server also offers the Database Copy Wizard. This allows a database to be duplicated from one database server to another or from one instance to another. After the copy process, both databases can still exist, but eventually one should be shut down. If the wizard is used to copy a SQL Server database into an instance of SQL Server 2000, the database will be upgraded in the process.

In order for the database copy to function properly, several prerequisites must be met:

- The database must be in read-only mode
- The database cannot already exist on the destination server
- The database source files must be readily accessible (shared)

To copy a database with the Database Copy Wizard, follow these steps:

In Enterprise Manager, select **Tools|Wizards**.

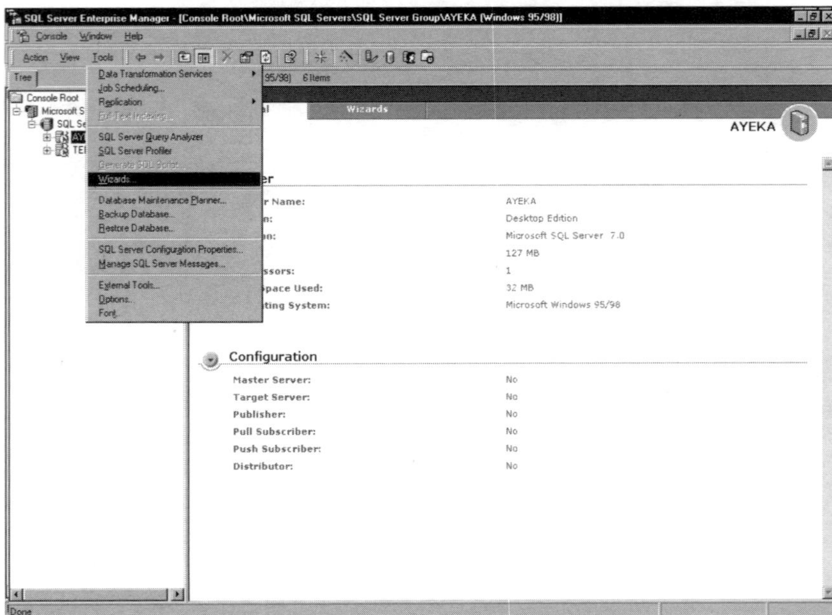

Expand the **Management** list and select **Copy Database Wizard**.
Click **OK**.

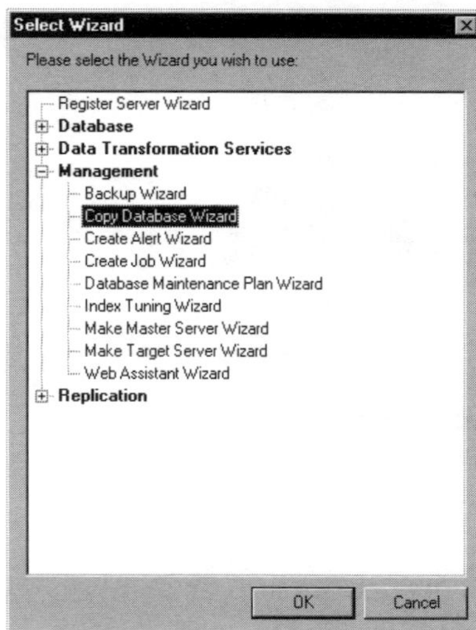

The first screen is an introduction to the process. Click **Next**.

Select the source server from which the database will be copied. Provide
any logins and passwords to access the database or select NT Authentication. Click **Next**.

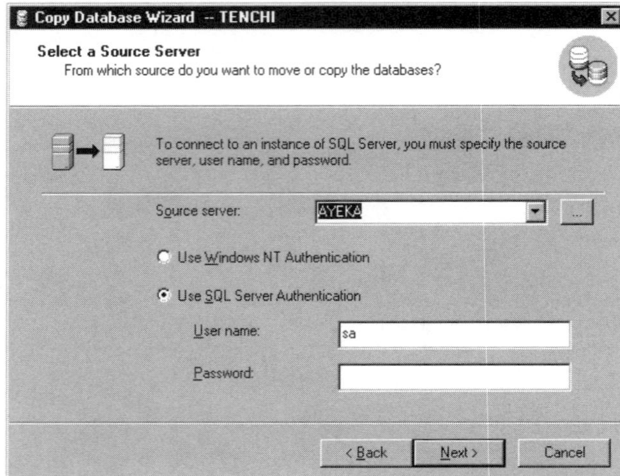

Select the destination server from which the database will be copied. Provide any logins and passwords to access the server or select NT Authentication. Click **Next**.

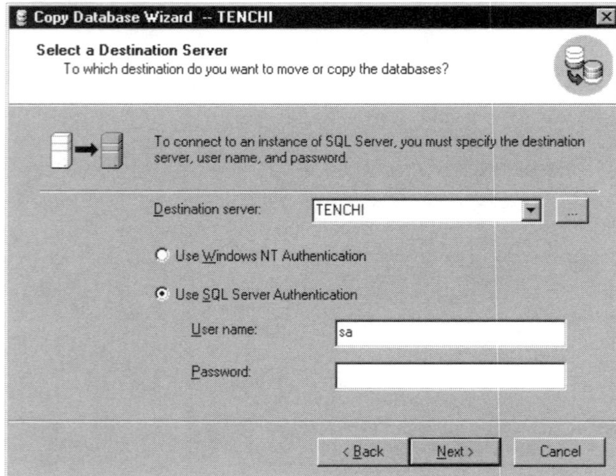

The next screen displays the databases on both servers and indicates which can be copied or moved. Select the database to be copied.

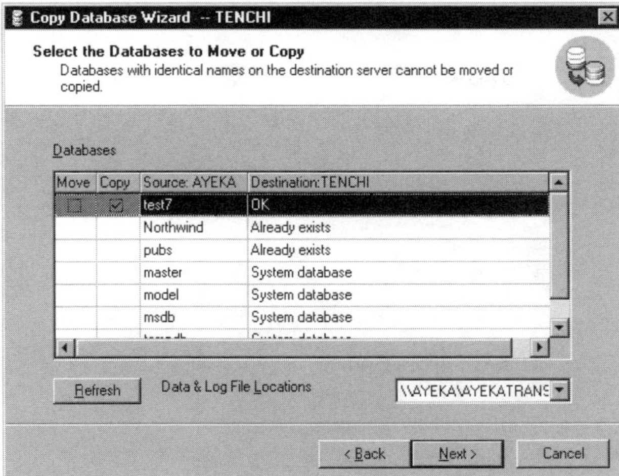

The database files should be readable (shared). Select the network drive from which they can be accessed in the Data & Log File Locations box. Click **Next**.

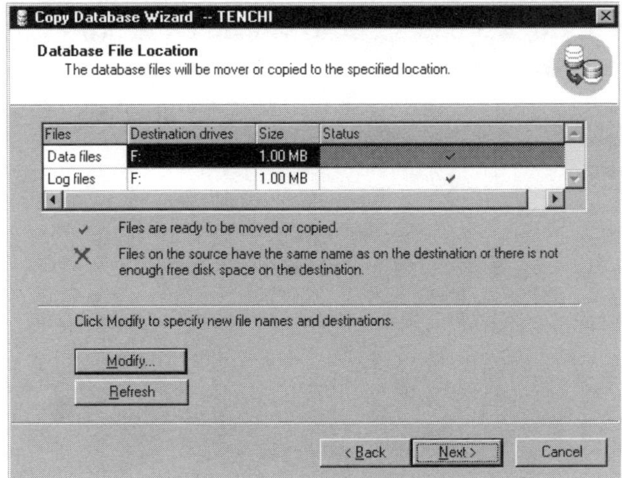

Verify the status of the database data and log files. If the Status column has a check, the file is ready to be copied. The destination location of the files can be changed with the Modify button. Click **Next**.

The next screen asks whether any logins, server-wide stored procedures, database jobs, or user-defined error messages will need to be copied with the database. The default is to copy all these objects. Click **Next**.

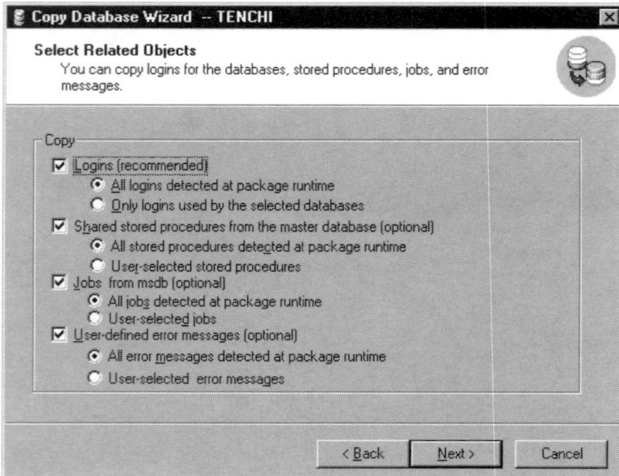

The screen displays the settings of the DTS (Data Transformation Services) package that will be run to copy the database. The options are to run it immediately to quickly start the upgrade, to schedule the package to run once at a specified date and time (this is useful if the database has to be upgraded during off hours), or to schedule the process to run repeatedly. Select **Run immediately**, and click **Next**.

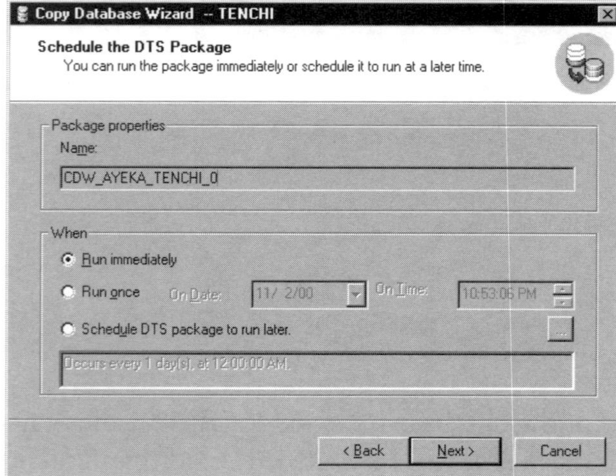

This screen summarizes the settings for the database copy process. To accept the settings and start the copy process, click **Finish**.

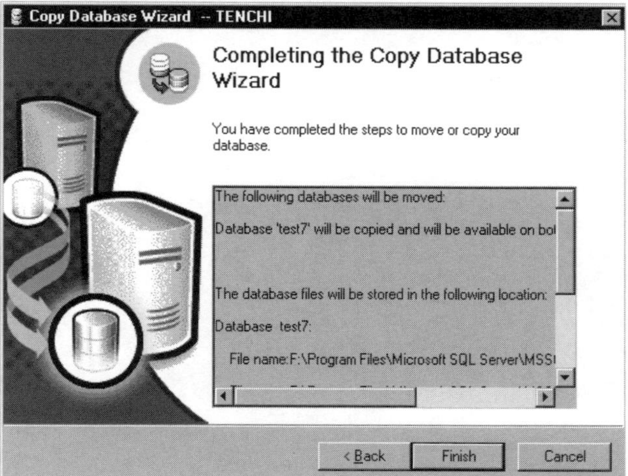

The database will start copying. During this process you will see a log of the copy progress.

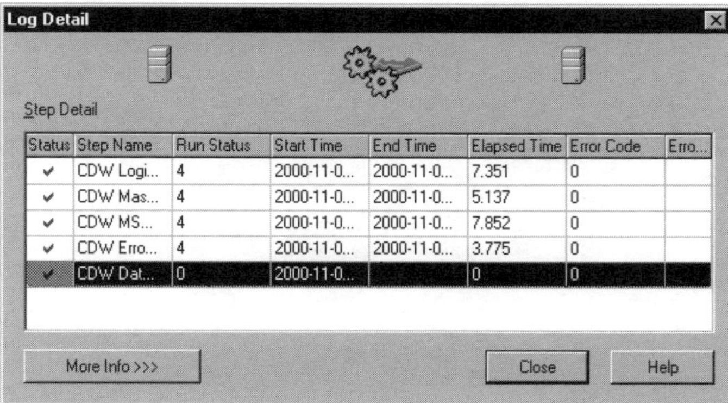

When the process is completed, the following window will appear. Click **OK**.

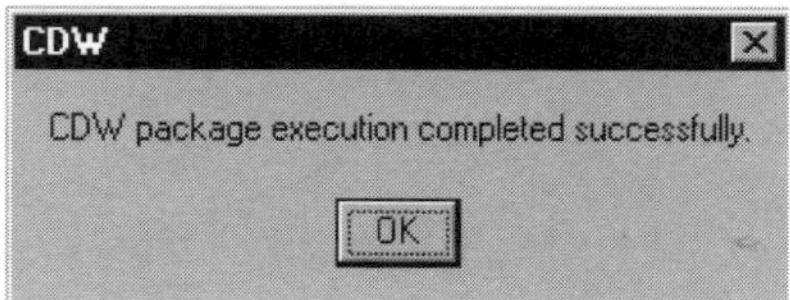

The database should now be copied to the new instance of SQL Server 2000. The old database can be disabled or deleted.

# Index

Let Soaring Eagle Consulting
Carry Your
Database Management Burdens
www.soaringeagleltd.com
888-289-8170

ibooks•com

information. unbound.

A full-service e-book source that gives you:
- browsing capability
- full-text searching
- "try-before-you-buy" previews
- customizable personal library
- wide selection of free books

**www.ibooks.com**